P
29/6/06

Cogn...

A Methods Companion

1

Cognitive Psychology
A Methods Companion

Edited by Nick Braisby

OXFORD
UNIVERSITY PRESS

Oxford University Press in association with The Open University

OXFORD
UNIVERSITY PRESS

Great Clarendon Street, Oxford OX2 6DP

Published by Oxford University Press, Oxford in association with The Open University, Milton Keynes

Oxford University Press is a department of the University of Oxford. It furthers the University's objective of excellence in research, scholarship, and education by publishing worldwide in

Oxford New York Auckland Bangkok Buenos Aires Cape Town Chennai
Dar es Salaam Delhi Hong Kong Istanbul Karachi Kolkata Kuala Lumpur Madrid
Melbourne Mexico City Nairobi São Paulo Shanghai Taipei Tokyo Toronto

Oxford is a registered trade mark of Oxford University Press in the UK and in certain other countries

Published in the United States by Oxford University Press Inc., New York

The Open University, Walton Hall, Milton Keynes, MK7 6AA

First published 2005.

British Library Cataloguing in Publication data available.

Library of Congress Cataloguing in Publication Data available.

Edited, designed and typeset by The Open University.

Printed in the United Kingdom by Scotprint, Haddington.

ISBN 0-19-928160-2

1.1

Contents in brief

Contents

Introduction

What is cognitive psychology? While it would be impossible to answer this question without describing its subject matter – the various topics that cognitive psychologists study – equally indispensable would be a description of the various methods that it adopts. What distinguishes cognitive psychology from, say, philosophy of mind or linguistics, is, in part at least, the range of empirically based methods that cognitive psychologists use. Over the past 20 years or so, there has been a sea change in that range of methods, with an ever-increasing reliance on methods that have some kind of neural basis.

This book focuses on the main non-experimental methods of cognitive psychology, though there are topics included that relate closely to the use of experiments, such as ethics and the use of quantitative methods.

Ethics

In Chapter 1, Bundy Mackintosh discusses the importance of adopting and adhering to ethical principles in conducting research. Although many cognitive psychological studies raise few major ethical concerns, it would be a mistake to think that none do, or that some studies raise no ethical considerations. In conducting studies with human participants, all researchers need to be aware of the ethical dimension that links them and their participants. Beginning with a philosophical distinction between deontological and consequentialist approaches to ethics, the author then outlines some of the key issues of which psychologists must be aware when conducting research. The chapter also discusses the ethical codes of the British Psychological Society (BPS) and the American Psychological Association (APA), and these are included in an appendix to this book.

Connectionism

In Chapter 2, Martin Le Voi introduces one of the methods of cognitive psychology that can lay claim to some kind of neural basis. Connectionism is an approach to modelling cognitive processes that is rooted in an understanding of the computational properties of neurons. By modelling these and their interconnections, albeit very simply, researchers have been able to develop models of cognitive processes that successfully reproduce certain aspects of human behaviour. The author discusses a number of different classes of model, demonstrating their properties, and illustrating their ability to simulate human data. Computer exercises are included to guide students in constructing connectionist models, entering training data, training and finally testing the models.

Connectionism exercises

The software for running these exercises can be found either (i) on the Course Software Resources CD-ROM for Open University DD303 students; students should follow the instructions on the CD-ROM packaging to install the software; or (ii) on the Oxford University Press companion web site; students should navigate to **www.oup.com/uk/booksites/psychology** and follow the instructions for downloading and installing the software.

Once installed, the software can be found on the
Start/All Programs/Cognitive Psychology/Connectionism menu.
(For Windows versions prior to Windows XP 'All programs' on the **Start** menu is
just labelled as **Programs**.) Detailed instructions for running each exercise can be
found in the chapter, under the relevant computer exercise.

Symbolic modelling

In Chapter 3, Paul Mulholland and Stuart Watt discuss a different type of cognitive
modelling, one that is predicated on two beliefs concerning the nature of cognition:
(i) that cognition is symbolic, and that mental representations are symbols or symbol
structures; and (ii) that cognition involves the rule-based transformation of symbolic
expressions. The authors illustrate the symbolic approach to cognitive modelling via
an in-depth discussion of ACT-R, and provide examples of how ACT-R can
successfully model human behaviour. In this chapter too, there are computer-based
exercises designed to aid students' comprehension of the key concepts involved in
this kind of modelling as well as the details of the ACT-R models themselves.

ACT-R exercises

The software for running these exercises can be found either (i) on the Course
Software Resources CD-ROM for Open University DD303 students; students
should follow the instructions on the CD-ROM packaging to install the software; or
(ii) on the Oxford University Press companion web site; students should navigate to
www.oup.com/uk/booksites/psychology and follow the instructions for down-
loading and installing the software.

Once installed, the software can be found on the
Start/All Programs/Cognitive Psychology menu. Start the program
called **ACT-R**. Within ACT-R, choose **File/Open** and select the appropriate file
name for the particular exercise, as follows.

- For Exercise 1, choose Exercise1.mod

- For Exercise 2, choose Exercise2.mod

- For Exercise 3, choose Exercise3.mod

- For Exercise 4, choose Exercise4.mod

Detailed instructions on what to do when running each exercise can be found in the
Instruction tab in each model's window.

*Note: If you have a copy of Cognitive Psychology, edited by Braisby and Gellatly
(the main volume to which this is a companion), you will see that Chapter 3 in this
volume is very similar, but not identical to, Chapter 16 in that volume. The main
differences concern the discussion of connectionism and the inclusion of the
computer exercises. Students who have read Chapter 16 in the main volume, may
just proceed to follow the exercises in this volume, or omit Chapter 3 altogether if
they do not wish to pursue the computer-based exercises.*

Neuroimaging

In Chapter 4, Ingrid Johnsrude and Olaf Hauk introduce another method that can lay
claim to a neural basis: neuroimaging. Neuroimaging is a rapidly developing field,

with many techniques having being developed and many in development. The authors describe a number of different techniques for imaging the brain's activity. Each depends on being able firstly to detect the activity of neurons by some means, and secondly to generate a measure of the activity. The measure can then be used to provide images displaying the spatial or temporal locus of neuronal activity and, perhaps more importantly, to support statistical analysis.

The authors outline six different techniques in all, though they concentrate primarily on EEG, MEG, PET and fMRI, outlining the limitations and advantages of these techniques.

Much controversy still surrounds the use of neuroimaging evidence. As becomes apparent in the course of Chapter 4, the different means for measuring neuronal activity are limited. For example, EEG and MEG have good temporal but poor spatial resolution – they are better at determining when neuronal activity takes place than exactly where. The reverse pattern holds for PET and fMRI. Such limitations – and many more are discussed in the chapter – remind us that neuroimaging techniques are informative only to the extent that we are prepared to draw *inferences* from the data they provide to the nature of cognitive processes, and that the validity of these inferences depends on many assumptions being satisfied. One thing that all the techniques have in common is that they measure *physical* qualities of neuronal activity. But cognitive processes are usually cast in terms of *information processing*. How can we be sure that physical activity is the vestigial trace of cognitive activity; that the physical signs we observe correspond to cognition?

Of course, researchers have developed strategies to make sure their inferences are reliable. By comparing the images deriving from the performance of tasks that differ in just one component, for example, researchers can be more confident that the physical activity they see reflects the cognitive activity required by that task component. However, you can perhaps sense the difficulties involved by trying a simple thought experiment. Imagine trying to produce physical images of a computer's activity. You could perhaps produce images of your PC or Mac's electrical or magnetic activity during a word-processing task; you might find that particular regions were active in certain tasks and not others. But it is hard to see how the images alone would tell you exactly what information processing the computer was performing. How would we know it was word processing and not calculating values and formulae in a spreadsheet? To draw those kinds of inference we would need some prior knowledge of the information-processing characteristics of the task and how those information-processing properties relate to the hardware involved. That is, the very least, we would need a good information-processing model. In psychology, neuroimaging data are similarly likely to prove useful only to the extent that we already possess good cognitive models. This is not to say neuroimaging data are not useful – they can help us discriminate between models that make different predictions concerning the locus and type of cognitive processes involved in certain tasks, and they may continue to throw up new data implying the involvement of processes in tasks that were previously unmodelled. Nevertheless, just *how* important neuroimaging data will prove for understanding cognition remains to be seen.

Cognitive neuropsychology

In Chapter 5, Ashok Jansari introduces the last of the three methods that arguably has a neural basis. Cognitive neuropsychology is a field with a long history, having developed from a mix of research- and clinically-related concerns. The chapter introduces the topic in the context of its historical development, indicating the evolution and multiplicity of the goals of neuropsychology, and the varied techniques that neuropsychologists use to understand a patient's impairment and its possible significance for models of cognition.

To sense some of the complexity involved, this time you might like to imagine trying to work out the information-processing characteristics of your PC or Mac, from an analysis of its errors. More often than not, it is extremely difficult to gain an understanding of information processing from observing just one (impaired) computer. Perhaps through observing many different computers, and systematically observing the patterns of impairment, one might ultimately begin to uncover some of the structure of their information processes. Whatever the inherent difficulties the strategy faces, this is the position of the cognitive neuropsychologist with regard to human information processing or cognition.

The difficulty of drawing inferences from patterns of impairment to the nature of cognitive processes is much reduced by making certain assumptions, and the author discusses a number of these – subtractivity, for example. The chapter also details many of the techniques used by neuropsychologists, such as standardized tests and the use of experiments. The chapter deliberately avoids in-depth discussion of some techniques that are being increasingly used by neuropsychologists, however. Cognitive modelling and neuroimaging are frequently used in conjunction with neuropsychological findings, providing researchers with (hopefully) converging evidence from different sources. However, these techniques are detailed in Chapters 2, 3 and 4, and so no involved discussion of them is offered here.

Quantitative methods

In Chapter 6, Martin Le Voi offers what can be described as a conceptual treatment of statistical techniques for analysing data. Most of the foregoing chapters assume that, at some point in the research process, data will be gathered and analysed, and the appropriateness of an interpretation will depend in large part on the results of that analysis. For many students, statistical analysis seems off-putting. For some, it is chock full of intimidating formulae and algebra; for others, the conceptual underpinnings of the techniques are obscure. In Chapter 6, the author attempts to introduce the key concepts needed by psychologists in a way that only minimally relies on mathematical competence or confidence. From these beginnings, a number of different types of analysis are introduced, as well as some of their accompanying assumptions and limitations.

Chapter 6 includes reference to two kinds of computer-based exercise: spreadsheet exercises and SPSS exercises. Both types have been designed to assist students' understanding of the material covered in the chapter.

Spreadsheet exercises

The software for running these exercises can be found either (i) on the Course Software Resources CD-ROM for Open University DD303 students; students should follow the instructions on the CD-ROM packaging to install the software; or

(ii) on the Oxford University Press companion web site; students should navigate to **www.oup.com/uk/booksites/psychology** and follow the instructions for down-loading and installing the spreadsheets. Two formats of spreadsheet are available: Excel and StarOffice. StarOffice is provided on the Open University On-Line Applications disk for those DD303 students who do not have MS Excel.

Once installed, the spreadsheets can be found on the **Start/All Programs/ Cognitive Psychology** menu. Invoke the menu item called **Quantitative methods spreadsheets** and a folder window will open, containing two sub-folders, **Excel** and **StarOffice**. Double click on the relevant folder, depending on your spreadsheet package. Having opened the folder, double-click on the file specified in the exercise to open it.

SPSS exercises

To run these exercises you will need access to a computer running SPSS. The SPSS data files for the exercises can be found either (i) on the SPSS CD-ROM for Open University DD303 students; students should follow the instructions on the CD-ROM packaging to install the software; or (ii) on the Oxford University Press companion web site; students should navigate to **www.oup.com/uk/booksites/ psychology** and follow the instructions for downloading and installing the data files. Note: it is assumed that the reader already possesses some familiarity with using SPSS, and the exercises in Chapter 6 do not give detailed guidance on how to conduct analyses in SPSS. If further guidance is needed, readers should consult one of the many SPSS guides available. Chapter 6 suggests the use of one such book, Brace, Kemp and Snelgar (2003) *SPSS for Psychologists*, Palgrave Macmillan.

Once installed, SPSS data files referred to in Chapter 6 can be found by default either (i) in the folder **C:\DD303\SPSS data** for Open University DD303 students or (ii) in the folder **C:\Cognitive Psychology\SPSS Data** if downloaded from the Oxford University Press web site.

An omission?

For some, there will appear to be one key omission in the above list of cognitive psychological methods: experimentation. However, there are a number of reasons why experimentation does not feature in this volume as a topic in its own right. While the experimental method is certainly central to cognitive psychology, it is also key to much of psychology quite generally. Many students will have encountered something of the experimental method prior to learning about cognitive psychology. Most students encounter the practicalities of the experimental method – learning how to design and conduct experiments – in the context of laboratory classes and project work. And arguably the best means of teaching experimentation is to supervise students in conducting their own experimental work.

Hence, the focus in this volume is on methods where supervision of practical work is not the prime means of teaching. This includes methods for which student practical work would be impracticable and/or unethical, such as neuropsychology and neuroimaging; methods that students can study with the aid of computer-based exercises, such as connectionism and symbolic modelling; and those aspects related to the experimental method that can be studied outside the laboratory, such as ethics and quantitative methods.

Using this book

This volume has been designed to accompany the Open University's level 3 course in Cognitive Psychology (DD303), and serves as a companion volume to the main text for that course, *Cognitive Psychology*, edited by Nick Braisby and Angus Gellatly, and also published by Oxford University Press. Both volumes have been designed to serve students taking other courses in cognitive psychology as well, either as essential or recommended reading, and possess a number of features that we hope will serve well both students learning about cognitive psychology and educators teaching the subject.

Chapter structure

Each chapter of this *Methods Companion* has been structured according to certain conventions.

- An **emboldened term** signifies the introduction of a key concept or term that is either explicitly or implicitly defined in the surrounding text. The locations of these defined terms are also flagged in bold in the index. Note: emboldening is also used to highlight key terms, actions and buttons in the computer exercises in Chapter 2.

- Each chapter contains a number of **activities**. Often these may be simple thought exercises that may take no more than a minute or so. Others are more involved. Each activity has been integrated into the design of the chapter, and is aimed at enhancing students' understanding of the material. We recommend that student readers attempt as many of these activities as possible and, where appropriate, revisit them after completing each chapter.

- A number of the chapters contain **computer-based exercises** that illustrate key concepts and models. Software is provided for these exercises – on CD-ROM for Open University students, and available for download from the OUP companion web site for other readers. Guidance for installing and getting started with the software is given above, while detailed guidance on the exercises is given in the relevant chapter.

- The chapters in this book also make use of **text boxes**. Each box has been written to amplify a particular aspect of the material without interrupting the ongoing narrative. Though the boxes illuminate a wide range of issues, some focus on aspects of **research studies** and **methods**. Students may find they wish to finish a section before reading a particular box.

- Each substantive main section finishes with a **section summary**, often a bullet point list reminding the student of the key points established in that section. We hope that students will use these as useful barometers of their understanding and re-read sections where the summary points are not clearly understood.

- Each chapter makes a number of explicit **links** to other chapters in the book, often to specific numbered sections, and sometimes to chapters in the main book to which this is a companion (i.e. to Braisby and Gellatly, *Cognitive Psychology*). It would be tedious in the extreme to continually follow each and every link, flicking to the relevant pages and reading the relevant 'linked' section. Rather, these links are intended to help students perceive the interconnected nature of cognitive psychology, and identify connections between topics that otherwise might seem disparate. Of course, we hope that students will be motivated to follow some of these links either on first reading, or on a later reading, perhaps as a revision aid.

- For convenience, references to chapters in the volume to which this is a companion (Braisby and Gellatly, 2005, *Cognitive Psychology*, Oxford University Press) are emboldened in the text; e.g. **Rutherford (2005)**.

- As well as a list of references, each chapter ends with some specific suggestions for **further reading**. While each chapter is designed to be self-contained, inevitably some issues get less attention than they deserve, and so interested readers may wish to pursue some of these suggestions for a more in-depth treatment. Moreover, it is always worth approaching a topic from more than one direction – consulting different texts, including other general texts on cognitive psychology, can help achieve a richer understanding and we recommend this approach to all students.

Supporting a course in cognitive psychology

There are few restrictions on how one might use this text to supplement the teaching of a course in cognitive psychology or in methods in psychology more generally. The chapters in this book may be tackled in a number of different orders. Depending on the focus of the course, particular chapters may be omitted. The book as a whole presupposes relatively little prior knowledge of cognitive psychology on the part of a student. However, in some instances, later chapters may presuppose some limited knowledge of related earlier chapters, though this is usually explicitly indicated. Similarly, while all chapters are designed to be taught at the same level, some chapters tackle issues that might be considered more complex.

Companion volume

Accompanying this book is a companion publication *Cognitive Psychology*, edited by Braisby and Gellatly, published by Oxford University Press, and designed as the main teaching text for the Open University's level 3 course in Cognitive Psychology (DD303). *Cognitive Psychology* is divided into five parts. The first four focus on broad and well-established topic areas within cognitive psychology, such as perceptual processes and memory. The fifth considers a range of challenges, themes and issues – topics that have been thought to present challenges to the cognitive approach, such as emotion and consciousness; themes such as cognitive modelling and modularity; and issues such as the relation of cognition to biology.

Companion web site

This book and its companion volume *Cognitive Psychology* are associated with a companion web site (at **www.oup.com/uk/booksites/psychology**) that contains much additional material that can be used to further students' understanding and may be used in presenting a course in cognitive psychology. Materials include electronic versions of figures, experiment files, and the software, spreadsheets and data files referred to above.

Acknowledgements

Developing the Open University's level 3 course in Cognitive Psychology (DD303) has been a major undertaking, involving the production of two books, various pieces of software and associated files, audio materials, web sites and web-based materials, and numerous other additional items and activities. To say that such a course, and that this text, could not have been produced without the help and cooperation of a large number of people is an understatement. The following page lists all those without whom this enterprise would not have been possible, and to each I extend my grateful and sincere thanks, as I do to anyone omitted in error.

Nick Braisby

Milton Keynes, January 2005

Cognitive Psychology Course Team

This book was designed and produced for The Open University course DD303 *Cognitive Psychology*. The editors gratefully thank all those people, listed below, who have been involved in the process (based at The Open University, unless otherwise stated).

CORE COURSE TEAM:
> **Course Chair:** Nick Braisby
> **Course Manager:** Ingrid Slack
> **Core Team Members:** Sandy Aitkenhead; Nicola Brace; Angus Gellatly; Alison J.K. Green; Martin Le Voi; Bundy Mackintosh; Peter Naish; Graham Pike

Course Manager (rights): Ann Tolley
Course Secretaries: Marie Morris; Elaine Richardson
Additional Authors: Jackie Andrade (University of Sheffield); Peter Ayton (City University); Chris Barry (University of Essex); Simon Bignell (University of Essex); Martin A. Conway (University of Durham); Graham Edgar (University of Gloucestershire); Simon Garrod (University of Glasgow); Gareth Gaskell (University of York); Ken Gilhooly (University of Paisley); Olaf Hauk (MRC Cognition and Brain Sciences Unit); Graham J. Hitch (University of York); Emily A. Holmes (MRC Cognition and Brain Sciences Unit); Ashok Jansari (University of East London); Helen Kaye; Paul Mulholland; Mike Oaksford (Cardiff University); Mike Pilling; John Richardson; Andrew Rutherford (Keele University); Anthony J. Sanford (University of Glasgow); Stella Tickle; Tony Stone (London South Bank University); Stuart Watt (Robert Gordon University); Jenny Yiend (MRC Cognition and Brain Sciences Unit)
Course Reader: Matt Lambon Ralph (University of Manchester)
External Assessor: James Hampton (City University)
Media Project Manager: Lynne Downey
Production and Presentation Administrator: Richard Golden
Copublishing Adviser: Jonathan Hunt
Lead Editor: Chris Wooldridge
Editors: Alison Edwards; Kathleen Calder; Winifred Power (Freelance)
Designers: Tammy Alexander; Alison Goslin; Diane Mole
Graphic Artists: Janis Gilbert; Sara Hack
Picture Researcher: Celia Hart
eMedia Quality Promoter: Roger Moore
Software Designers: Ian Every; Maurice Brown; David Morris
Rights Adviser: Alma Hales
Contracts Executives: Katie Meade; Sarah Gamman
Compositors: Pam Berry; Lisa Hale; Phillip Howe
Print Buyer Controller: Lene Connolly
Assistant Print Buyer: Dave Richings

This publication forms part of an Open University course DD303 *Cognitive Psychology*. Details of this and other Open University courses can be obtained from the Student Registration and Enquiry Service, The Open University, PO Box 625, Milton Keynes, MK7 6YG, United Kingdom: tel. +44 (0)1908 653231, e-mail general-enquiries@open.ac.uk

Alternatively, you may visit the Open University website at http://www.open.ac.uk where you can learn more about the wide range of courses and packs offered at all levels by The Open University.

To purchase a selection of Open University course materials visit the webshop at www.ouw.co.uk, or contact Open University Worldwide, Michael Young Building, Walton Hall, Milton Keynes MK7 6AA, United Kingdom for a brochure. Tel. +44 (0)1908 858785; fax +44 (0)1908 858787; e-mail ouwenq@open.ac.uk

Ethics

Chapter 1

Bundy Mackintosh

1 Introduction

Debate about the values and ethical concerns of research that makes use of animals or human participants, or may impact their mental or physical well-being, has a long history and a continually evolving influence on the research community. Perhaps confusingly, many texts in fields such as psychology, medicine or the biological sciences will contain references to studies that seem very disturbing to the reader by current standards and would almost certainly fail to pass the scrutiny of modern ethical screening. As a result, reading about the studies of other, possibly eminent, investigators cannot be guaranteed to provide a guide to designing suitable research in the present, let alone research which would meet the needs of any future requirements (see, for example, Box 1.1).

1.1

Famously unethical? Milgram's studies on obedience

In the 1960s and 1970s at Yale University in the USA, Milgram completed a series of experiments to explore obedience in ordinary volunteers recruited from the community by newspaper advertisements (Milgram, 1963, 1974). During the course of the study, volunteers were induced to deliver what they thought to be dangerously intense electric shocks to a fellow participant. If you are not familiar with these studies, then it might be worth reflecting at this point on what obedience rates you might predict. What proportion of ordinary men (Milgram's participants were all male) do you think would obey instructions in a university experiment that they believed would involve delivering an electric shock that was both painful and possibly injurious or even lethal to a fellow participant? Milgram asked just this question of staff and students at Yale. In case these individuals were not sufficiently expert at judging human behaviour, he also asked 40 psychiatrists the same question. The former thought 1 per cent and the latter thought only 0.1 per cent would continue the experiment to its conclusion. The surprising and controversial outcome was that 65 per cent of participants complied with *all* conditions of the experiment. Even after relocating the entire study to run-down premises in a nearby town and repeating the procedure without the authority imparted by a prestigious university and university professor, obedience rates remained at a staggering 50 per cent.

In brief, the design of Milgram's experiment was as follows:

Participants were recruited to take part in an experiment on 'learning', for which they were paid. On arrival they thought they were drawing lots with another participant to decide who would be 'learner' and who would be 'teacher' in the experiment (in reality the draw was rigged so that the participant who had answered the advertisement would become the 'teacher'; the other participant, an actor working with the experimenter, became the 'learner'). The 'teacher' was to test the 'learner' on a paired-associate learning task. Errors were to be punished with an 'electric shock' through electrodes attached to the hands of the 'learner'. After each error the level of the electric shock was to be increased using switches on an elaborate 'hoax' electric generator console on which the higher levels of shock had labels such as 'danger', 'severe shock' and 'XXX' at the extreme end. The actor made many errors and cried out and protested as if they were receiving real electric shocks until the higher levels were reached, after which they fell silent. The experimenter instructed the participant to treat 'no response' to the paired-associate question as an error, which necessitated a further increase in shock level. That is, if the participant continued to the highest level of shock then the behaviour of the actor should have led the participant to believe that they might have electrocuted their fellow participant to the point of rendering them unconscious or even killing them. To be fair to the participants, many did question whether they should continue to the high levels of shock. At these points the experimenter instructed them to continue, with graded prompts to the effect that the experiment would be ruined if the participant did not continue. At the close of the session participants were fully debriefed. Despite the obvious distress that participants suffered in the course of this study, Milgram felt that the end justified the means. He felt his work provided profound insights into human nature and our understanding of the ability of ordinary humans to engage in, for instance, military atrocities, in the name of obedience.

ACTIVITY 1.1

Do you think Milgram's experiment (Box 1.1) would satisfy current ethical codes?

COMMENT

The answer is almost certainly 'no'. Participants were distressed by the experiment well beyond what they might have expected in their everyday lives. They were not able to give informed consent because they were misled about the procedures. They were not informed that they could withdraw at any point – on the contrary they were coerced into continuing.

Notions of informed consent and absence of harm lie at the centre of considerations about the ethical appropriateness of research. Those invited to participate in research should possess enough information to judge whether they wish to take part and, as a result of their participation, should not be left in a worse condition than when they began, either physically or emotionally. In the case of studies employing vulnerable participants, such as children, the elderly and those with learning disabilities, these safeguards should also extend to any carers. Such studies additionally raise issues concerning who should give informed consent to planned procedures.

Good ethical practice is not solely about making sure participants (and where relevant their carers) are treated with respect and protected from harm. The reputation of, and people's respect for, the researcher, their institution and the disciplines of psychology and the neurosciences in general are at stake. Adherence to ethical codes should not be seen as a hurdle to be jumped over. Ethical considerations force researchers to think about the *process* of conducting research, and not just research questions themselves. They therefore play a role in ensuring that research is professionally conducted and that participants not only enjoy the process but feel they are helping in some small way to further our knowledge and push back the frontiers of science. As with many enterprises, word of mouth has a powerful effect, so it is also in researchers' interests to pay attention to their participants' experience. Many areas of research could not proceed at all without the help of human participants. It would be foolish, therefore, to squander such a valuable resource; paying attention to ethical issues should ensure that both individual researchers and the profession as a whole do not do so.

The British Psychological Society (BPS) and the American Psychological Association (APA) publish ethical codes of conduct for psychologists which include sets of principles for conducting research with human participants (the BPS and APA guidelines are included as Appendix 1 to this book). Each organization expects its members to adhere to their guidelines, and the journals of each require all research accepted for publication to comply with these codes. Other countries, of course, have similar codes but at present the requirements of these two appear to dominate North American and European research in psychology and the neurosciences.

There has been a burgeoning of institutional structures to oversee ethical issues and most, perhaps all, universities and other institutions (such as hospitals and prisons) that carry out research with human participants or animals have their own ethical committees. These usually consist of a panel of experts, often also including laypersons, which may set rules that are more stringent and specific than those of the BPS or APA. Although it may be suggested by some that research ethics committees serve as much to protect institutions from litigation as to protect the interests of participants, their express purpose is to ensure that only worthwhile research that pays proper regard to the well-being of all concerned takes place. Funding bodies almost invariably insist on adherence to their own codes as well as requiring that local ethical clearance has been obtained before releasing funds, so that researchers must submit details of their project proposals (sometimes to several committees simultaneously) and obtain ethical approval before their work can go ahead. The complexity of this process is further confounded by the limited consensus about practice between different sets of guidelines and the sometimes quite idiosyncratic interpretation of them by ethics panel members. See Box 1.2 for discussion of some of the issues an ethics committee would expect to consider in deciding whether to approve a proposed research study.

1.2

Gaining approval from an ethics committee

Proposed studies have to be considered by at least one ethics committee; that is, a panel of experts (often including lay people) who are there to ensure that the study is worthwhile and that participants will not come to any harm as a result of participating in the research. Ethics committees are normally found in hospitals (for research with patients), universities (for research involving both students and community volunteers), and prisons (for research with offenders). Research with children, the disabled or the elderly may fall under one of these or may involve additional bodies. Overlapping interests may mean permission has to be sought from more than one committee. For instance, if a university lecturer is conducting research with patients with brain injury, both the university and local NHS panels would be involved. Before a piece of research can proceed, researchers have to submit for approval a summary of their research proposal to their own and any other relevant ethics committee.

The proposal will usually indicate:

- details of the host institution

- the background and rationale of the study

- the proposed methodology

- the participant recruitment, payment and data collection procedure

- methods for obtaining informed consent

- the duration and number of sessions with each participant

- the materials that will be used

- any physical or psychological risks or distress the researcher expects the participant might encounter as a result of taking part in the study, and what measures will be taken to deal with them.

- the proposed statistical analysis of the data

- who will have access to the data in original and/or anonymized form

- details of compliance with data protection legislation

- proposed dissemination of results

- specification of responsibilities for public indemnity

- the qualifications and experience of the investigator and/or research supervisor.

It is up to the researcher to submit to and obtain ethical clearance from an ethics panel. Once the proposal has been submitted the researcher may be invited to a meeting with the ethics committee where s/he would be asked to summarize the study and explain why it should be given ethical clearance. Ethics committee members can quiz the researcher on any aspect of the study and require that part (or all) of the study be amended before it can go ahead. If, however, the study appears to be straightforward and non-controversial, ethical clearance may be granted by post.

When getting to grips with the relevance of ethics to research and how to assess the ethical issues raised by particular studies, it is helpful to try to look at research proposals in the way that ethics committees do. This also helps to sharpen critical awareness of the whole research process.

Students are most certainly not immune from this scrutiny; indeed, it is a vital aspect of training to be a psychologist that students demonstrate sensitivity to ethical issues, and understanding of and compliance with all relevant guidelines.

It should be noted that this chapter does not attempt to consider the ethics of animal experiments in any detail. The ethics of using animals in research are both complex and controversial. The special conditions for research with, and the housing of, research animals in the UK and elsewhere is covered by stringent legal frameworks. Regulations are designed to minimize unnecessary discomfort to the animals commensurate with the benefits expected from the research. A full discussion of ethics in animal research probably also requires considering other forms of animal exploitation including methods of animal husbandry in food production, the treatment of working animals, the pet trade, and the effects on wild animals of disturbance, pollution and the destruction of natural habitats. These are very important issues. However, consideration of them would detract from the chapter's main aim of illuminating ethical questions as they relate to cognitive psychology – though cognitive psychology does make reference to work conducted with animals, research using human participants is the primary focus of study.

Summary of Section 1

- Ethical concerns have a long history and continue to influence the research community.
- Notions of informed consent and absence of harm lie at the centre of considerations about the ethical appropriateness of research.
- Adherence to ethical codes is important for the reputation of researchers and the discipline of psychology, and professional organizations such as the BPS and APA publish guidelines that their members are expected to follow.
- Before commencing a project, researchers must consider ethical aspects of their proposals and gain approval from one or more ethical committee.

2 Ethical approaches: deontology and consequentialism

A **deontological** approach to ethics focuses on the process of research itself and the intent and conduct of the investigator. This implies a set of principles that have a universal form driven by notions of honesty, justice, integrity and respect, that should be adhered to regardless of the place and circumstances surrounding any particular investigation. For example, consider the notion of 'informed consent'. Ethical considerations suggest that participants should freely give their agreement to the research process, understanding what processes will be involved. In addition, this might be assumed to encompass any consequences that could follow from publication or release of information into the public domain. In reality, some research questions require that participants cannot be fully informed of all details of the research procedures without, in the process, nullifying the potential outcomes.

Also, whilst an investigator certainly ought to take all possible steps to protect the identity and respect the sensitivity of their participants, it is not possible to anticipate all potential outcomes. It is also not reasonable to guarantee complete confidentiality if the participants themselves transgress laws or moral or ethical codes. Indeed there is a legal requirement on the part of researchers (and others) to pass on information concerning, for example, the abuse of children or other vulnerable individuals.

A **consequential** approach to ethics does not assume an inviolate set of rules, but regards the situation and the consequences of actions as of primary relevance. Concentrating on the outcomes of research, such as increased knowledge or later advantages, for instance relief of suffering, moves the researcher towards making a cost–benefit analysis. In the extreme, however, a position in which the ends justify the means could allow a dangerous precedent, opening the potential of justifying real harm to a few individuals in the knowledge that information thus obtained may bring substantial benefit to many. In effect, this is the legal standpoint that most Western cultures currently take towards research on animals, although it is clear that many individuals within these cultures strongly object to this position.

In reality, the tension between the deontological and consequential standpoints is usually resolved by taking a somewhat middle position, but the conflict between them can and does arise concerning some sensitive issues. The requirement therefore falls upon researchers, academics, and students to consider the full context of the ethical position within which research can take place and the often conflicting rights and responsibilities of a potentially wide range of affected parties extending well beyond the immediate confines of the research situation.

Summary of Section 2

- A deontological approach to ethics focuses on details of the research process itself, and whether underlying ethical principles have been adopted.
- A consequential approach to ethics considers the consequences or outcomes of research to be of primary relevance.
- Most ethics committees will combine both approaches when reaching their decisions.

3   Ethical issues

Ethical questions have become so central to thinking about research methodology that, even when only reading about the work of others, consideration of ethics will help make sense of particular design choices and maintain an awareness of the complex and ever changing ethical climate within which psychologists necessarily work. Before embarking on research at any level, it is vital to consult and satisfy appropriate ethical guidelines and codes of conduct. In order to do so you will have to plough through the detailed and technical prose in which they are (necessarily) written. This chapter aims to highlight some of the important principles for research involving human participants whilst avoiding the minute detail and precise language that these guidelines need to employ.

Box 1.3 discusses a task, paired-associate learning, which is uncontroversial in itself but uses materials that raise ethical questions.

1.3

An uncontroversial task?

In a research procedure, the task itself may be uncontroversial but the choice of material may be sensitive. For example, examine the following sample instructions and materials for a paired-associate memory task that ask the participant to form mental images of the 'to be remembered' items. (Of course, instructions for the experiment proper would fully explain the purpose of the experiment and the requirement to later recall words.)

Sample instructions

In this study we are exploring the effects of different types of imagery on memory for pairs of words. We would like you to produce a vivid mental image of yourself associated with each of these word pairs and afterwards you will receive a list of the first words of the pairs and we will test your ability to recall the second word from each pair.

Sample materials

(a) 'Neutral' materials	(b) 'Emotional' materials
baby – bath	murder – rape
kettle – drink	death – grief
nail – hit	spider – face
pork – roast	torture – agony
sandwich – bite	slaughter – holocaust
pedestrian – crossing	
kitchen – sink	
bat – ball	
bleach – dustbin	
match – burn	

Comment

Other and more controversial materials could be used, such as swear words, sexually explicit words, racist insults and so on. Here we have chosen not even to provide examples in these categories – would it be ethical to do so?

For the task described, forming a mental image of oneself associated with the emotional items described might cause distress (as might imaging oneself associated with swear words, racist or sexually explicit words). Would some other task using this same material be more acceptable? Perhaps an emotional Stroop task might prove acceptable instead – in this task, participants try *not* to

→

read the words but are asked to name the colour of the ink in which the words are printed. (See, for example, **Yiend and Mackintosh, 2005**.)

However, any of the words listed above, and many in the categories where we have not listed words, are likely to appear with some regularity in the media. It should therefore be acceptable to make (careful) use of them provided participants have some warning of their nature. But as will already be clear there are no hard and fast rules about what is acceptable and what is not. In addition, different types of participant will vary in their sensitivity to materials; a spider phobic might be particularly vulnerable to the 'spider – face' example, for instance.

ACTIVITY 1.2

(a) Deciding whether material is ethically suitable is not at all straightforward, as Box 1.3 shows. Indeed, some of the words in the 'neutral' list might take on quite different meanings if the pairings were rearranged. Suppose a researcher wanted to conduct a similar experiment, but their 'neutral' materials consisted of the following paired-associates:

bleach – drink

baby – burn

bat – bite

pedestrian – hit

Would asking participants to form mental images for such materials raise ethical concerns? Try to consider the arguments for and against, and judge whether you would wish to approve the study.

(b) Ethical objections were made by one ethical committee when the word 'pork' appeared in a list of words to be learned outside awareness on the grounds that it might offend some religious beliefs. Because presentation was to occur outside awareness the committee felt that the participants would be unable to object and therefore more than usual care was required. What would be your decision in this case?

3.1 Competence

Researchers are expected to work within the boundaries of their own competence. This applies not just in the context of administering certain research procedures, but also in terms of anticipating and dealing with their potential consequences. For example, when dealing with complex equipment, such as described in Chapter 4 on neuroimaging techniques, it is clearly vital that the researcher is able to attach electrodes safely and efficiently, or screen and prepare a participant for a brain scan. These procedures are often so specialized that, although the researcher must have a good notion of what is involved and the necessary safety issues, detailed aspects of the procedures might be devolved to other members of a research team, such as radiologists in the case of PET scans. The researcher's competence must therefore extend to knowing who else will be essential, or perhaps on call, before investigations can begin.

At the other end of the spectrum are procedures that require relatively trivial technical competence such as issuing questionnaires or observing behaviour. Since it is deceptively difficult to conduct good research using these methods, ethical considerations should also include whether there could be flaws that risk wasting the participants' time. It is often difficult, especially for those outside the research area, to judge whether the value of the research warrants the participant time spent. Ethics committees are therefore more likely to concentrate on how questionnaire length, content or wording, or the nature of the observations, might affect those involved. Appropriate competence in this sphere includes some anticipation of what might upset or offend – for instance, in the context of religious or local cultural values, or in terms of emotional reactions to materials.

Investigators need to be competent and professional in setting up and conducting their own research but it is equally important that they refrain from claiming or implying that they have qualifications, affiliations or skills that they do not possess. The general public are inclined to misunderstand the nature of a psychologist's specialist knowledge. Frequently, they mistakenly assume that psychologists are medically trained. Many are not entirely clear of the distinctions, if any, between psychiatry, psychotherapy, and psychology. As anyone calling themselves a psychologist or admitting to studying the topic is likely to have discovered, the uninitiated can often assume they have almost magical abilities. Psychologists may be expected to offer insights on problems ranging from 'how to train my dog', 'how to solve family relationship problems', or 'how to be happy' to 'how to stop my child misbehaving at school'. In addition, psychologists are not infrequently expected to possess a superhuman ability to mind-read and uncover people's innermost thoughts and motives. These expectations provide a powerful tool for potential harm or loss of dignity. Caution should be exercised if advice is sought where the investigator is not qualified to help. Even allowing a participant to pour out their heart, without offering advice, could lead to embarrassment and loss of dignity when they later discover that psychology does not, after all, mean therapy. The boundaries of expertise need to be very cautiously applied.

3.2 Informed consent

Investigations or interventions should not normally be carried out without the valid and informed consent of those taking part. Steps should be taken to ensure that the nature of the process, and any anticipated consequences, have been understood. Undue coercion should not take place through inappropriate financial inducement, or unequal positions of perceived power or status of those involved. In the case of patients, or those in care or in prison, it should be made clear that participation will in no way influence their future care or treatment prospects. Full disclosure of research procedures should generally occur. Information should only be withheld as part of a necessary aspect of the investigation, in which case information should be provided retrospectively. The rights of those with reduced or no capacity to give free informed consent, such as children, the elderly, those with learning disabilities, or those in care or in prison, should be specially safeguarded. In these cases, consent should instead be obtained from relevant others such as carers, guardians, close family members and/or those who have appropriate legal authority. In observational research, it is only deemed acceptable to proceed without prior consent in situations in which an individual might normally expect to be viewed by others, such as in a public space. Sample consent forms are provided in Box 1.4.

1.4

Three examples of consent forms

(A)   Informed consent form for an experiment with adult participants

Attentional Processes in Cigarette Smokers

I agree to take part in the above investigation. The purpose of the investigation has been explained to me, and I understand that confidentiality will be maintained at all times and that I can withdraw at any time.

The investigation will involve me taking part in a short test of reaction times on a computer, providing a sample of saliva and completing a questionnaire about my feelings.

☐ I have read the information sheet

☐ I have had the opportunity to ask questions and discuss the study

☐ I have received satisfactory answers to my questions

☐ I have received sufficient information about the study

☐ I am willing to take part in the study

Researcher
Signed   *Date*
....

Participant
Signed   *Date*
....

Name
....

Study approved by .... Ethics Committee

(B)   Parental consent form for an experiment with children

I have received the information leaflet explaining the nature of this study and my child's contribution to the research. By signing below I indicate that I give consent for my child to take part, and for any data I and my child provide to be used for research purposes. I understand that our contribution will remain completely anonymous and that I am free to withdraw my child, or my child's results, from this study at any time without giving a reason.

Child's name: (please print)...

Parent/guardian's name: (please print)..

Parent/guardian's signature:...........................date:.................

Please note: In order to maintain anonymity this consent form will be retained separately from any data that you or your child contributes

(C)   Consent form for an online research study

After an explanation of the nature of the task, including the time required to complete it online, the following consent section appeared, requiring a mouse click to continue:

The nature and purpose of this study has been explained to me and by pressing the 'consent' button below I am giving my consent to take part. I understand any information that I provide will remain anonymous and that researchers will not be able to identify the contribution of any particular volunteer. I understand that I am free to withdraw from this study at any stage without giving reasons. I can simply close the browser window to abort my responses without any information being sent.

This study has been approved by the Open University Human Participants and Materials Ethical Committee (Ref: ....) and conforms to the ethics code of the British Psychological Society.

3.3   Withdrawal

Signing a consent form does not diminish the right that all participants have to withdraw from the research process at any stage. Indeed it is important that investigators make this clear from the outset and it is frequently a required clause within any consent form. Not only do participants have the right to terminate any session or agreement as they wish but they should retain their right to withdraw their own data, including such material as video/audio recordings, even retrospectively.

Participants might wish to withdraw for reasons ranging from distress to boredom, from misunderstanding of the requirements of the study to disdain for the potential outcomes of the research. Retrospective withdrawal of consent could arise, for example, when parents realize that an apparently innocent video of their small child snatching a toy from playmates was a precursor to serious bullying. If a child sadly dies or suffers serious illness, parents may find it distressing to think of researchers pouring over an early snapshot of their lives. Box 1.5 discusses other cases of withdrawal from research.

1.5

Withdrawal from research

When the nature and duration of a study is realistically explained to volunteers, it is rare for them to withdraw before completion. If the session is very nearly finished it might be reasonable to point this out to the withdrawing participant, but they should not be coerced into finishing the task. It is important to bear in mind that participants may not wish to explain the real reason for withdrawal, which could be quite unrelated to the tasks they are completing (they could be suffering from indigestion rather than objecting to the investigation).

Just as rare is the case where it may be necessary to withdraw the research from the participant (this problem is somewhat more likely to occur when payment is given for participation, attracting some recruits who are not primarily interested in helping with research). The following are examples of problems that could arise:

- The researcher could find themselves testing someone who swears and complains about the task and that this type (or all types) of psychological research is valueless.

- The participant may be very lonely and more interested in a friendly chat than concentrating on the task.

- The previous evening's, or the current day's, intake of drugs (alcohol or otherwise) may render the participant comatose in front of a less than exciting computer task, so they fall asleep.

Under such circumstances, a 'strategic retreat' is recommended – one that curtails the session without loss of dignity to the participant. The session could end early with only some tasks completed, or 'equipment failure' could terminate the session more abruptly. If payment was promised, then it should be given for the full amount of time that the participant expected to attend, regardless of how long the session actually lasts.

Withdrawal at a later date

Imagine that a parent has consented to their child being filmed as part of an observational study on pre-school cooperative play. During testing the child is possessive and has a tantrum which the parent finds a little embarrassing. Nevertheless, they agree that the researcher can use a video clip of their child as an example in illustrating their research findings in journal articles, talks and conference proceedings. A year or two later the same child is diagnosed with autism. Looking back to the earlier incident the parent is now anxious that the early signs were already visible. The thought of qualified psychologists pouring over such details of their child's early problems is upsetting to the parent who then withdraws consent for the researchers to make further use of the video clip.

3.4 Deception

Deception can take many forms. For instance, the following are all examples of deception of one kind or another:

- misleading participants about what their involvement will entail, either with respect to the nature of the tasks to be fulfilled, any discomfort they may feel, the time that they will take

- failing to acknowledge the nature or extent of any possible consequences of the study

- introducing confederates of the experimenter as if they are fellow participants or ordinary members of the public

- making dishonest claims about the value of the outcomes of the investigation.

Withholding of prior information about procedures may sometimes be justified when such knowledge would interfere with or invalidate the purpose of the investigation, but thorough debriefing is essential. On the whole, methods are not acceptable if participants are consistently left feeling they would have withdrawn or never taken part had the full procedure or true purpose been revealed earlier. Box 1.6 discusses a hypothetical case of deception.

1.6

Deception: is it acceptable to lie or mislead in the interests of science?

Box 1.1 provided you with a clear example of participants being misled about the nature of an experiment in which they agreed to take part. Below is a further example. You might consider whether you would find it acceptable if you were a member of an ethics committee and, if so, whether you would require any extra safeguards or procedures as a condition of your acceptance. As part of your considerations you need to think about whether the study could have been conducted equally successfully if fuller information about its true nature had been given beforehand.

Incidental learning

During a statistics lecture the lecturer made an excuse to his class of undergraduates and left the room, apparently to collect some handouts he had asked his secretary to copy. During his absence, two 'workmen' entered the lecture room, and unscrewed the whiteboard from the wall and removed it from the room. A 'porter' wearing distinctive uniform walked into the room during the procedure and walked behind the whiteboard. He rapidly reversed his jacket whilst behind the board and emerged wearing a different coloured uniform. He appeared to check some details with the two 'workmen' and they then all left the room. On his return, the maths lecturer explained that there had been a theft and handed out questionnaires asking the class to recall all they could about the incident. He asked everyone to put their name on the questionnaire and later the same day interviewed several students about their recollections, including questions aimed to determine whether they had noticed the change in uniform of the porter.

Note: Research has shown that it is quite likely that the students would not have noticed the change of clothes – indeed experiments suggest that the porter could have been substituted for another individual and even this gross change could have gone undetected.

ACTIVITY 1.3

Box 1.6 describes a study on incidental learning. As described, the study could not have taken place if students had been forewarned as to its purpose. But was this deception ethical? Take a few moments to consider whether the study was ethical, and how it might have been modified to circumvent ethical concerns.

COMMENT

Your consideration of this case may well generate more questions than answers. However, those questions can, in turn, help in deciding whether to grant ethical approval. Some questions that you might have considered are:

- Is it acceptable to deceive the students at all?

- How long can they be left thinking that a theft has taken place? Should they be debriefed immediately?

- Will belief that a theft has taken place under their very noses be distressing?

- Can the experimenter make use of these results without first getting the students to consent to having their data used this way?

- Would it be more acceptable if the class were psychology students for whom participation in such a study, and the time taken to do so, might be justified in terms of a learning experience?

3.5   Confidentiality and privacy

Information about research participants must be considered highly confidential, particularly if it includes anything of a sensitive nature. Data that include personal identifiers cannot be shared with other researchers without the consent of the participants. When research is disseminated it should not be possible to identify individual participants either directly or through the use of a thin disguise. Where it is necessary to retain personally identifiable information, where possible this should be held separately from other data which should be rendered anonymous as soon as possible. This is commonly achieved by providing individuals with an identity code. This code is used to distinguish participants' data, but the key to the code is held, along with any other necessary personal information, in a separate encrypted file.

Investigators should be careful not to divulge information obtained during sessions, even where this was not necessarily relevant to the research enterprise. If you recall from the discussion on competence in Section 3.1, some participants divulge all sorts of personal information thinking that this is relevant and/or appropriate. This privileged information should never be shared with others in a way that risks identifying the participant or anyone else that they mention (except in rare cases where there is danger of actual or potential harm to the participant or others). In the UK, specific rules associated with personal information are enshrined in the Data Protection Act (see Appendix 2), and equivalent legislation is in place in many other countries. Researchers need to be aware of current requirements surrounding storage and sharing of data. There are limited occasions when the breaking of confidentiality is not only acceptable but actually required by law. These are generally situations in which a participant divulges information about actual or intended criminal offences such as domestic violence or child abuse.

3.6   Risks

Investigators have a responsibility to ensure that taking part in their study will not expose participants to unnecessary risks that could have been anticipated. Of course, crossing the street or walking down stairs bring with them a small but recognizable risk of accident. What is deemed acceptable in a research setting is a degree of risk that a participant might expect to willingly encounter in their normal everyday, but not necessarily working, life. This distinction between working and everyday life is crucial of course, since those in the armed forces, for example, who may be regularly at risk, even of death, in the course of their duties, cannot expect a lesser standard of care in comparison with others when they freely volunteer in a research setting. Participants should not be coerced into taking risks that they would normally be reluctant to undertake, nor should they be induced to do so through the offer of financial reward. Participants must receive sufficient information to judge risks for themselves and be asked about factors that might make them vulnerable. Risks fall broadly into three categories: physical, emotional and social.

Potential physical risks are clearly paramount when using drugs or invasive or highly technical methods, such as electrophysiology or brain-imaging techniques, but basic health and safety issues must be considered in all situations. The testing environment as well as the equipment must be safe for its purpose. Physical risks can be created or exacerbated by pre-existing conditions, an issue that may be especially relevant if testing patients. Magnetic resonance imaging (MRI) techniques provide particularly emotive examples. Because of the very high strength of the magnetic field generated in this imaging technique, considerable force will be exerted on any metal substance in or on the body. As an example, MRI safety courses give dire warnings about walking into the scanning room carrying anything metal, say a hammer. Such items are liable to be snatched out of one's hand by the force of the magnetic field and travel at high speed towards the centre of the scanner and smash into it, and/or its occupant, causing potentially devastating damage and harm. Any metal lodged or implanted within the body of the potential participant, such as shrapnel, metal clips, valves or plates could be in danger of being dislodged, and any electronic device, such as a pacemaker or implanted hearing aid, may catastrophically malfunction. Clearly, researchers must be fully aware of these issues. Participants, and anyone else present, must be carefully screened and questioned, and any removable metal items set aside before they are allowed near the scanner.

Most procedures are far less risky, but still require routine precautions such as ensuring that electrical equipment is regularly tested for safety, that noise levels are not too high, that wires do not present a danger by trailing across floors, and so on. However, even sitting quietly at a computer screen can constitute a hazard for some. For instance, a rapidly flickering computer screen can impose risks for those vulnerable to epilepsy. It is up to the researcher to be as informed as possible about any likely problems.

Emotional risks are potentially always present, particularly when participants might be upset or feel humiliated when they find tasks difficult or tiring, especially as they are unlikely to realize that tests are often specifically devised to ensure relatively high error rates to avoid ceiling effects. But special care is required when testing involves deliberately manipulating emotions or includes vulnerable populations. For example, the elderly, highly anxious or depressed individuals, or patients with neurological damage (and particularly someone who is all of the above) may be especially sensitive to making errors, or become confused or react strongly to the use of emotional materials (see, for example, Box 1.3). Emotion research may necessitate using materials that are deliberately emotional such as pictures or videos showing threatening or distressing scenes, or may include inducing negative mood as part of a procedure (see, for example, **Yiend and Macintosh, 2005**). Emotional risks may also follow if cultural or religious values are violated, or if participants feel they, or their gender, sexual orientation, racial or religious affiliations are being demeaned or discriminated against by the process or materials used in the investigation. It is not always easy to anticipate what might raise concerns for participants, and investigators may need to seek advice. When these types of risk are inherent in the research, it is particularly important that potential recruits to the study are fully informed of the nature of the study and the materials at or before the stage at which they consent to participate. It is also vital that procedures are in place to deal sympathetically and appropriately with any distress that might arise (see Section 3.8 on debriefing).

Social risks are often hard to define and can be quite subtle, but could include encouraging, or potentially creating, discriminatory attitudes or behaviour by appearing to provide support for these attitudes in the materials used or the behaviour of investigators or their collaborators.

3.7   Recruitment and payment

Recruitment and initial contact with potential participants should follow the same guidelines as the research process itself. That is, any message conveyed during the recruitment procedure should provide honest information about what is expected and should not make exaggerated claims for the effectiveness of the research (or products, if any, to be tested). Some research requires participants to have particular characteristics, such as being within a specified age range or educational background, being bilingual, having English as a first language, or having a history of specific physical or emotional disorder. In these cases investigators should seek neither to cause offence, upset or alienation of any particular group nor to inadvertently give negative labels to target groups.

Payment for time and expense should not be offered in such a way as to coerce potential participants into taking greater risks than they might otherwise agree to within their normal lifestyle. Some ethics committees do not think it appropriate to pay participants who have been recruited because they have particular medical conditions, since this is seen to constitute inappropriate pressure to take part.

3.8   Debriefing

In all studies, participants should expect to receive some general information about the study to which they are contributing and its purpose. Where deception or an unexpected aspect of the procedure was involved this should be explained and reasons for the deception or withholding of information justified. In cases where there may be specific risks, the debriefing procedures should be carefully thought out. For instance, some experiments in emotion research include procedures intended to induce either a negative or positive mood during the session. It is important to check that participants' moods have returned to pre-experiment levels, and if necessary use procedures to repair mood before they leave. The most obvious danger is that a negative mood will persist, causing distress and disruption, but it is possible to imagine that inducing an overly positive mood could present just as great a problem. For instance, leaving the testing session with 'not a care in the world' could be a danger if it encouraged rash or risky behaviour. A euphoric individual could feel invincible, or convinced that this was their lucky day for a hefty bet at the races, or a purchase on the stock market. Debriefing and especially mood repair may require time that should be allowed for in the testing schedule. Additionally, it may necessitate organizing back-up from clinically qualified personnel or providing information directing participants towards professional help. The particular requirements of the debriefing period should be part of the risk assessment for the study. Investigators should attempt to anticipate problems that might arise due to their research intervention and make contingency plans to take account of them. Participants, and if necessary their relatives or carers, should be given a route to contact the investigator or their team if problems should persist or arise some time after the testing session.

3.9 Feedback and conveying specialist information

Debriefing about the purpose and significance of the research project is a separate issue from giving feedback to participants about their individual level of performance or scores on tests and questionnaires. Where, for instance, children's developmental milestones are estimated, or IQ or personality tests or questionnaires measuring emotional vulnerability are given, caution should be exercised about whether feedback should be provided, and if so how. In many cases it is best to withhold detailed feedback to avoid the information being misused or misinter-preted. However, it is often desirable to explain why this will be the case, or the investigator could (with honesty) indicate that not enough is known about the tests to be able to make a valid comparison with the scores of other people. In brain-imaging procedures, consideration should be given as to how to proceed if a scan should reveal abnormalities, such as brain tumours, about which the participant was not previously aware, or deterioration of an existing condition beyond that expected.

3.10 Colleagues and students

It is an investigator's responsibility to ensure that any assistants, students or colleagues working with them on a project also adhere to the appropriate ethical guidelines. They should encourage fellow researchers to follow ethical guidelines and bring the guidelines to their attention if they consider that they are not doing so.

3.11 The safety of the researcher

The sections above concentrate mainly on the experience of the participant in research. However, the safety and well-being of the researcher themselves must be an additional focus of attention. Although often falling within the more general remit of 'health and safety at work', the researcher's own well-being must not be overlooked. This will include their response to the research situation or materials, the reaction to participants' responses, or the risks associated with testing participants alone outside working hours or in the participant's own home.

3.12   Personal conduct

It is imperative that investigators ensure that their research procedures are ethically sound and this includes how they themselves behave towards all those they contact in the course of their research. They must conduct themselves in a professional manner that in no way takes advantage of their privileged position in terms of access, status or presumed power over their participants (or participants' relatives, carers and so on). This includes being polite, punctual and considerate in their dealings, and refraining from any practices that might impair their ability or professional judgement (such as taking drugs or alcohol). Hopefully, it goes without saying that those undertaking research should never exploit the research setting for financial or political advantage nor gratification of personal desires.

3.13   Internet-mediated research

Increasing use of the Internet as a tool for research opens new areas of ethical consideration. Most, if not all, of the issues discussed in this chapter still apply when researchers contact their participants over the Internet. It is often only the format that must change. However, new issues are created by the absence of direct contact between investigator and participant. This can be highly relevant to the outcome of the research enterprise as there can be no control over the circumstances prevailing whilst the study takes place. The researcher cannot be sure who is participating, or whether they are providing honest information about themselves. This merely exaggerates an existing problem in human participant research, but in face-to-face contact it is usual to be able to verify at least the sex of the participant and their approximate age. Even the accuracy of these simple statistics cannot be assumed over the Internet. There are separate methodological issues also. It is up to the researcher, for instance, to arrange (or attempt to arrange) to debar repeat attempts by the same participant, or a group of friends contributing together. Special techniques may be required to compensate for the lack of the experimenter. For instance, to thwart obvious cheating in a memory experiment, the online 'back' button may need to be effectively deactivated or bypassed to prevent a return to the 'to be remembered' material once recall is required. These are essentially practical rather than ethical issues.

From an ethical standpoint, as with all research formats, it is important that the participant is properly informed about the nature of the study, including how long it will take; that they understand they are free to withdraw and that their information is held confidentially (and preferably anonymously); and that they are offered information and debriefing at the end of the study. After receiving the relevant information, consent must be sought by a device such as clicking on a 'consent' button (see Box 1.4(C)). Because researchers cannot be sure of the age of any potential participants, they need to be cautious about the material presented. In the absence of the investigator in person, some mode of contact should be provided, usually an email address, in case worries or concerns arise from the research. Harvesting information from newsgroups and web pages requires care over confidentiality, and infiltrating discussion groups and 'seeding' them with the investigator's own information raises the usual issues of deceit and manipulation that arise in many non-Internet studies. These issues are, to some extent, variations on themes that arise when questioning the ethics of observing people in public places without their consent, or when researchers act as participant observers and their own behaviour alters that of the group.

Internet methods allow interesting alternatives on the theme of deception. For instance, because there is no personal contact it is a simple matter to investigate the influence of the apparent sex/race/religion/disability, etc. of the investigator merely by adapting the text or providing (misleading) pictorial information. Of course, the participant may suspect the deception and, in any case, ease of deception means that the honesty of the respondent can be equally suspect! However, there is some evidence that the anonymity of the computer, in comparison with an investigator present in person, is helpful when completing sensitive questionnaires. Participants may be prepared to reveal more personal information via a computer keyboard than with pencil-and-paper methods.

Box 1.7 discusses the related issue of ethical considerations in relation to the media, and specifically in connection with 'reality' TV programmes.

1.7

Ethics and the media: anything goes?

Not uncommonly, researchers and students alike will complain that the ethical codes that constrain research seem to go out of the window when the media are involved, when public entertainment or public 'information' are the criteria rather than scientific endeavour. Invasion of privacy, intrusion, embarrassment, loss of dignity, deliberate distress or humiliation are not uncommon, and whilst some of these are entered into with willing consent (perhaps aided by the promise of fame or financial coercion), many are not.

A well-known social psychology experiment by Zimbardo (1975, 1999) was recreated for a television series in which recruits took the part of 'prisoners' or 'guards' and lived in a specially created set. This is not unusual and there have been many 'reality' TV shows requiring participants to live on set, to obey strict rules of conduct, to complete tasks and challenges that have not been explained in advance, to be constantly on camera and to be denied contact with their family and friends. It would be extremely unlikely that these procedures would be accepted by a research ethics panel, yet there are panels that consider the ethics of TV productions and these programmes must have been scrutinized. This is not, by any means, the only area where such an obvious double standard applies. In the ethics of animal welfare, the rules applied to the care and conditions of animals maintained for research insist on standards (space per animal, temperature regulation, cleanliness, air conditions and so on) that far exceed those of farm animals maintained for food. You may consider whether it is appropriate that ethical rules differ depending on whether science, entertainment or food is the aim. However, these contrasts merely serve to highlight the many inconsistencies in all human activities. Ethical considerations change with context, culture and time; one thing we can be fairly sure about is that the debate about what is appropriate in research, and elsewhere, is not about to end soon.

ACTIVITY 1.4 ────────────────────────────────

Consider a 'reality' TV programme with which you have some familiarity. How well does the programme stand up to ethical scrutiny? For each of the main issues discussed in Section 3, try to decide whether the programme deals with the issue satisfactorily. If you are unsure, think about what further information you would need.

Summary of Section 3

- Before embarking on research at any level, researchers must ensure that their proposed research will satisfy appropriate ethical guidelines, concerning at least the following issues:
  - competence
  - consent
  - withdrawal
  - deception
  - confidentiality and privacy
  - risks
  - recruitment and payment
  - debriefing
  - feedback and conveying specialist information
  - colleagues and students
  - the safety of the researcher
  - personal conduct.
- Internet-mediated research raises additional practical and ethical questions.

4 Special cases

Whilst the sections above should apply equally to all studies, it is worth highlighting the kinds of special issues that might be particularly relevant to some of the studies mentioned in this and its companion volume. This helps to increase awareness of the types of issues that might arise in any investigation.

4.1 Work with patients

Ethical issues surrounding work with patients begin well before they are even invited to participate in research. Procedures for identifying those who might fulfil the criteria for inclusion in a study, and then making initial contact with them, must not breach the confidentiality of the medical records held by health professionals. Once contact has been made, are patients able to give informed consent to help with the research? If not, who will act in their best interests and make a decision on their behalf? Is it possible to research brainwave sensitivity in coma patients, for instance, if no relatives are visiting who might provide consent? Special care must be taken not to exacerbate patients' condition, overtax their ability, humiliate them, nor insensitively bring to their attention deficiencies or abnormalities of which they were previously unaware. Patients who agree to help with research should not be 'over tested' by a whole series of researchers. Thus researchers and their colleagues must seek to make arrangements to space out testing sessions to avoid exploitation. Special consideration and respect needs to be given to those caring for these patients. See Box 1.8 for further discussion of such issues.

1.8

Exploitation or valuable contribution? The use of patients in research

Most psychologists have heard of HM whose memory problems are almost invariably reported in introductory texts (see **Rutherford, 2005**). Consider the ethics of asking HM to take part in a research project. He won't remember who you are even if you have met previously. He won't remember any previous testing sessions. Within a short time of describing the procedures he will forget you even mentioned them. How can he give consent? If someone gives consent on his behalf, are they allowing researchers to exploit his disability in a way that is demeaning? What alternative activities would occupy his time if researchers were denied the opportunities to include him in their research? Is his quality of life (or that of those who care for him) enhanced or diminished by his contribution? There are no straightforward answers to these questions. HM has contributed many hours of his time in the interests of research and without doubt his contribution has been very valuable. There are a number of other patients who are 'in demand' for research purposes; some are too handicapped by their disability to take up normal paid employment, but many seem to enjoy taking part and the interest shown in them; they often build up strong personal relationships or friendships with researchers for whom they give very generously of their time.

Patients who are sufficiently rehabilitated (or working towards this) to have gained some independence may be held back if testing sessions take up their valuable time, or leave them too tired to cope with their own everyday tasks. On the other hand, sometimes carers welcome the arrival of a researcher, who will 'occupy' their 'charge' for a time, or at least provide someone with whom a normal conversation can take place, and a break in an otherwise constrained routine. Each case must be treated as unique, and the pros and cons of contributing to research assessed for all those involved. When 'one more patient with frontal lobe damage' is required for a project, it is important not to take advantage of their goodwill and coerce the patient or family into taking part when this may be disruptive to their routine or harmful to their well-being.

4.2 Brain imaging

Participants in either PET (positron emission tomograpy) scanning or MRI (magnetic resonance imaging) must be screened before they participate. Potentially intrusive questions must be asked and researchers need to exercise sensitivity whilst doing so even though the process may be routine from their standpoint. For instance, for PET scanning, only women beyond the menopause can take part since exposure to even the minute doses of radioactive substances used might constitute a risk for an unborn foetus. Women may be embarrassed or insulted if asked for this information insensitively. Likewise, screening questions that are used before MRI procedures can take place involve asking about previous brain and other operations, the presence of clips or metal fittings in the body, pacemakers, the possible presence of shrapnel and the possession of tattoos (which apparently contain metal). The scanning experience itself can be lengthy and the participant has to remain very still for quite long periods. PET involves injection of radioactive substances, whilst the MRI scan involves potentially claustrophobic confinement within the bore of the apparatus and when scanning is taking place the machine is very noisy. Participants may find these conditions unacceptable, particularly if they have an anxious disposition (see Chapter 4 for more details of these techniques).

4.3 Emotion research

Some of the sections above have considered a few of the special issues that become relevant when researchers work with individuals who are within or close to the clinical range for emotional disorders, such as anxiety and depression. Special care has to be taken that the testing situation itself is neither unduly upsetting nor likely to trigger an emotional episode after the event. When emotional material is presented, participants need to be warned ahead, and sufficiently early in the recruitment process that they feel able to withdraw without guilt or embarrassment. It is good practice to show them examples before they begin if the material is extreme. Participants need to be fully warned if they are to be asked about their feelings during the course of the study. They should not be made to feel belittled or vulnerable by being overtly categorized as falling within a particular emotional grouping (e.g. by being labelled as 'high in neuroticism' or 'depressed'). Procedures may need to be put into place to ensure that the participant's mood has returned to normal at the end of the session and that contact details are provided in case problems arise later. Researchers themselves may need to be given special support if they habitually deal with participants who become upset during the course of investigations.

4.4 Researching with children

The ethical issues discussed in this chapter raise special problems when conducting research with children. In particular, the researcher needs to acknowledge the power relationships that exist between adults and children. In many societies, adults teach and children learn. In a sense, in conducting research with children, the researcher reverses this relationship by asking the children to share their experiences, and tell the researcher what they think. Child participants are entitled to the same sort of respect as adult participants. This means the researcher must gain consent, respect anonymity, maintain the right to withdraw and give feedback. It can be difficult to achieve informed consent with younger children. For example, how do you explain what might be complex research aims? Can children appreciate what it means to agree to take part in a research study? It is difficult to provide general answers to these questions because how the study is explained will depend on the child and the situation. In any event, the researcher must get the consent of the child's parent or guardian and if at all possible the consent of the child her/himself. They should also be sensitive to the child's behaviour during the research. It may be that because of the power relationships referred to above the child does not say that s/he is experiencing distress. The researcher will need to be vigilant and, if the child is uncomfortable, bring the activity to a close. Again, in giving feedback about the research, both the child and the parent must be treated with respect.

Summary of Section 4

- Particular kinds of research study raise special ethical questions. These include:
  - work with patients
  - brain-imaging studies
  - emotion research
  - research with children.

5   Conclusion

Ethical issues involve complex and evolving considerations that attempt to protect the well-being of research participants, and the reputation of institutions and the discipline and professions of psychology and the neurosciences. Ethical decisions are frequently difficult and involve weighing up both the procedures proposed and the potential benefit of the research outcomes to others. Research in psychology and the neurosciences is governed by sets of guidelines designed to ensure that participants in research do not emerge from the research experience harmed physically, emotionally or financially by their participation. On the contrary it is hoped that they will feel appreciated, informed and have a positive attitude towards the research enterprise to which they have contributed, towards the institution where it took place and towards psychology and the neurosciences as professions. It is up to all who are involved in research to attempt to further this aim.

Further reading

Ethical codes are frequently updated, so you may wish to search for and consult sources on the Internet. However, the following general texts provide further exploration of some of the issues raised in this chapter.

Bersoff, D.N. (ed.) (2003) *Ethical Conflicts in Psychology* (3rd edn), Washington, DC, American Psychological Association.

Nagy, T.F. (1999) *Ethics in Plain English: An Illustrative Casebook for Psychologists*, Washington, DC, American Psychological Association.

Sales, B.D. and Folkman, S. (eds) (2000) *Ethics in Research With Human Participants*, Washington, DC, American Psychological Association.

References

Milgram, S. (1963) 'Behavioural study of obedience', *Journal of Abnormal and Social Psychology*, vol.67, pp.371–8.

Milgram, S. (1974) *Obedience to Authority*, London, Tavistock.

Rutherford, A. (2005) 'Long-term memory: encoding to retrieval', in Braisby, N. and Gellatly, A. (eds) *Cognitive Psychology, The Open University/Oxford University Press.*

Yiend, J. and Mackintosh, B. (2005) 'Cognition and emotion', in Braisby, N. and Gellatly, A. (eds) *Cognitive Psychology, The Open University/Oxford University Press.*

Zimbardo, P.G. (1975) 'Transforming experimental research into advocacy of social change', in Deutsch, M. and Hornstein, H. (eds) *Applying Social Psychology*, Hillsdale, NJ, Lawrence Erlbaum.

Zimbardo, P.G. (1999) *Stanford Prison Experiment: A Simulation Study of the Psychology of Imprisonment Conducted at Stanford University* [online] http://www.prisonexp.org [accessed 10 August 2004].

Connectionism

Chapter 2

Martin Le Voi

1 Inspirations for cognitive modelling

Cognitive modelling is an essential part of theorizing in psychology. It consists of generating representations of knowledge, mechanisms of processing and organizational structures that are capable of processing information and producing outputs that psychologists believe model not only human behaviour, but also the cognitive processes on which that behaviour depends. There are many forms of cognitive modelling. This chapter focuses on connectionist modelling; symbolic, or rule-based modelling, is discussed in Chapter 3.

Cognitive models do not appear out of thin air. They are inspired by well-understood physical systems of the day. Before electricity was discovered, models of the brain, believe it or not, used systems of pumps and valves to explain behaviour! Later models likened the brain to gigantic telephone exchanges or used flow diagram models derived from computer programming. Recently, inspiration for cognitive models has come from successes in computer programs that attempt to create Artificial Intelligence, and also from an improved understanding of brain microstructure, or 'neural networks'. These kinds of models are generally 'tested' by implementing them in a computer and seeing how well their behaviour can then reproduce or 'simulate' certain aspects of human behaviour.

1.1 The rule-based approach

Computer modelling attempts to create behaviour in a computer (an Artificial Intelligence) that mimics (simulates) the behaviour of a natural intelligence: namely ourselves. One modern approach has attempted to do this by programming the computer with a large collection of rules, and it is the sequential activation of these rules that produces behaviour more or less like that of the intended target, such as an expert medical diagnostician (an example of an expert system). More general models like ACT-R, based on systems of production rules, are used to develop models of how human beings learn, think and solve problems (see Chapter 3).

In these models (also known as procedural models), large and complex collections of production rules process incoming information, adding to and subtracting from internal memory systems and in so doing they are able to simulate human behaviour in areas of memory, language and problem solving. Chapter 3 describes how Anderson's ACT-R model simulated human memory (Section 3) and also arithmetic skills (Section 4), showing that known psychological phenomena can be produced by rule-based simulations.

1.2 'Neural' networks

To try and devise models that offer alternative insights into human behaviour, exponents of connectionist models turned away from the capability and potential of the rule-based approach whose inspiration lay in the power of familiar computational, but essentially artificial, machines (i.e. computers). The connectionist approach took a much closer look at the micro-structure of the brain itself, to see if insights into the power of a natural information-processing engine (such as the brain) might provide a better, and hopefully more realistic, modelling system. Most psychologists are familiar with the general structure of the brain, consisting of individual neurons with dendrites, axons and synapses, but researchers in connectionist modelling were most interested in how these individual components might operate collectively to provide an information-processing capability.

Figure 2.1 shows how inspiration from known brain structure is used by psychologists to form 'neural' models. Signals arrive on incoming axons and project onto a collection of six neurons (in this case), forming a network. If only it was possible to fathom the information-processing properties of such **neural nets**, a model of human cognition based on inspiration from a natural, rather than artificial, intelligence could be developed. When models such as these were developed, they were found to have some remarkable properties, many of which are known to be characteristic of human behaviour. For example, connectionist models were found to be intrinsically capable of generalizing from many specific cases, a property that underlies some models of concept formation (see Section 3). This intrinsic **generalization** didn't require extra add-ons to the model so that it could 'do' generalization, rather, generalization was one of the natural behaviours of connectionist models. If you build a connectionist model, as we shall see, it is automatically capable of generalization. There are other remarkable properties that are inherent in connectionist models, such as content-addressable memory, which is explained later. All these characteristics are known to be natural properties of human cognition, so psychologists were immediately attracted by a class of cognitive models whose intrinsic properties seemed closely related to the known properties of natural intelligence. Psychologists immediately wanted to know more about the full capabilities of such cognitive modelling systems, and I shall present here the foundation of the systematic exploration of those information-processing properties.

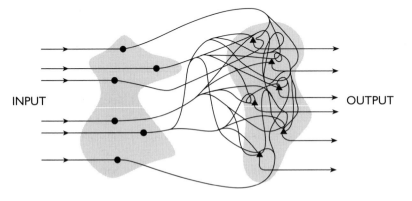

Figure 2.1   A typical 'neural network'

Source: based on Anderson et al., 1977

Summary of Section 1

- Computational models of the brain began with models based on the rule-based approach, exemplified by ACT-R (see Chapter 2), which by and large used localized, serial (one rule at a time) computation.
- Some psychologists wanted to develop models that bore a closer resemblance to the neural architecture of the brain, so they developed 'neural' network models based on connectionism.

2 Local and distributed representation

The adult human brain loses thousands of neurons every day but, despite that loss, our cognitive processes continue unaffected. We don't generally wake up unable to speak or with large areas of vision lost, unless there is massive damage to the brain through accident or disease. The brain is robust to the loss of parts of its information-processing potential, and increasing levels of damage usually produce a slowly increasing loss of performance rather than a sudden, catastrophic impairment. This slow loss of performance is called **graceful degradation**, and is one of the hallmarks of distributed, rather than local, representation.

2.1 Local representation

Neural models can be local. An example of a local representation in perception is provided by the 'grandmother cell hypothesis'. Work pioneered by researchers Hubel and Wiesel (1959, 1962) has shown that neurons in cats' brains selectively respond to more and more complex visual attributes as recordings are made 'deeper' in the visual cortex. Beginning with cells in the retina responding to areas of light, subsequent layers of cortical neurons respond to more complex patterns of light falling on the retina, progressing through so-called complex and hyper-complex cells that respond to more complex aspects of the retinal image. It is as if each layer is taking the processing outputs of the previous layer and processing them to a higher level of representation. Could it be that cells would be found that respond selectively to highly specific complex stimuli, such as your own grandmother? In other words, when your grandmother comes into your field of vision, the neurons would process the information up through levels of progressively greater complexity until one neuron fires in recognition: the so-called 'grandmother cell'. This single cell would therefore selectively respond to your grandmother as a stimulus and, by extension, other cells would respond to other complex stimuli, such as your father, the neighbour's cat and so on. This could lead to the conjecture that the perception of these objects is localized within the single neuron.

Although this is a clear example of a local model of perception, there were many problems with this view that meant it never gained much ground. Apart from the fact that the discovery of neurons selectively responding to ever more integrated or abstract parts of the scene seemed to run out of steam after a certain level, and that experiments such as these could never be done on humans, the whole idea of the perception of objects being confined to the response of a single cell such as the 'grandmother cell' seemed fundamentally unsound.

Consider an alien coming to Earth, who hears that the final of the Lawn Tennis Championship is being played. The alien wants to know where. At Wimbledon, you say. 'Where in Wimbledon?', 'On the centre court'. Although you think that may suffice, the alien, ignorant of the game of tennis, continues 'Where on the centre court'. Well, all over, you say. 'But I want to know exactly where on the centre court: was it on this blade of grass or that?'

These questions are absurd because tennis is played all over the tennis court, not just on some individual blade of grass. Play is distributed over the whole area. In the same way, perception and memory (and other human behaviour) probably arise from the functioning of much of the brain, indeed much of the organism, and attempts to localize them to single cells are simply inappropriate (see, for example, Tulving, 1991).

ACTIVITY 2.1

If the idea of your grandmother was governed by the activity of a single cell in your brain, would you need one for every grandmother, indeed every person you know? How would the general concept 'grandmother' be represented? What would happen if these cells died?

COMMENT

You would probably need one for every person you know. The concept of 'grandmother' would also be represented by a single cell: otherwise how would the brain know whether what is represented is a physical object (person) or an abstracted concept? If the cell for your grandmother representation died, presumably you would be unable to recognize her.

2.2 Distributed representation

Let us look at an example of a distributed representation. We have all seen digital watch faces or digital clocks in public places such as railway stations. Instead of using complete single digits for each number as on a traditional clock, individual numbers are represented in such a display by activity across the seven segments (or units) that make it up (see Figure 2.2). Every unit is involved in the representation of each number, either by being on or off. Depending on activity in other segments, each one may form part of an edge, an angle or a closed loop. Representation of each number is **distributed** over all seven segments: no single unit uniquely represents one of the numerals. In the same way, it is suggested that representation of memories in the human brain are distributed over a collection of individual units and their connections. These units in the brain would be the neurons (units) and their synapses (connections). Connectionist models of the way knowledge is distributed over a collection of neuron-like units are sometimes known as 'neural networks'.

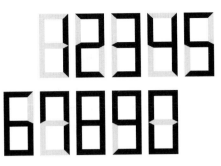

Figure 2.2 Figures from a digital watch face

2.3 What are the advantages of distributed representations?

Distributed representations have a number of advantages. In the digital figure example, seven units are used to represent the ten numerals. This is an improvement over a system that needs a separate unit for each numeral. So there is some *economy* in a distributed system.

Another advantage of a distributed system is that all is not lost if there is any deterioration in the stimulus signal or loss of individual units. Suppose there is a single unit that represents the numeral 7. If this unit is damaged, or its input signal is deteriorated, then it may not represent the numeral 7 at all. However, if the representation of the numeral 7 is distributed over seven units (as in Figure 2.2), then even if one of these units fails, the others still stand a chance of getting the message across. This capability to continue correct operation despite the loss of parts of the information results from the fact that the original representation encoded more information than was required to maintain the representation: this is known as **redundancy** in the encoding. Figure 2.3 shows how some of the redundancy in the representation of the digital figures means that, although some information might be lost, enough is still available distributed over the seven units to allow recognition in certain circumstances of damage (but not all).

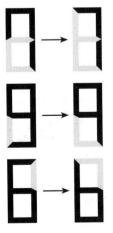

Figure 2.3 Resistance to some damage: the figures on the right can still represent the same numerals as the figures on the left

When very large numbers of units are involved, such as might be the case for neurons in the brain, distributed representations are highly robust to damage, which is just as well considering thousands of brain cells die every day in the adult human. The gradual deterioration in performance of a distributed system (graceful degradation), in contrast to the catastrophic failure that occurs in most conventional computers when even a single critical instruction or component is faulty, is one of its strengths. This also seems to be a characteristic of the human brain, since impairment from disease, damage, stress, aging or shock is generally very gradual, or partial, rather than catastrophic.

Summary of Section 2

- Local representation in neural models, such as the 'grandmother cell' hypothesis, has generally been rejected as implausible.
- Distributed models generally have redundant encoding. Information is not confined to particular locations, and good performance is still possible when the network receives incomplete information. These models exhibit graceful degradation when damaged, which is also a characteristic of the human cognitive system.

3 Parallel processing

People can use the similarity between multiple stimuli to generalize from those instances to form an organizing concept (see **Braisby, 2005**). Such generalization is a very important aspect of human cognition and, in this section, we shall show how connectionist models can display generalization from simple cues to general schema, using simple mechanisms of pattern matching and pattern association.

3.1 Pattern matching

As we shall see, connectionist models are particularly good at 'pattern matching', especially when only the 'best fit' match is needed rather than an absolutely precise match. However, pattern matching is an essential component of many cognitive models, for example, Braisby discusses how pattern matching is a feature of certain models of categorization (**Braisby, 2005**). In the classical view of concepts, instances are matched to a concept on a list of common properties, a successful match on every property in the list meaning that the instance may be judged a member of the concept. Matching properties to a feature list of a concept is also important for prototype theories, which we shall look at more closely later.

3.2 Pattern associators

In any memory system in which the desired response or memory is retrieved by means of some cueing process, this pattern matching process is vital. The retrieval process has to check the cue against all the memories stored, and produce the most appropriate one: in other words, the response that is correctly associated with the cue. For example, when you see a friend's face, you have to use that cue to retrieve the correct name associated with that face. We shall see that this pattern matching and association is handled elegantly and neatly by connectionist models. In these models, the match is performed against all the previously stored patterns in a single step, producing direct retrieval of the associated pattern by parallel processing. The first such connectionist model we will consider is called, conveniently, the **pattern associator**. A pattern associator is simply a device that takes particular (specified) input patterns and associates them with desired (specified) output patterns. For convenience these patterns are conventionally represented as number sequences (e.g. 00 or 01). (See Box 2.1.)

2.1

Representation in connectionism I

Much of the success of any cognitive model rests on how it solves the problem of representation. This is particularly important for connectionist models, since the translation from input representations to output representations holds the key to how the neural network will learn.

Representation in connectionist models is based around feature sets (see **Braisby, 2005**). We shall use an example of a three-element feature set used to represent features of animals for a little 'toy' problem. Each feature element can take one of two values, either 0 or 1. We shall define three features:

1   Animal type, coded as Mammal (0) or Bird (1)

2   Ability to fly, coded as 0 (not able to fly) and 1 (able to fly)

3   Lives North or South of the Equator, coded as 0 (North) and 1 (South)

Thus, these three features combined together can be used to encode some of the features of animals. Since there are two values for each feature, there are eight possible different combinations of them (2 x 2 x 2). Table 2.1 displays those combinations with one example of each. Note that, in a connectionist model, there can be more than one example of each type, as we shall see in a later exercise.

Table 2.1   Combinations of three binary-coded features

Animal type		Flies?		Lives		Code	Example
	Code		Code		Code		
Mammal	0	No	0	North	0	0 0 0	Polar Bear
Mammal	0	No	0	South	1	0 0 1	Weddell Seal
Mammal	0	Yes	1	North	0	0 1 0	Horseshoe Bat
Mammal	0	Yes	1	South	1	0 1 1	Ipanema Bat
Bird	1	Yes	1	South	1	1 1 1	Spangled Kookaburra
Bird	1	Yes	1	North	0	1 1 0	European Robin
Bird	1	No	0	North	0	1 0 0	Great Awk
Bird	1	No	0	South	1	1 0 1	King Penguin

So for this example, a pattern of three digits, each either 0 or 1, defines the input.

Output patterns follow the same principle. Often, for a pattern associator, the neural network may act as a classifier, so that the output defines into which class each pattern should fall. The output is often called a 'teacher' because it is the ideal output and can be used to 'teach' the network to produce actual outputs that are close to the ideal. The task of the connectionist model is to use the 'teacher' output to modify its connections so that eventually the presentation of the input patterns results in an output that correctly corresponds to the defined (ideal) output. We shall see that this works by a process that compares the network's actual, calculated output with the defined (teacher) output. Any difference is used to change the connections in such a way that this difference is gradually reduced, eventually allowing the network to produce an output that correctly corresponds to the 'teacher' output, for all the inputs it is trained on.

Pattern associator exercise 1

Simple pattern associator

In this computer exercise you will try out a very simple two-layer pattern associator (see Figure 2.4). It demonstrates learning and the association of patterns. You will 'train' a small network to learn a simple set of patterns, and you will see the connections between 'neurons' change as they learn the associations. A graph displays how training proceeds by reducing the error through learning each pattern one at a time (however, your computer will be much too fast for you to see this graph build slowly as the network 'cycles' through the patterns one by one).

In this exercise the simple pattern associator is trained on the following patterns (see Table 2.2), similar to those in Box 2.1:

Table 2.2   Pattern set for exercise 1

Pattern number	Input pattern	Ideal output pattern ('teacher')	Label (not used by network)
1	0 0 0	1 0	A1
2	0 0 1	1 0	A2
3	0 1 0	1 0	A3
4	1 1 1	0 1	B1
5	1 1 0	0 1	B2
6	1 0 0	0 1	B3

You can see that the input consists of three elements, each of which is a 0 or 1. Each of these elements will be presented to one of the three input nodes of the network. The output is two elements, each of which is 0 or 1. These will be tested at the two output nodes of the network. This table of patterns is usually called a **pattern set**.

So the network will have three input nodes and two output nodes and will look like Figure 2.4.

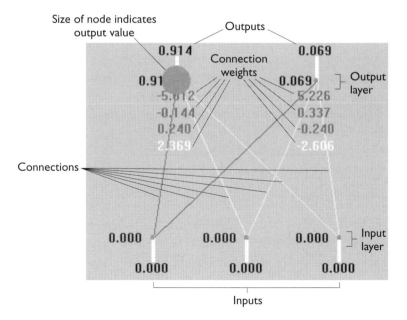

Figure 2.4   A simple two-layer pattern associator

In depicting neural networks, the input layer (a layer is a collection of nodes that perform the same function) is traditionally placed at the bottom, and the output layer at the top. The input layer sends information forwards to the output layer. You can see that every input node sends a connection forwards (upwards) to every output node: this is usually called a **fan-out** or **feed forward**. At the end of the exercise we'll look at exactly what happens at the output nodes.

Step 1: build network and pattern set

1 Run the program *Pattern Associator.* You should find this in the **Start** menu, once you have installed the software.

2 Click on the **File** menu.

> COMPUTER The **File** menu drops down.

3 Click on the **New Network**... submenu.

> COMPUTER The **New Network** dialog appears, see Figure 2.5.

4 Make sure the check box labelled **For existing data** is *not* selected.

5 Type '2' into the box labelled **Output Layer**:

6 Type '0' into the box marked **2nd hidden**:

Figure 2.5   The **New Network** dialog

33

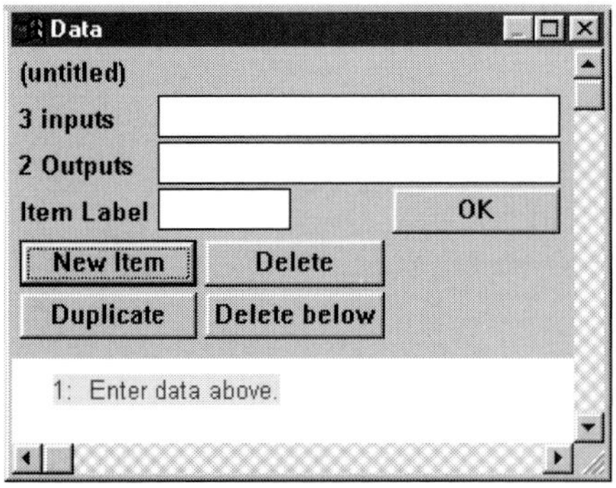

Figure 2.6 The **Data** window

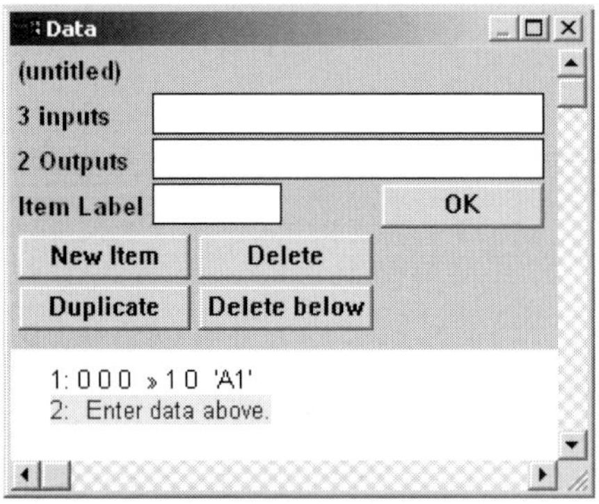

Figure 2.7 A new item will appear at the bottom of the list

7 Type '0' into the box marked **1st hidden**:

8 Type '3' into the box marked **Input Layer**:

9 Click on **OK**.

COMPUTER The **New Network** dialog disappears, and the **Network** window on the right should display a network something like Figure 2.4.

Now we need to enter the training data (i.e. the pattern set from Table 2.2). To do this, you use the **Data** window (in the middle of your screen). You can see it already expects three inputs and two outputs, see Figure 2.6. Here is what you do for the first two patterns:

10 Click in the box called **3 Inputs** and type the numbers '0 0 0' (we are working through the six patterns in Table 2.2). Spaces between the digits are optional.

11 Click in the box **2 Outputs** and type the numbers '1 0'.

12 Click in the box **Item Label** and type the label 'A1'.

13 Click on **OK**.

COMPUTER A new item will appear in the list (see Figure 2.7). The item you have entered appears as: **1: 0 0 0 » 1 0 'A1'**

The input values are on the left of the » sign, and the output values are on the right. A1, a label for the pattern, is not used in processing: it is there only to help you identify patterns and what is happening during and after learning.

14 Click on the button **New Item.** A new item will appear in the list (see Figure 2.7).

15 Click in the box called **3 Inputs**. Type the numbers '0 0 1' (this is the second pattern in Table 2.2 above).

16 Click in the box called **2 Outputs** and type the numbers '1 0'.

17 Click in the box **Item Label** and type the label 'A2'.

18 Click on the button **OK**.

COMPUTER The pattern in the list updates to show your edits.

19 Repeat steps 14 to 18 for the remaining four patterns in Table 2.2 above (in step 16 you will need to type '0 1' for patterns 4 to 6). If you make any errors, you can always click on a pattern in the list and re-edit it, or even delete it with the **Delete** button if necessary.

COMPUTER The data set should look like Figure 2.8.

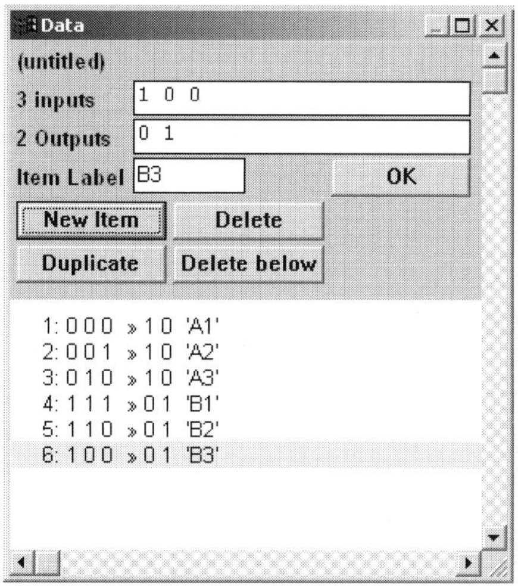

Figure 2.8 How the entered training data should look

At the moment, the computer doesn't know that it needs to learn these items. We must tell the computer which items to use for training.

20 Click just to the left of the first pattern.

COMPUTER The letters **Tr** (for training) should appear next to the pattern.

21 Repeat Step 20 for the other five patterns.

The list of patterns should look like Figure 2.9:

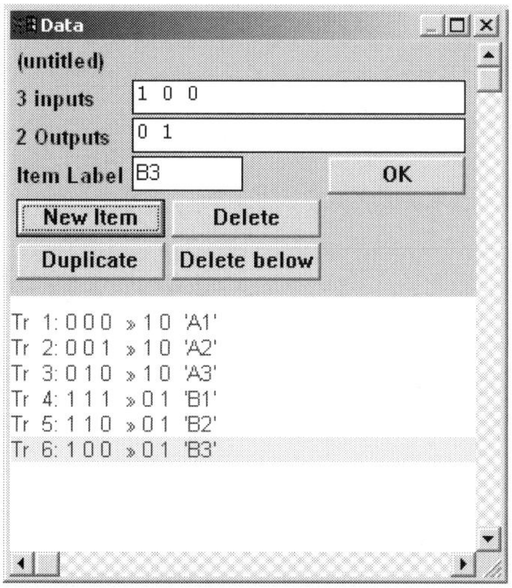

Figure 2.9 Click to the left of each pattern and the letters 'Tr' should appear

Now we are ready to train the network. In the **Training** window (see Figure 2.10) there are a number of parameters, such as **Learning coefficient** and **Match threshold**. We can leave these as they are for the moment. The learning coefficient alters how fast the network learns, and the **Reduce error to** value tells the network when to stop: it refers to the error values in the top of the window. **Match Threshold** isn't used in training, so we'll look at it later.

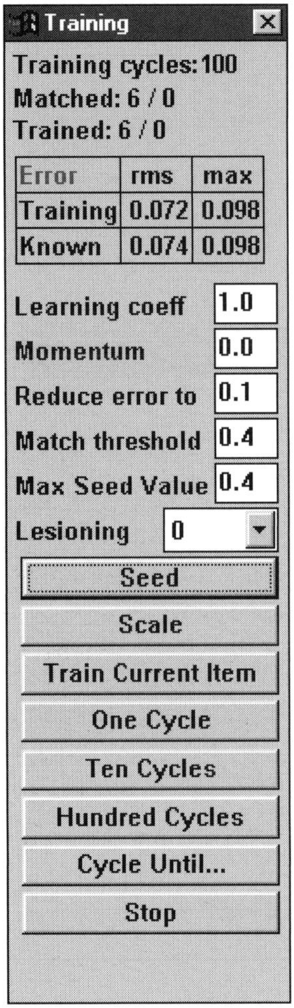

Figure 2.10 The **Training** window

Step 2: train network

22 Click on **Seed**. This prepares the network for learning. It does this by setting the strengths of the connections to random values (this process is called 'seeding').

23 Click on **Cycle Until**....

COMPUTER The graph in the **Network** window (Figure 2.11) will show the error declining as the network cycles through the six training patterns. The declining error is also shown in the **Error** box in the **Training** window. When the error reaches (nearly) zero, the network is said to have learned the

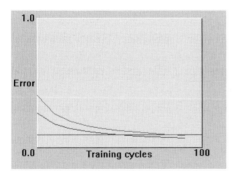

Figure 2.11 Reducing errors in a six-pattern data set

training set. For a small network like this, training will be so fast that all you will see is the final graph. The network will usually learn in less than 100 complete cycles through the whole pattern set. This may seem a lot but even slow computers will cycle through faster than the display can keep up.

Step 3: test network

The trained network can respond to tests. All you do to test the network is click on the pattern you want to use as input.

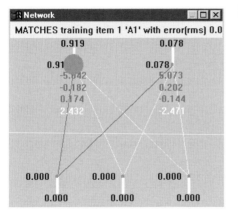

Figure 2.12 **Network** window

24 Click on the first pattern in the **Data** window.

COMPUTER The **Network** window shows values for the two output nodes, and these you will see are similar to the output pattern '1 0' in the A patterns in Table 2.2 (see the values at the two output nodes at the top of Figure 2.12). Indeed, the computer has checked the patterns (using the **Match threshold**) and lists the output it most strongly resembles: A1 is listed as the match since this is the first with the output pattern 1 0.

25 Click on the other two A patterns (these should be patterns 2 and 3).

COMPUTER In each case, the pattern should match A1: these three patterns all correspond to output A: i.e. because the output for both A1 and A2 is the same (1 0), then the match is to pattern A1, simply because it is the first in the list. It could equally well be a match to pattern A2.

26 Click on the B patterns (these should be patterns 4, 5 and 6).

COMPUTER Each of these should match B1 pattern (the first with the output 0 1).

So the network has learned these patterns, such that patterns 1 to 3 all have similar outputs and should be classified as 'A', and patterns 4 to 6 all have similar outputs and should be classified as 'B'.

The most interesting test is to see what happens if we give the network previously unseen patterns. Let's enter two new patterns from Table 2.3:

Table 2.3

Pattern number	Input	Output	Label
7	0 1 1	1 0	A4
8	1 0 1	0 1	B4

27 Click on the button **New Item**.

> ⟨COMPUTER⟩ A new item appears in the list (look back to Figure 2.7). This is a duplicate of the selected item.

28 Click in the box called **3 inputs** and type the number '0 1 1'.

29 Click in the box called **2 outputs** and type the number '1 0'.

30 Click in the box **Item Label** and type the number 'A4'.

31 Click on the button **OK**.

> ⟨COMPUTER⟩ The new pattern updates to show your edits.

32 Click on the button **New Item**.

> ⟨COMPUTER⟩ A new item appears in the list below.

33 Click in the box called **3 inputs** and type the number '1 0 1'.

34 Click in the box called **2 outputs** and type the number '0 1'.

35 Click in the box **Item Label** and type the number 'B4'.

36 Click on **OK**.

> ⟨COMPUTER⟩ The new pattern updates to show your edits.

What happens if we test with these items? Click on each one and find out using steps 24 to 26.

You should find that pattern 7 (A4) matches pattern A1, and pattern 8 (B4) matches B1. The network has responded with matches to patterns it has never been trained on. This is known as **spontaneous generalization**. We will see more examples as we learn more about connectionism, and these examples will be more powerful than the one looked at here.

ACTIVITY 2.2

Can you see why the pattern associator in Pattern associator exercise 1 has associated the new pattern 0 1 1 with A and pattern 1 0 1 with B?

You can see from the pattern set that, in this case, the classification of the pattern is based on a very simple, indeed trivial, matching. The first feature in the input series is the one that determines the output classification. The second and third features are redundant (irrelevant). Look at your network once it has learned. It should look like Figure 2.4, which is also a picture of the network after learning. On your screen, you can see the connections in the 'fan-out' are different colours. The connections from the leftmost input are strong (they should be a strong blue or red colour), while the connections from the other two inputs are very weak (they will be a pale grey). This reflects the fact that the categorization is entirely due to the leftmost input, and the other two are redundant. The strength of these connections is known as **weight**.

The same information (connection weights) is presented as a column of numbers by each of the output nodes. The first number in each column is the 'weight' given to the leftmost input. The one below it is the weight from the node to its right, and so on. The last weight (which is in white figures rather than in black) is the weight from a 'bias' node, which is always on (i.e. has the value of input = 1). It is necessary because of the way we have numbers between 0 and 1, so we have to bias results to that range. You can see that the weight from the leftmost node is high (it should be numerically greater than 4) while the weight from the other nodes is small (numerically much less than 1). The left output node will have a high negative weight (e.g. −4.5) while the right output node has a high positive weight (e.g. +4.5). Note that the output is held to be less than one by something called a 'squashing function', which, as its name suggests, 'squashes' output values into the range 0 to1.

In other categorization tasks, as we shall see, the discrimination is not as trivial as this, and the weights construct an output value from some combination of many of the inputs. Sometimes it is instructive to see what those input combinations are for a given output.

So even this most simple pattern associator can store multiple associations, such that various cues presented at the input give rise to various responses at the output. What is interesting is how such networks behave when they have many units with lots of weights attached.

ACTIVITY 2.3

How did the network learn in Pattern associator exercise 1?

COMMENT

The network learned by changing the values of the connections. In step 22, the network cycled through all the patterns one by one, making small adjustments to the connections until it learned them all. However, it did this so fast that you won't have seen the connections changing gradually. You might like to try Pattern associator exercise 1 again, except, instead of clicking on **Cycle Until**... in step 23, you click on **One Cycle**. If you click on this repeatedly, you will see the connections in the **Network** window changing gradually as the network learns the patterns. This is discussed more in Sections 3.4 and 5.1 below.

3.3   The auto associator

Pattern associators are useful when we want to form an association between one complete pattern and another (e.g. to link one, perhaps visual, pattern into another, perhaps olfactory, like the association of the sight of a rose with its smell). In Section 5, we will look at a large network that associates graphemic (written word) information with phonetic (spoken word) information. For a model of memory, however, one of the most common uses is when a complete set of information, such as memory for an event, has to be held in memory, and then later retrieved using just a small part of the recorded information as a **cue** for recall of all the rest. Generally, any part of the information may form part of the cue, and there is no way of knowing which part of the information will be used as a cue, or which part of the information will need to be recalled. As an example, suppose I ask you questions about your home. I could ask you to tell me what you have in your living room, or I could ask you where you keep your books. Whether or not part of the answer to one of these questions was the cue used in the other, the point is that your knowledge about your home needs to be encoded in a system in which any kind of information can be used for recall of any other. That is, asking about what you keep in your living room may lead you to recall books as part of the answer, and one of the answers to asking where you keep books may be your living room.

This is an important feature of human memory. If we are presented with a partial cue, such as a picture of a face or the scent of a rose, we will recall other information to complete the cue, such as the name of the face or the sight of a rose. The memory system has been cued with part of the *content* of the memory trace in order to produce recall. This capability is known as **content addressability** (see Auto associator exercise 1). When you see a friend, just the image of the face (part of the memory's content) usually is sufficient for recall of the name or other information about that person. However, alternative computational models, based on computer analogies (such as rule-based models) find it difficult (though not impossible) to model content addressability, since conventional computers are designed to address memory by *location*, not content: information is looked up in a computer by knowing *where* it is stored. The same is true of finding books in a library: to find one you need to know where it is stored and finding it will require a search path based on the library's storage scheme. Content addressability is such a central feature of human memory that any cognitive model of memory must adequately reproduce it.

The connectionist model most suited for this capability is the '**auto associator**'. First we need to understand how to extend the analysis of a pattern associator to a simple auto associator.

Auto associator exercise 1

This computer exercise will demonstrate another form of network called an auto associator. You will see that it too learns by cycling through input patterns but, instead of having inputs at one layer and outputs at another, the whole pattern is both the input and the output. You will find that the pattern can be 'cued' by any part of the pattern, and the rest of the pattern will be completed by the network: this process is called content addressability.

Consider a child learning which animals are called dogs, and which are cats. The child is attempting to create the correct representation in semantic memory that identifies dogs as dogs and cats as cats. What the child actually sees is numerous individual dogs and cats (these are known as 'exemplars') that are often correctly named by a nearby adult. From these exemplars the child has to progressively build a 'picture' in semantic memory of the general characteristics of dogs as opposed to cats, or indeed any other animal or thing. This learning process is something that connectionist models are particularly well suited to. We shall now look at how connectionist models can learn or 'memorize' inputs and respond to cues. This is achieved by altering the weights or connection strengths in the model so that the network responds correctly to cues.

2.2

Representation in connectionism II

Each pattern is two letters together, e.g. A – B, C – D, E – F, G – H, where each letter is represented in terms of three elements. So each pattern has six inputs, three for each of the two letters. The network is intended to learn the four patterns listed in Table 2.5. The computer display separates the parts of the pattern with an underscore (_).

In this example, the representation chosen does not define the features that each input represents, as is done in Table 2.1. Instead, arbitrary but unique input patterns are assigned to each 'letter'. So A is represented by 0 0 0 across three inputs, but what feature of letters each of those inputs represents is not defined (such features could be straight lines, closed segments, etc.). The intention is to examine the network as it learns unique input patterns and its behaviour under cued recall, using an arbitrary representation scheme. The argument is that the behaviour of the network will be much the same under most (if not all) representation schemes you might try, so it is unnecessary to specify a pre-determined feature representation system. This arbitrary form of representation is commonly used in demonstrations of connectionist model behaviour, as we shall see again in Auto associator exercise 2.

Table 2.4 Representation codes for eight letters

Letter	Representation code
A	0 0 0
B	0 1 1
C	0 0 1
D	0 1 0
E	1 1 0
F	1 0 1
G	1 1 1
H	1 0 0

Table 2.5 Pattern set for exercises

Actual patterns to be learned	Label
0 0 0 _ 0 1 1	A – B
0 0 1 _ 0 1 0	C – D
1 1 0 _ 1 0 1	E – F
1 1 1 _ 1 0 0	G – H

Overview of Auto associator exercise 1a

Use the program *Auto Associator* to open the file **AA1a.nnd**. Click on **Seed**, then **Cycle Until**..., and watch the network learn the training patterns (marked with **Tr**). You can then test the network with parts of the training patterns, this is easily done by clicking on the incomplete patterns (numbered 5 to 12). See what the network does with the incomplete part of the pattern. Does it complete it correctly?

Step 1: build network and open pattern set

1   Run the program *Auto Associator*. It should be in the **Start** menu, as a sub-menu.

2   Click on the **File** menu.

|COMPUTER| The menu drops down.

3   Click on the **Load...** submenu.

|COMPUTER| **Load Network and Training** dialog appears, see Figure 2.13.

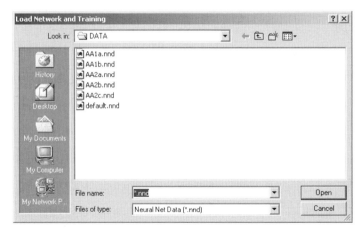

Figure 2.13   The **Load Network and Training** dialog

4   Find the file **AA1a.nnd**. Select it and click on **Open**.

|COMPUTER| The **Load Network and Training** dialog disappears, and the network appears in the right hand (**Network**) window, with the pattern set in the middle (**Data**) window (see Figure 2.14).

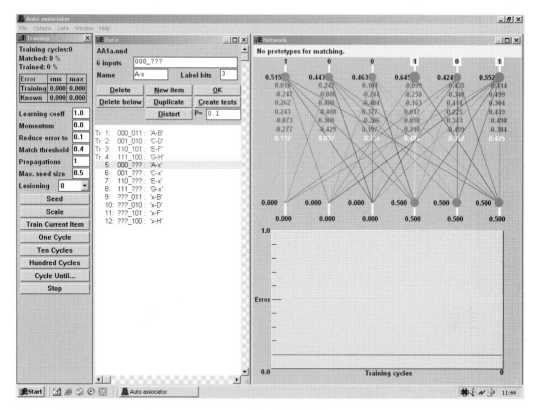

Figure 2.14   The *Auto Associator* program with a file loaded

Step 2: train network

5   Click on **Seed**.

6   Then click on **Cycle Until…**.

COMPUTER   The training graph shows the reduction in error during training.

Step 3: test network

Now we can test the network with the incomplete patterns. These will contain question marks, like this: **000_??? : 'A − x'**

The question marks are undefined parts of the pattern.

7   Click on incomplete pattern **'A − x'** (it should be number 5). What does the output look like on the three right-hand outputs? The auto associator will 'translate' the output into 1 or 0, presented in a little white box (e.g. **[1]**). Does this correspond to the representation of the letter B (011)? It should look like Figure 2.15.

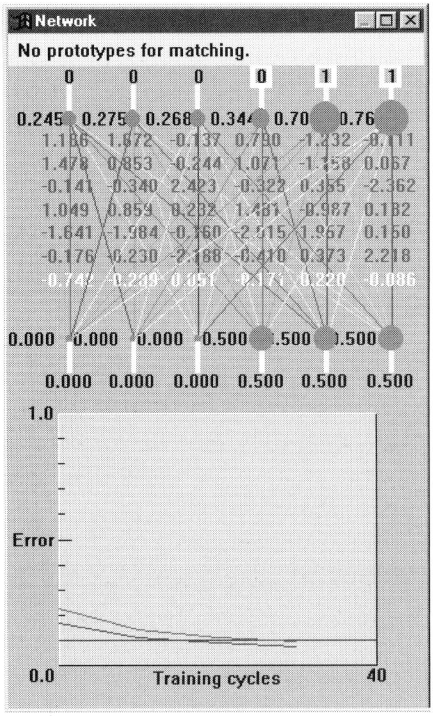

Figure 2.15 The **Network** window showing the 'translated' outputs

Try other incomplete patterns and see how the network completes the pattern. It does it equally well if the pattern is incomplete on either the left-hand side or the right-hand side. Note that any pattern of incompleteness would work (e.g. 0?0_?1?) and the network would try and fill in the missing parts (though it may not always make sense). That is, it is simply a matter of convenience to divide the patterns in half, and label each half with the representations in Table 2.4.

Overview of Auto associator exercise 1b

For this exercise load the network **AA1b.nnd**. You will see that it is a five-node auto associator. As you did above, click on **Seed**, then **Cycle Until...** in order to learn.

The network has learned the six patterns with **Tr** against them. Only these patterns were 'seen' by the network in training. You can try testing the network with the partially defined patterns you can see in the **Data** window. How well does it complete the patterns?

Particularly interesting are the partial patterns **x – C2: (??_110)** and **x – D2: (??_011)**. The network has not been trained on these patterns, so it has never 'seen' them. But if you test the network with them, it will reply with the 'correct' output (10 for **x – C2**, 11 for **x – D2**). This is another example of *spontaneous generalization* – the network has correctly generalized from the six patterns it has seen to another two patterns it has never seen.

In the network presented in Auto associator exercise 1, the auto associator is drawn as a two-layer network, in which the output is constrained to be the same as the input. Often, auto associators are drawn as a single layer of neurons, in which the neurons send connections to each other (i.e. other neurons in the same layer). This has the effect of automatically ensuring that the output is the same as the input. Computationally, however, the network works the same as the network you have tried. If you see diagrams of auto associators looking like this (Figure 2.1 is an example), think of them as like the network you saw in Step 4 above (Figure 2.14).

3.4   Learning by error reduction

In the last exercises, it is important to note that learning took place on the basis of purely local operations. That is, the alteration of a weight (connection) in any part of the network is due to a comparison between the actual output and desired output at that precise point of the network; no information about how well the pattern fits the target anywhere else in the network is either used or required. If you want to see how this process works, the network simulators have buttons called **One Cycle** and **Ten Cycles**, which will do the learning in small steps. With one of the network problems from the pattern associator or auto associator exercises loaded, after clicking on **Seed**, try clicking on **One Cycle** or **Ten Cycles** instead of **Cycle Until**..., then you can see the weights (connections) of the network change gradually, and the error (shown in the **Training** window) also comes down slowly. How it works is that the network compares the output of each output node with the expected output value (we called this a 'teacher' in Box 2.1) for that node, and calculates a change in the weights across all its inputs which will make that error less. The change in weights is scaled (altered) by the learning coefficient (labelled **Learning coeff** in your program, it is in the **Training** window): larger coefficients usually mean faster learning, though in some networks learning becomes unstable (it tends to oscillate or bounce back and forth) if the learning rate is set too high.

Note that this error calculation occurs for every different pattern seen during training. So the weights will move in different directions to try and accommodate the error for every pattern, until eventually the overall error across all the nodes and all the patterns (this is the figure shown in the **Error** box in the **Training** window) reduces to a small value once the patterns have been learned.

The fact that connectionist networks can learn from such purely local operations is also a major desirable feature of a model that purports to mimic operations in the brain. In the brain, it may be surmised that neurons can only learn by altering their connections based on the activity in adjacent neurons with which they are in direct communication. It seems unlikely that a connection between neurons could be *directly* modified by activity elsewhere in the brain, so the brain probably learns by means of purely local operations, too.

Summary of Section 3

- Pattern matching is a fundamental process in many computational models of human cognition.

- The pattern associator, a simple two-layer connectionist model, is well suited to doing pattern matching and generating associations in parallel between different input and output patterns. It is capable of *spontaneous generalization*.

- The auto associator also performs pattern matching and storage, and is appropriate where there is no obvious definition of the input and output parts of the pattern: any part of a stored pattern may be used as a cue for retrieval of the rest. Retrieval of the whole pattern from a fragment of its content is known as *content addressability*.

- Connectionist networks can learn from input patterns presented to them by a process of gradual modification of connection weights, which are changed in the direction that reduces the error between the network's calculated output and the pre-defined (teacher) output. This process is called learning by error reduction.

- The learning process proceeds using purely *local* information for each connection weight: calculation of the change in weight for one connection does not need information about the error anywhere else in the network.
- Large networks can learn several different patterns simultaneously, storing information about each pattern in one set of weights: the information is distributed over all the connection weights.

4   What can connectionist models do for us?

4.1   Emergent properties of associative networks

Even with simple networks as in the last computer exercises we can illustrate some properties of these associative networks. The first property is content addressability. In Auto associator exercise 1, if we interrogate the network with a *cue* consisting of only part of the input pattern, such as (001_???) we can see if it responds with the missing part. The result is indeed that the network responds with (001_010), completing the pattern. The network recalls the missing fragment of the input pattern using only the cue to start its activity. This cue comes from part of the *contents* of the original pattern and is used to *address* the network for recall of a particular pattern, hence the term content addressability. This is an important **emergent property** of connectionist models. It has long been known that an important feature of human memory is its ability to respond to partial cues to recall whole memories (patterns). In rule-based computer models content addressability has to be 'programmed in', whereas for auto associators based on connectionist models it is a natural response of the network to partial cues. The extent to which various properties of human memory are naturally found in connectionist models (i.e. are emergent properties), rather than having to be explicitly programmed in to a computer model, is behind much of the debate as to the intrinsic worth of connectionist models as opposed to rule-based models of human cognition (see Chapter 3; and **Stone, 2005**).

The second property is that we didn't have to restrict ourselves to presenting one input pattern to learn. We used many. Both exercises showed the result of presenting multiple different patterns to the network. If we go on presenting the patterns, eventually the weights *converge* on a set that successfully stores *all* patterns perfectly: you should recall seeing the error measure falling to (nearly) zero in each case.

It might strike you as odd that one set of weights, each of which is involved in the storage of both traces, can store more than one pattern. It does work though. Any system where the pattern encoding is distributed over many units can do this.

An example is holographic recording. You may have seen holograms on credit cards, where they are used to try to defeat fraudsters by making the fabrication of credit cards a complicated matter. Holograms work by storing the light pattern from a source (my credit card uses a bird in flight) as an interference pattern across a suitable substrate. This substrate consists of millions of points that record the local interference. These points can record the interference from more than one pattern, so that more than one image can be stored. Which image you see depends on the direction of the light shone on to the hologram and the direction in which you view it: so with some holograms as you move them the picture changes from one object to another. It is a little like the children's display toys with little ridges on them, which show cartoon animals moving from one view to another. As in the neural network, which depends on the cue used to determine the pattern that is recovered, the toy or hologram depends on the angle of light used (the cue) to determine which image is recovered. If it helps, you can consider neural networks as holographic memory systems (since multiple memories are stored over one set of connections). In the past, psychologists have proposed other holographic memory models (e.g. CHARM, Composite Holographic Associative Recall Model proposed by Metcalfe Eich, 1982).

4.2   An example of a connectionist model of learning and memory

In **prototype theory** (see **Braisby, 2005**), a concept has a **prototype**, which is a kind of idealized 'master' concept, and all the instances of the concept (called exemplars) are similar to the prototype, but not identical. Some of the features are different. Indeed, there is probably no exemplar that is absolutely identical to the idealized prototype, but depending on the number of features that differ from it, an exemplar can be closer to (a good exemplar) or further away (a bad exemplar) from the prototype. So, for example, in Auto associator exercise 1 we discussed a child learning the concepts of cats and dogs by seeing many individual examples. According to prototype theory, each of these would be similar to, but not identical to, an ideal cat or dog prototype. As the child sees all the different exemplars (s)he builds a concept of the prototypical dog, with which future exemplars can be compared in order to categorize them.

McClelland and Rumelhart (1986) used a connectionist model based closely on this example to demonstrate the behaviour of a distributed model of memory. The network was based on a 24-unit auto associator.

McClelland and Rumelhart used this model to demonstrate several character-istics of memory. In each demonstration, several input patterns, designed to represent exemplars or instances of concepts in the real world, are presented to the network, which learns from each one, using a learning procedure just like the one presented in the Pattern associator and Auto associator exercises. After learning, the network is cued with pattern fragments, and the output response is examined to see if it corresponds with the input patterns or with ideal prototypes.

The first demonstration was designed to model the situation when someone (e.g. a child) sees a number of different exemplars of a concept, such as a dog, and learns the prototype of a concept without ever seeing the 'pure' prototype on its own, as it were: only particular individuals are seen. The main idea is that categories are organized around a prototype, to which all the exemplars are related to a greater or lesser degree. For some psychological models (such as Rosch, 1978) the prototype is a distinct entity, an abstraction that comprises the most typical properties. Exemplars of the concept are compared with the prototype in order to determine whether they are members of the category. The models can be refined in such a way that the abstracted prototype is not so much a 'perfect' exemplar, but instead a collection of salient attributes or features. If enough of these features are present in an exemplar, this leads to its categorization as one of the concepts. According to prototype theory, the concept of dog is represented as an abstraction made up of the most typical dog properties.

The psychological problem is how the concept is created, since people never see the 'abstract' concept itself, rather all they experience is a set of individual examples. For many concepts it is hard to imagine what a perfect prototype could be: consider the concept furniture for instance. So it would be most interesting to see what a connectionist network, designed to learn from input patterns in the way set out above, makes of a whole series of individual exemplars, and whether it can respond to them as a category in a meaningful way.

Auto associator exercise 2

Learning a prototype from exemplars

McClelland and Rumelhart (1986) explored this with an auto associator network of 24 units. In this exercise you will see that a fairly simple network, with simple arbitrary representation schemes, can construct a prototype that it never sees (i.e. is never presented with), can learn multiple prototypes simultaneously (even if those prototypes are correlated or overlap), and can also learn to extract a prototype while simultaneously able to remember specific examples presented to it.

2.3

Representation in connectionism III

McClelland and Rumelhart's simulation divides up the input pattern over the 24 units into two groups, the first group consists of eight inputs and the second group consists of 16 inputs. The pattern over the first eight units is set up to 'represent' the name of an individual dog (e.g. Fido, Rover etc.) and so differs completely on each presentation (we are pretending the child sees each individual dog once only). The last 16 units represent the individual dog itself, rather like a collection of features (such as waggy tail, pointy ears, lolling tongue). Three examples of input patterns are shown in Table 2.6.

Here are three examples (examples of real-life dogs in brackets):

Table 2.6

'Individual name' part	(e.g.)	'Individual dog' part	(e.g.)
11100011	(Fido)	1011010111111000	(Cocker Spaniel)
10110101	(Rover)	1011000010101000	(Alsatian)
00101110	(Spot)	1001001001101000	(poodle)

As in Auto associator exercise 1, the *actual* features represented by the 24 inputs are not specified. The exercise is to see how the network learns the arbitrary patterns, and responds to cues.

The 'name' parts of these individual patterns, over the first eight units, are all quite different: they are uncorrelated. This is intended to reflect the fact that names of dogs (Fido, Rover) are arbitrary and don't generally have features in common. However, the patterns of the last 16 units in each exemplar, the 'dog' part, are similar to the other exemplars: they are correlated. This is intended to mimic the fact that various dogs do have similar features because they are not arbitrary objects but, well, dogs. Dogs have four legs, two eyes etc., and also more unique 'doggy' attributes such as tail-wagging and barking. In fact each pattern is a slight distortion of the pattern, which is defined as the dog 'prototype'. The 'prototype' of dog (never shown to the network) was arbitrarily defined as the following pattern of 16 inputs:

1011000011111000

This is, if you like, the representation of the abstract 'typical' dog. So each individual 'dog' pattern was created by distorting this prototype by 'flipping' each unit's sign (from 1 to 0 or vice versa) with a small probability (0.2). The result is that each individual instance of 'dog' was based on or similar to the prototype pattern above, with a few (between two and seven) of the 16 units 'flipped'. Flipping a unit might be similar to seeing some dogs with black ears and some with white. The name pattern over units one to eight was entirely random in each case.

Overview of Auto associator exercise 2a

The network is presented with fifty different 'dogs', each with a new random name, and each a new distortion of the prototype.

Run the *Auto Associator* program and open the file **AA2a.nnd**. You will see the 50 different 'dog' input patterns used for training marked with **Tr** in the **Data** window. This time, we are not going to cycle through the list many times to learn all the patterns. This is because in our simulation a child sees a new dog once only. That is why we have 50 examples. Instead we will cycle once through the whole list. Set the **Learning coefficient** to 0.01. Set the maximum seed size to 0.01. Select **Use Cross-Entropy** in the **Options** menu. 'Cross-entropy' is a better learning algorithm when ouputs are 0s and 1s. It is an alternative way of calculating the error that is used to adjust weights. Click on **Seed** the network, then click on **One Cycle** in order to let the network 'see' each input exactly once.

You can try testing the network with the prototype pattern marked **Pr** in the **Data** window. Does the network give a strong response to this pattern (remember it has never seen it before)? That is, does the output over the last 16 units correspond to the input (being a series of 1s and 0s, or at least close enough)? Try the patterns it **was** trained on. Is the network responding as strongly to the other patterns (that it actually did see)?

Figure 2.16 shows output after one-cycle training with the prototype input.

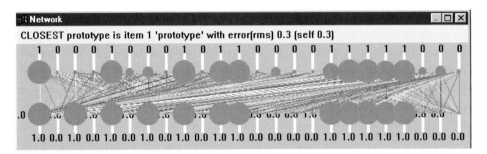

Figure 2.16 Output of the network after one cycle of training with the prototype

You can see the output strongly corresponds to the prototype over the right-hand 16 units, which is where the dog 'features' are coded.

2.4

Representation in connectionism IV

Two new prototypes were created for the concepts 'cat' and 'bagel', again using 16 units:

cat:	1011000010101101
bagel:	1101011010011110

These additional prototypes were chosen so that the cat, being a small mammal, shared some 'features' with the dog prototype: in fact its correlation with the dog prototype is 0.5. It wouldn't share the more 'doggy' attributes, e.g. barking. The bagel, however, is not correlated with either of the other prototypes, since as a piece of food rather than a small furry mammal it is an entirely unrelated object. McClelland and Rumelhart were interested in the capability of the network to simultaneously learn three different prototypes, of which two were related to each other to a certain extent.

In this case the prototypes themselves were given prototype 'names' (e.g. 'cat', 'dog' or 'bagel'). That is, for each of the three prototypes, a unique pattern was defined over the first eight units that was always associated with the individual examples of that prototype. In other words, the 'name' part of the pattern did not vary randomly but was designed to see if the network could learn to associate three pre-defined, fixed name patterns with an abstraction derived from the presented individual distortions of the three prototypes (see Table 2.7). In Auto associator exercise 2b, the distortions have been created by flipping the inputs with a probability of 0.1.

Table 2.7

Name pattern		Original Prototype representation
(Does not change when presented)	(e.g.)	(always distorted when presented)
10101010	(Dog)	1011000011111000
11001100	(Cat)	1011000010101101
10011001	(Bagel)	1101011010011110

Overview of Auto associator exercise 2b

So, as you have seen from Auto associator exercise 2a, the model seems to be capable of generating for itself a representation of the original (but never seen) prototype. This is another form of spontaneous generalization. Even more interesting is the model's behaviour when more than one prototype is presented.

Run the *Auto Associator* program and open the file **AA2b.nnd**. You will see the different 'dog', 'cat' and 'bagel' input patterns that are used for training marked with **Tr** in the **Data** window. Once again, we are not going to cycle through the list many times to learn all the patterns. Instead we will cycle once through the whole list. Set the **Learning coefficient** to 0.2. Set the maximum seed size to 0.01. Make sure **Use Cross-Entropy** is selected in the **Options** menu. Set **Propagations** to 4. Click on **Seed**, then click on **One Cycle** in order to let the network 'see' each input exactly once.

You can try testing the network with the six test patterns (the patterns that contain question marks) near the top of the pattern set in the **Data** window. The test patterns are partial cues with either the name part of a pattern, or the prototype part of the pattern. How does the network respond to these patterns? You should find that cueing with the prototype name accurately produces the response of the correct prototype. This should be true even for the cat and dog prototypes, which are correlated with each other (correlated patterns are often hard to discriminate). Figure 2.17 shows the output from presenting the network with the 'dog' name pattern. Remember the network simulation has never seen any of these prototypes: they are all abstractions from the data.

This is a harder problem than Auto associator exercise 2a, and will begin to give you a feeling for the way connectionist models sometimes need 'coaxing' to give the best results. For this problem, it works best if the value for **Propagations** in the left-hand **Training** window is set to 8. This helps 'tidy up' the network response by recycling output back to input eight times. Even with this, you may find you need to cycle through the data set four to eight times to get good results.

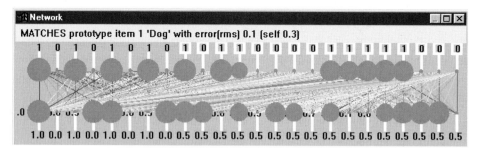

Figure 2.17 The Network window showing ouput from the 'dog' name pattern

This is an especially interesting result for the dog and cat prototypes, whose prototype patterns were correlated. It shows that a connectionist network accurately learns to discriminate three prototypes from the presentation of many individual exemplars, all different. And the network has no idea, prior to or during learning, how many prototypes lie behind the individuals it is presented with, nor is it informed at presentation how 'good' an exemplar each stimulus is. The underlying prototype structure is derived from commonalities in the input patterns as an automatic consequence of learning by error reduction (Section 3.4).

Learning specific and general information simultaneously

Even more impressive is McClelland and Rumelhart's final demonstration. In this, they wanted to see if the model could simultaneously learn a general prototype and specific exemplars. Suppose a child has a neighbour with a dog called Rover, a grandmother with a dog called Fido and also sees several other unspecified dogs in the park, which are identified generically as 'dogs' (i.e. not given names). Will the child (or rather the network!) learn to associate both the specific and the general concepts in this case so that he or she (or it) can recognize that dogs are dogs, and also recognize and name Fido and Rover correctly, with no prior knowledge?

2.5

Representation in connectionism V

Table 2.8

Name pattern		Original representation
(Never changes when presented)	(e.g.)	(only the prototype is distorted when presented)
10101010	(Dog)	10110000111111000
10001000	(Fido)	10010000111111100
10011101	(Rover)	11110000111111000

The situation uses three different 'name' patterns; one each for 'Fido' and 'Rover', and one for the class name 'dog' (see Table 2.8). The individual 'dog' patterns for Fido and Rover are two particular distortions of the prototype 'dog' pattern. Fido differs from the dog prototype at input positions 11 and 22 (remember, the first eight input positions are the name pattern); Rover differs from the dog prototype at input position 10.

Now the pattern set has the particular Fido and Rover patterns repeated exactly several times (these patterns have repeated presentations, the child 'sees' Fido and Rover many times). Several other (non-repeated) different distortions of the dog prototype make up the rest of the pattern set (the child sees many other dogs once only). The other distortions which are not considered to be the particular dogs Fido and Rover, were paired with the 'dog' name pattern.

Overview of Auto associator exercise 2c

Run the *Auto Associator* program and load the file **AA2c.nnd**. You will see the 'dog', 'Fido' and 'Rover' input patterns that are used for training marked with **Tr**. Once again, we are not going to cycle through the list many times to learn all the patterns. Instead we will cycle once through the whole list. As in Auto associator exercise 2b, set **Propagations** to 4 in the **Training** window. Set the **Learning coefficient** to 0.2. Set the maximum seed size to 0.01. Make sure **Use Cross-**

Entropy is selected in the **Options** menu. Click on **Seed** the network, then click on **One Cycle** in order to let the network 'see' each input exactly once.

This is the hardest task in these exercises. You may need to cycle through the pattern set more than once for good results. Sometimes the network fails to learn properly even doing this. You will then need to start again by clicking on **Seed** and cycling through the training set again.

You can try testing the network with the test patterns near the top of the pattern set in the **Data** window. The test patterns are partial cues with either the 'name' part of a pattern, or the 'dog' part of the pattern. How does the network respond to these patterns? You should find that cueing with the prototype name accurately produces the response of the dog prototype. What happens if you cue with a particular 'dog' pattern like 'Fido'? You should find the correct particular dog pattern is recalled.

Figure 2.18 shows the output from presenting the network with the 'Fido' name pattern.

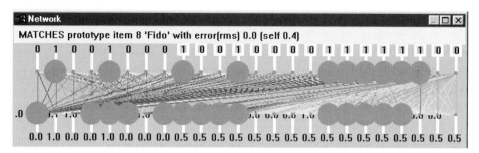

Figure 2.18   The **Network** window with the 'Fido' name pattern as input

So cueing with the 'dog' name pattern or prototype 'dog' pattern produces the appropriate prototype pattern response. Yet cueing with specific Fido or Rover name patterns produces recall of the appropriate specific Fido or Rover 'dog' pattern and vice versa. The sensitivity of this distributed memory system is indicated by the fact that the Rover 'dog' pattern differs from the 'dog' prototype at only one point (see Table 2.8), yet recall of the name from it as cue (and its recall from the name as cue) is essentially perfect.

So, a distributed memory system such as the one in the last computer exercise, learning simply from a set of individual exemplars presented to it, can simultaneously learn specific information about the exemplars and automatically generalize (spontaneously generalize) across those exemplars to extract knowledge about prototypes. It can learn and store many different patterns simultaneously in the same network, using one set of connections. It is this multiple use for a single set of connections, over which several different knowledge patterns are distributed, that makes connectionist models stand out from other approaches. Procedural models such as ACT-R (see Chapter 3) can be made to generalize across stimuli and are designed to perform pattern matching, but the knowledge of the instances in ACT-R is not distributed over a common set of parameters. Further, the interrogation of the connectionist network by the cue produced a single response pattern in one process: as if all stored patterns had been processed in parallel to produce the appropriate response. In no sense were the individual stored patterns examined serially, one-by-one, for the best fit. The model performs true parallel distributed processing. It is not simply a categorizer or prototype extraction device; it is a much more general-purpose information processor capable of powerful and flexible processing.

It also gives an interesting insight into the semantic/episodic memory distinction (see **Rutherford, 2005**). The specific information about individual dogs, i.e. each one's name and perhaps where it was seen, is analogous to memory for individual 'episodic' events, while the ability to generalize over those individuals so as to classify them all as dogs is an operation associated with what is usually called semantic memory. This single connectionist processor is capable of learning the specific and the general information simultaneously: episodic and semantic memory operations are combined into one connectionist model. This 'leads naturally to the suggestion that semantic memory may be just the residue of the superposition of episodic traces' (McClelland and Rumelhart, 1986, p.206). In other words, perhaps in human memory there is no fundamental separation of semantic memory from episodic memory, which is a view gaining ground among some psychologists. There are some models of memory that attempt to explore this idea systematically, e.g. MINERVA (Hintzman, 1986) or CHARM (Metcalfe Eich, 1982). It does seem that connectionist models very much blur the need for a separation of episodic and semantic memory into two more-or-less independent memory systems.

Summary of Section 4

- An auto associator network can be trained to respond to collections of patterns with varying degrees of correlation between them.
- When the input patterns being learned are highly correlated, the network can generate the central tendency or *prototype* that lies behind them, another form of spontaneous generalization.
- A single auto associator network can learn more than one prototype simultaneously, even when the concepts being learned are related to each other. Cueing with the prototype name will give recall of the correct prototype (which was never presented to the network complete).
- An auto associator network can extract prototype information while also learning specific information about individual exemplars of the prototype.
- Thus, the network's capability to retrieve specific information from cues (content addressability) means that, given a specific enough cue, it can retrieve the specific information of the individual exemplars from which the prototype generalization is constructed.
- Such behaviour is an example of a unitary memory system that can support both 'episodic' and 'semantic' memory within the same structure.

5   More powerful connectionist models: the simulation of human cognitive behaviour

The connectionist models described above (pattern matching, auto associators, and prototype learning from exemplars) are really 'demonstration' models. They show what these models can do when appropriately configured or trained, and their behaviour is described as simply having various useful characteristics, such as spontaneous generalization and content addressability, which are known to be characteristic of human performance, in a general kind of way. The behaviour of the models, however, is not directly compared with the behaviour of humans in a way that makes a specific comparison with human performance in a given task (for example, per cent correct recall or reaction time data). Connectionist models are much more powerful when they attempt to precisely model or simulate human performance on a given task, and the example we now turn to does just that in the field of reading, in particular the characteristics of the memory store of words that forms the lexicon.

There is enormous psychological interest in the mechanisms of reading. The ability to read and pronounce an enormous corpus of words is clearly a considerable feat of learning and memory. English words with similar letter sequences can have quite different pronunciations: consider *gave – have, rose – lose, root – soot, bomb – comb – womb*. Clearly the rules of pronunciation are quite complex. Words are usually divided into 'regular' words and 'exception' words. Regular words have pronunciations that might be expected from simple rules based on the letter strings within them: words such as *tint, gave* and *rose* are regular. Exceptions to these pronunciations would be *pint, have* and *lose*. A simple (but not foolproof) way to work out the regular pronunciation of a letter string is to add a letter to make a non-word. Adding *b* to – *ave* produces *bav*e, a non-word that most people pronounce like *gave*, so we think of that as the regular pronunciation.

This ability to pronounce non-words, that generally we have never seen before, means that we haven't just learned a list of all the correct pronunciations for every word we have seen: we must have internalized some mechanisms for translating letter strings into pronunciations.

Perhaps there is a way of presenting words, along with their correct pronunciation, to a neural network so that, without any further constraints, the network simply learns the 'rules' of pronunciation and performs word and non-word pronunciation just like we do. However, there is a major qualification, indeed stumbling block, to constructing models of cognition based on two-layer pattern associators (described in Section 3). They cannot learn to associate patterns that are not 'linearly predictable'. This means that there are some pattern associations that cannot be modelled using one set of output units, in which the patterns are learned by changing weights at the output set of nodes only. The prototype patterns in Section 4 could be learned like this because they were linearly predictable: they were bound to be because the prototypes were designed to be slightly related (cat and dog) or completely uncorrelated (bagel), and the exemplars were small distortions of these prototypes. It is perhaps easier to see what linear predictability means by looking at an example of patterns that are not linearly predictable.

Table 2.9 An example of pattern association that is not linearly predictable

Input	Response (output)
1 1	0
0 0	0
1 0	1
0 1	1

Table 2.9 shows an example set of pattern associations that are not **linearly predictable**. Note that the pattern 0 0 is in the same category as its converse 1 1, (both produce the response 0) and similarly 0 1 is categorized with 10 (both produce the response 1). The two-layer pattern associator in Pattern associator exercise 1 cannot in principle learn this discrimination: there is no set of weights and thresholds that this network can use that would work (see Pattern associator exercise 1).

This is because the categorizations (0 0 with 1 1) and (0 1 with 1 0) cannot be done on the basis of the individual 'features' acting independently (each 'feature' being each 0 or 1 in the pattern) but it has to be done on the basis of *combinations* of features. Another example of this is the reading of English words. Take the letter string 'ave': the pronunciation of this string can only be determined from its context. A common pronunciation would be as in *gave*. But this differs from the pronunciation found in *have*. Before you think that a simple rule for the pronunciation of 'ave' could be constructed according to the preceding letter (a preceding 'h' means pronounce as in *have*), consider these words: *shave, haven, gavel*. And then how would you cope with *weaver*? Pronunciation of English letter strings comes from a complex analysis of the surrounding word context, sometimes depending on the sentence context itself (consider the two pronunciations – and meanings – of *read*). These analyses cannot be done by simple two-layer pattern associators such as that in Pattern associator exercise 1.

5.1 Hidden layers

To perform this association we require an extension to the two-layer pattern associator model. We need an extra layer. Because this layer is in the middle of the network, so it can't 'see' the inputs directly, and also can't 'see' the outputs, it is known as a **hidden layer**, and the units in it are called **hidden units**.

Pattern associator exercise 2

Learning configural patterns

In this exercise, you will find that a seemingly simple problem is impossible to learn with a two-layer network, and that hidden units are necessary for the computation of associations between configural patterns.

2.6

Representation in connectionism VI

The representation of the patterns is in Table 2.9. Again, we are using 'arbitrary' patterns, to illustrate the problem of pattern sets that are not linearly predictable. Another adjective for this problem is **configural**: since the discrimination between the patterns relies on the total *configuration* of the inputs.

Run the *Pattern Associator* program and open the file **PA2.nnd**. You will see the four input patterns that are used for training marked with **Tr**. As in Pattern associator exercise 1, we are now going to cycle through the list many times to learn all the patterns. Take a close look at the network in the **Network** window: it has two layers as in Figure 2.4. As we've said, this network will be incapable of learning this problem.

Overview of Pattern associator exercise 2a

Don't spend more than 30 seconds on this exercise!

Click on **Seed** the network, then click on **Cycle Until...** in order to let the network try and learn the problem. It won't. You can sit in front of your computer till the cows come home, but the error (shown in the graph in the **Network** window) will never fall below 0.5. Click on the **Stop** button (in the **Learning** window) before it drives you mad!

Overview of Pattern associator exercise 2b

Now we will add a layer to the network, using the **File** menu, **New Network...** submenu. Add another layer by specifying '2' in one of the **hidden layer** boxes. The network should look like Figure 2.19. Can this network now learn the problem? A step-by-step guide follows.

Step 1: build network and load patterns

1   Run the program *Pattern Associator* as in Pattern associator exercise 1.

2   Click on the **File** menu.

     COMPUTER **File** menu drops down.

3   Click on the **Load**... submenu.

     COMPUTER **Load Network and Training** dialog opens.

4   Find the file **PA2.nnd**. Select it and click on **Open**.

     COMPUTER The two-layer network and pattern set appears in the middle and right windows. We need to change it to a three-layer network.

5   Click on the **File** menu.

     COMPUTER **File** menu drops down.

6   Click on the **New Network**... submenu.

     COMPUTER **New Network** dialog appears, see Figure 2.5.

7   Make sure the check box labelled **For existing data** is selected.

8   Type '1' into the box labelled **Output Layer** (this is what it should contain anyway).

9   Type '0' into the box marked **2nd hidden layer** (this is what it should contain anyway).

10   Type '2' into the box marked **1st hidden layer**.

11   Type '2' into the box marked **Input Layer** (this is what it should contain anyway).

12   Click on **OK**.

> COMPUTER The **New Network** dialog disappears, and the **Network** window on the right should display a network something like Figure 2.19:

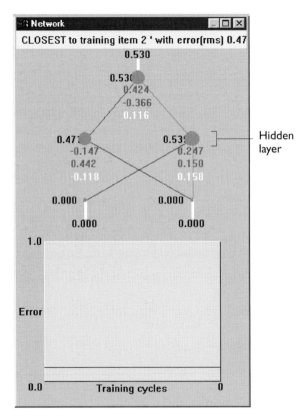

Figure 2.19 The **Network** window displaying the hidden layer

Step 2: train network

Now we are ready to train the network. In the **Training** window there are a number of parameters, such as **Learning coefficient** and **Match threshold**. We can leave these as they are. The **Learning coefficient** alters how fast the network learns, and the **Reduce error to** value tells the network when to stop: it refers to the Error values in the top of the window.

13   Click on **Seed**. This prepares the network for learning.

14   Click on **Cycle Until....**

Did your network learn? The error in the graph should fall to nearly zero when it does. Perhaps it didn't. This problem is so 'hard' that even a three-layer neural network (which is known as a 'universal approximator') can sometimes fail to learn it. If it didn't learn, try **Seed** again, which changes the initial conditions of the network, then click on **Cycle Until...** again in order to let the network have another go. The network should learn successfully about two times out of three.

In these connectionist models, the network compares its output with a target output, and any difference or error is 'propagated back' to the input weights, which are altered in a way that reduces the error. If you step through the task one cycle at a time, you can see the weights changing on each of the two upper layers.

This exercise showed how the computation of new weights *propagates backwards* down the network from the output units to the input units, and as it is based on the calculation of error in the highest layer, it is known as the **backward propagation of error** method of learning (or **backprop** for short). One major feature of this learning scheme is that it preserves the situation that the network learns by purely local actions: modification of the weight of any connection is calculated from information local to that connection: that is the input transmitted from the lower layer unit and the errors in the direct connections above it. The weight calculation requires no knowledge of the state of any part of the network beyond the local connections. In networks with hidden units it is the dominant mechanism used for creating connectionist models capable of learning useful processing capability.

5.2 An example of a powerful multi-level connectionist model

We shall now look at a connectionist model with hidden units designed to simulate the reading of English words.

Seidenberg and McClelland (1989) set up a connectionist model based on a three-layer network with hidden units (see Figure 2.20).

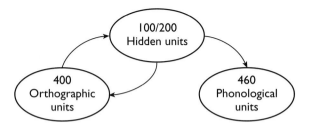

Figure 2.20   Seidenberg and McClelland's model for word reading

Source: Seidenberg and McClelland, 1989

2.7

Representation in connectionism VII

Input orthographic units

Table 2.10   Example coding over first three (of 400) units for input triple _ma

Letter position in triple	Input unit with letter sets		
	1	2	3
First position set	_ a c d e f k n p v	_ a b f h j k m n v	_ e j k n q s u w y
Middle position set	b c e g j m n p r z	a d e k n p r s t w	h j k m p q s t v x
Last position set	a d g h k n s u v x	a c g h k o t u w _	a b e g k m t v y _
Code for triple _ma	1	0	1
	(all three match)	(only two match)	(all three match)

Four hundred 'orthographic input units' take an input based on letter strings from words. The input is not a simple presentation of individual letters. Instead, the letter strings are encoded as triples, based on a scheme devised by Rumelhart and McClelland (1986). The letter string *make* is represented as the set of letter triples _ma, mak, ake, and ke_ (the underscore indicates the beginning or end of a word). Further, each individual input unit will respond to a range of different triples (see Table 2.10). In the scheme used, each unit has a set of ten possible first letters, a set of ten possible middle letters and a set of ten possible final letters. Any letter triple whose first letter corresponds with any letter from the first position list *and* whose second letter corresponds with any letter from the second list, *and* whose final letter corresponds with any letter from the final position list will cause that unit to respond (see Table 2.10: matches are in bold outline). So each individual unit will respond to many different input triples (1000 in all). However, as every unit has different letters in its three sets, across the input network of 400 units only a small set of units is activated by a given letter triple. Each unique triple activates about 20 units in all. It is the different *pattern* of activation over the 400 input units that uniquely encodes each triple.

This pattern feeds through connections to the hidden units and on to the 460 output 'phonological' units.

Output units

These have a similar representational scheme, derived from Wickelgren's (1969) triples scheme. Of course, since the aim is to represent phonology, the encoded features are phonetic ones such as vowel, fricative or stop (rather than written letters of the alphabet): the finer details can be found in Rumelhart and McClelland (1986). Once again, there is a set of first position phonetics, second position phonetics and third position phonetics, so every output unit responds to a large set of different phoneme triples. However, each unique phoneme triple corresponds to a unique pattern of excitation of about 16 of the 460 output units, so the network as a whole has unique representations for every possible phoneme triple. The important point is that both input and output use *distributed representation* over many units, so that a given input word, or a given output pronunciation, produces a unique *pattern* of activation.

After deciding on the representational scheme, some more steps are required before starting on the training process. Two thousand eight hundred and ninety seven monosyllabic words, chosen largely from the Kucera and Francis (1967) word count, had to be coded into a computer according to their true pronunciation, and a training regime decided. The network model was to be trained to learn the pronunciations of these words in a way that reflected the uneven experience that we have with English words: the Kucera and Francis word count reveals that the most common word 'the' occurs in English texts over 69,000 times more often than the rare word 'rake'. The training scheme ended up as a set of 150,000 learning trials, in which the most common words appeared 230 times in all, while the least common words were presented about 14 times.

Each of these 150,000 learning trials worked the same way. For the word being 'presented' on that trial, an orthographic string is derived from the letter triples (see the examples in Box 2.7 above) and presented as a unique pattern of excitation to the orthographic input units. Activation spreads forward along the connections to the hidden units, which in turn respond and send activation along the second set of connections to the output phonological units. The phonological output units respond to this activity and produce an output pattern or response. This pattern is compared to the previously determined correct phonological definition (the 'teacher', see Section 3.2). Any difference between the network's response and this definitive 'pronunciation' is propagated backwards through the network and used to adjust all the weights on the connections in such a way that the difference or error between what the network produces as a response to the presented 'word' is reduced.

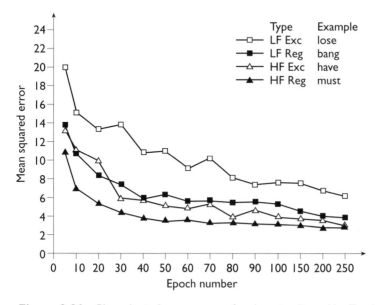

Figure 2.21 Phonological error scores for the stimuli used by Taraban and McClelland
Source: based on Seidenberg and McClelland, 1989.

So, after 150,000 learning trials, what did this network learn? The performance of the network is measured by its ability to produce the correct, defined phonology. A measure of this difference is called the **mean squared error** (see Section 3 in

Chapter 6). Figure 2.21 shows how this error reduces over the course of training. The learning is plotted for four groups of words (as taken from Taraban and McClelland, 1987), these are regular (Reg) or exception (Exc) words of high (HF) or low (LF) frequency. Regular words contain letter strings that occur in many words, always with the same pronunciation. For example, *Must* contains the sequence *–ust*, which is pronounced the same in other monosyllabic words with that ending (*just, dust*, etc.). Exception words are words pronounced differently from the majority of words with the same letter sequence: *have* is pronounced differently from *gave, shave, wave*, etc.

Figure 2.21 shows how the network learns the pronunciation of all the words, though even at the end substantial error is found on the low frequency exception words. You can see that regular words and high frequency words give rise to fewer errors. For the low frequency words, the network has received a lot less training, presumably in much the same way as humans would.

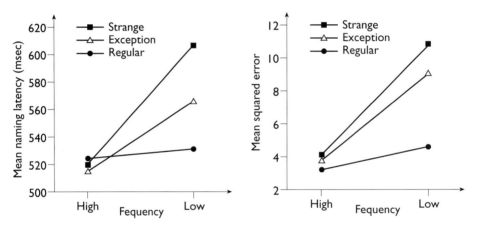

Figure 2.22   Results of the Waters and Seidenberg studies: experiment (left graph) and simulation (right graph)

Source: Seidenberg and McClelland, 1989 (after Waters and Seidenberg, 1985)

The difference between regular and exception words has been well explored by psychologists interested in the processes of reading (a good account can be found in Ellis, 1993). Psychologists have measured the speed with which people name the words when presented with them (this is known as **naming latency**). Results from an experiment by Waters and Seidenberg (1985) are shown in Figure 2.22. As well as looking at regular and exception words, they looked at 'strange' words: these are words like 'corps' or 'aisle', which have letter sequences that occur in few other monosyllabic words, and they also have quite idiosyncratic pronunciations. The results for the naming latencies found by Waters and Seidenberg are in the left half of Figure 2.22.

Seidenberg and McClelland's simulation of these results works by presenting to the connectionist network the same actual words used by Waters and Seidenberg (1985), and measuring the error in 'pronunciation' after it had undergone training as described above. This error is the extent to which the phonological output of the network differs from the pre-determined correct phonological representation of the word. They assume that this error would somehow be transformed into an effect on naming latency if the model had the capability of transforming the 'phonological' output into actual speech.

The right of Figure 2.22 shows the mean squared error produced by the connectionist network for the various groups of words. The type of word and its frequency appears to have much the same effect on the network's error as they do on the naming latency of human subjects. The connectionist model appears to be a good *simulation* of human behaviour. Some more results are shown in Figure 2.23. Brown's (1987) experiment used 'unique' words, such as *soap* or *curve*, which have letter sequences not found in other monosyllabic words, but are less eccentric than the 'strange' words, and their pronunciations are less idiosyncratic.

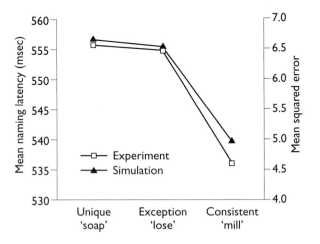

Figure 2.23   Naming latency for unique, exceptional and consistent words

Again, the simulation proceeds by presenting the same words used by Brown (1987) to the connectionist network and measuring the phonological error. Once again, the type of word has an effect on the network's output error that closely mimics the effect on human naming latency.

Seidenberg and McClelland (1989) explored a whole range of experiments, comparing the naming latency found in human subjects on various groups of words with the error output of their connectionist model. By and large, the agreement was very good.

Seidenberg and McClelland do not claim that their connectionist model is a complete or final model of the reading process. The most they would want to claim is that the successful simulations show that this approach is probably along the right lines, and is worth pursuing and refining in order to increase its match with behavioural results. Extending the model to allow it to produce actual speech output would also be valuable. The main theoretical contrast they emphasize is with common psychological theories of human reading. These have concentrated on the likelihood of the existence of several, largely independent, routes that are used to pronounce written words (see for example Ellis, 1993). In such models, regular words are pronounced by using a *rule-based system*, which converts spellings more-or-less directly to sound. However, such a route could not work for exception words, so for these a second route, independent of the first, looks up the meaning of the word in a semantic system (the **mental lexicon**), which can then be used to look up an unambiguous pronunciation of the word.

Seidenberg and McClelland's model dispenses with this multiplicity of routes, and indeed the simple model that we have looked at dispenses with the semantic lexicon itself. In their connectionist model, pronunciation is computed directly from each word's orthography, in a way that is identical for high and low frequency, regular and exception words and even non-words. The differences found in the naming latencies of these various groups of words are predicted by this single mechanism model of reading, without recourse to semantic lexicons and multiple routes. At the very least, psychologists wishing to argue that multiple routes are involved in human reading have to provide new evidence not based simply on naming latency to justify their position. Such evidence may be based on the impairment to reading caused by brain damage in otherwise healthy adults who were formerly skilled readers (**acquired dyslexia**). However, the Seidenberg and McClelland model can then attempt to simulate such evidence also: Ellis (1993) provides a brief account. There is no doubt that the successful simulation of human behavioural data by connectionist models, even if it does not provide immediate solutions to the analysis of human behaviour, at least presents a challenge to conventional psychological models.

Summary of Section 5

- Patterns that cannot be discriminated on the basis of their simple, individual features treated independently are not linearly predictable. The discrimination has to be done on the basis of complex combinations of features. A real-life example is the computation of the pronunciation of English words from their spellings.

- Pattern associators based on connectionist networks can only perform discriminations on stimuli that are not linearly discriminable by incorporating extra layers of computational units. These layers, which have no direct external input and produce no external output, are made up of hidden units.

- Connectionist networks with layers of hidden units learn associations by backward propagation of errors. The final output of the top layer is compared with the target output, and the error is used to calculate error in the previous layer, generating a correction factor each time, and so on backwards down the network.

- A three-layer pattern associator, designed by Seidenberg and McClelland (1989), with an appropriate distributed representational scheme for input orthography (spelling) and output phonology (pronunciation) can learn the correct 'pronunciations' of a set of English words.

- This pattern associator, trained on the pronunciation of English words, simulates the results obtained from psychology experiments that measure human responses to naming various types of words, such as high and low frequency regular and exception words.

- The successful simulation of human behaviour by a connectionist network model that computes its output in a single step, has no built-in rules and was configured by simply training the network on correct pronunciations, challenges conventional psychological models that rely on multiple pronunciation mechanisms, and are frequently dependent on explicitly specified rule-based systems.

6   Conclusion

Connectionist models take an entirely different approach from rule-based (procedural) computational models, such as ACT-R. The big advantage of such models, both connectionist and procedural, is that the models are forced to be explicit about the computational architecture, and in particular about the representation of input and output information. What did you think of the representation scheme used by Seidenberg and McClelland (1989) in Section 5? It was complicated, but even so was it a good way to capture the input and output information? A neural network model can stand or fall by the accuracy or otherwise of its chosen representation scheme. Later studies with the Seidenberg and McClelland model (e.g. Morris, 1989) showed problems with it, and alternative schemes have been used (e.g. Plaut *et al.*, 1996: this data set is available in your software as 'reading.nnd'). For both approaches, the comparison with human behavioural data is crucial, and one way to expand this is to 'lesion' models by deleting connections (in the case of the connectionist models) or rules (in the case of procedural models. You might like trying to lesion the models you have used in Section 3.3 of this chapter (use the **Lesion** menu in the **Training** window). How many connections need to be lost before the networks lose all functionality? What is the behaviour of the model as it gradually loses more and more connections?

  As psychologists improve their understanding of the nature of information handled by real brain neural connections, and the transformations that are applied to that information, better and better connectionist simulations of human performance should result.

Further reading

For an especially good analysis of critiques and responses see:

Bechtel, W. and Abrahamsen, A. (2001) 'Are rules required to process representation?' in Bechtel, W. and Abrahamsen, A. *Connectionism and the Mind*, (2nd edn) Oxford, Blackwell.

Bechtel, W. and Abrahamsen, A. (2001) 'Are syntactically structured representations needed?' in Bechtel, W. and Abrahamsen, A. *Connectionism and the Mind*, (2nd edn) Oxford, Blackwell.

For more on the Seidenberg and McClelland model presented here see:

Patterson, K.E., Seidenberg, M.S. and McClelland, J.L. (1989) 'Connections and disconnections: acquired dyslexia in a computational model of reading processes' in Morris, R. (ed.) *Parallel Distributed Processing*, Oxford, Clarendon Press.

For a forceful critique of connectionist models see:

Prince, A. and Pinker, S. (1989) 'Rules and connections in human language' in Morris, R. (ed.) *Parallel Distributed Processing*, Oxford, Clarendon Press.

References

Anderson, J., Silverstein, J., Ritz, S. and Jones, R. (1977) 'Distinctive features, categorical perception, and probability learning: some applications of a neural model', *Psychological Review*, vol.84, pp.413–51.

Bechtel, W. and Abrahamsen, A. (2001) *Connectionism and the Mind: Parallel Processing, Dynamics and Evolution in Networks* (2nd edn) Oxford, Blackwell.

Braisby, N. (2005) 'Concepts' in Braisby, N. and Gellatly, A. (eds) *Cognitive Psychology*, Oxford, Oxford University Press/The Open University.

Brown, G.D.A. (1987) 'Resolving inconsistency: a computational model of word naming', *Journal of Memory and Language*, vol.26, pp.1–2.

Ellis, A.W. (1993) *Reading, Writing and Dyslexia* (2nd edn.) Hillsdale, NJ, Lawrence Erlbaum Associates.

Hintzman, D.L. (1986) 'Schema abstraction in a multiple-trace memory model', *Psychological Review*, vol.93, pp.411–28.

Hubel, D.H. and Wiesel, T.N. (1959) 'Receptive fields of single neurones in the cat's striate cortex', *Journal of Physiology*, vol.148, pp.574–91.

Hubel, D.H. and Wiesel, T.N. (1962) 'Receptive fields, binocular interaction and functional architecture in the cat's visual cortex', *Journal of Physiology*, vol.160, pp.106–54.

Kucera, H. and Francis, W.N. (1967) *Computational Analysis of Present-Day American English*, Providence, RI, Brown University Press.

McClelland, J.L. and Rumelhart, D.E. (1986) 'A distributed model of human learning and memory' in McClelland, J.L., Rumelhart, D.E. and the PDP Research Group (eds) (1986).

McClelland, J.L., Rumelhart, D.E. and the PDP Research Group (eds) (1986) *Parallel Distributed Processing: Explorations in the Microstructure of Cognition, Vol.2, Psychological and Biological Models*, Cambridge, MA, MIT Press/ Bradford Books.

Metcalfe Eich, J. (1982) 'A composite holographic associative recall model', *Psychological Review*, vol.89, pp.627–61.

Morris, R. (ed.) (1989) *Parallel Distributed Processing*, Oxford, Clarendon Press.

Plaut, D.C., Seidenberg, M.S., McClelland, J.L. and Patterson, K. (1996) 'Understanding normal and impaired word reading: computational principles in quasi-regular domains', *Psychological Review*, vol.103, pp.56–115.

Rosch, E. (1978) 'Principles of categorization' in Rosch, E. and Lloyd, B.B. (eds) *Cognition and Categorization*, Hillsdale, NJ, Lawrence Earlbaum.

Rumelhart, D.E. and McClelland, J.L. (1986) 'On learning the past tense of English verbs' in McClelland, J.L., Rumelhart, D.E. and the PDP Research Group (eds) (1986).

Rutherford, A. (2005) 'Long-term memory: encoding to retrieval' in Braisby, N. and Gellatly, A. (eds) *Cognitive Psychology*, Oxford, Oxford University Press/The Open University.

Seidenberg, M.S. and McClelland, J.L. (1989) 'A distributed, developmental model of word recognition and naming', *Psychological Review*, vol.96, pp.523–68.

Stone, T. (2005) 'Theoretical issues in cognitive psychology' in Braisby, N. and Gellatly, A. (eds) *Cognitive Psychology*, Oxford, Oxford University Press/The Open University.

Taraban, R. and McClelland, J.L. (1987) 'Conspiracy effects in word recognition', *Journal of Memory and Language*, vol.26, pp.608–31.

Tulving, E. (1991) 'Memory research is not a zero-sum game', *American Psychologist*, vol.46, pp.41–2.

Waters, G.S. and Seidenberg, M.S. (1985) 'Spelling–sound effects in reading: time course and decision criteria', *Memory and Cognition*, vol.13, pp.557–72.

Wickelgren, W.A. (1969) 'Context-sensitive coding, associative memory, and serial order in (speech) behaviour', *Psychological Review*, vol.76, pp.1–15.

Symbolic modelling   Chapter 3

Paul Mulholland and Stuart Watt

1   What is cognitive modelling?

Cognitive modelling involves building a working model of a cognitive process and then comparing the behaviour of that model against human performance. If the model behaves in the same way as humans, then the structure of the model and the way it works may give some insight into how humans perform the task.

Cognitive modelling is very like the kind of technique that car designers or architects use to make it easier to see and test their designs. Psychologists use models in the same way: to make it easier to understand and to test their theories. Generally speaking, there are two different approaches to cognitive modelling. First, there is a high-level approach. To follow the car analogy, a high-level model should look and behave as much like a car as possible, without necessarily having the same internal workings. A high-level model might state that there is an engine, but might not say exactly how it worked, or what it was made of. But there is also a low-level approach, where a modeller would look at representing the kinds of bits that cars were made from (wheels, axles, pistons, valves, and so on) and try to understand how the behaviours of these components could work together to behave like a car. In cognitive psychology, Parallel distributed processing (or connectionism) (see Chapter 2) can be thought of as a low-level modelling approach and rule-based systems can be thought of as a high-level approach.

1.1   Rule-based systems

A **rule-based** system models cognition as an explicit set of rules – for example, production rules – that provides a recipe for how the model should behave. **Production rules** contain two parts – a condition and an action. They are structured in the form 'IF condition is met THEN perform action'. The **condition** specifies what must be true in order for the rule to be applied. The **action** is what the production rule should perform if the condition is true. If a production rule matches its condition and performs its action, then the rule is said to have **fired**. A rule-based model is constructed out of a set of production rules that together can produce the desired cognitive behaviour. The production rule written in an English-like form in Figure 3.1 could be used in a model of how to make a cup of tea. A complete model of tea making might contain production rules for boiling the kettle, warming the pot, adding tea bags to the pot, adding sugar and stirring the tea. Each production rule would fire when the current state of the tea-making process matched its condition. The rule in Figure 3.1 would only fire once the milk had been added to the cup and the tea was ready to pour.

> **IF** the cup just contains milk **AND** the tea in the pot is ready
> **THEN** pour tea into the cup

Figure 3.1   A production rule from a model of tea making

It is possible to model complex cognitive processes using production rules. For example, a rule-based model of how humans produce grammatical sentences may have production rules for selecting an appropriate verb depending on the meaning of the sentence, and for selecting an appropriate ending for the verb depending on the tense to be used.

Unlike PDP models, rule-based models focus on how the cognitive tasks humans perform can be understood as the processing of information without considering how such processing might be realized in the brain. The relationship between the approaches taken by PDP and rule-based systems can be understood in terms of Marr's (1982) levels of explanation. Marr argued that psychological explanations can be understood at any of three levels: computational, algorithmic and hardware. The PDP approach places a greater emphasis on the hardware level, arguing that if the model reflects some basic properties of the human brain, interesting psychological behaviour will emerge. On the other hand, a wholly rule-based approach places virtually no emphasis on the actual brain, effectively saying that the way the brain works is more a matter for biology than psychology. Instead, it argues that psychological phenomena can be most appropriately explained at the computational and algorithmic levels.

PDP models being closer to Marr's hardware level are described as being sub-symbolic. A **sub-symbolic model** does not contain any explicit representation of symbols such as rules. Instead, PDP models are constructed out of neural-like units. Conversely, rule-based systems can be described as **symbolic models** as they explicitly model cognition using symbols such as rules.

1.2 Cognitive architectures

Newell (1973) argued that it was not sufficient to develop a collection of discrete models to describe a broad range of psychological phenomena. Instead, there should be some integration and consistency across the models being developed. For example, playing chess, recognizing objects and producing grammatical sentences are all psychological processes that use long-term memory. If rule-based models of these three psychological phenomena contained completely different ways of representing, organizing and retrieving from long-term memory, this would clearly be a problem. Humans use the same cognitive processes across a range of tasks.

This led to the development of rule-based cognitive architectures that could account for a range of cognitive processes using the same modelling components. A **cognitive architecture** is an overarching framework that can account for a number of phenomena using a fixed set of mechanisms. As well as maintaining consistency across a set of models, cognitive architectures have another important advantage. Cognitive architectures distinguish clearly between the cognitive model and the computer (and any associated programming languages) on which the model is running. When a cognitive model is developed using a standard programming language (such as the C programming language) there is a need to distinguish which parts of the program are psychologically relevant and which are just dependent on the programming language being used. For example, a programming language has facilities for storing information but the model developer is not necessarily claiming that the way this information is stored in the computer bears any relation to the way humans store information in memory. A rule-based cognitive architecture is 'emulated' on a computer, but there is a clear distinction between the working of the model and the working of the computer. By this, we mean that the cognitive architecture is run on a computer but has its own self-contained set of processes, such as production rules. It does not directly use the general purpose processes of the computer that are used to provide the computer user with all kinds of facilities from email to word processing.

PDP is itself a cognitive architecture comprising a fixed set of artificial neural mechanisms. Two of the most well known rule-based cognitive architectures are ACT-R (Anderson and Lebiere, 1998) and Soar (Newell, 1990). In the next three sections we will look in detail at ACT-R, as a rule-based cognitive architecture and some of the empirical data it has been used to model. Particular consideration will be given to the extent to which ACT-R meets Newell's (1990) goal to develop a cognitive architecture that can provide an integrated and consistent account of a wide range of psychological processes.

Summary of Section 1

- Cognitive modelling involves building a model of a cognitive process and then comparing the behaviour of the model against human performance.
- Rule-based systems provide symbolic models of cognition comprising explicit rules, called production rules.
- Rule-based cognitive architectures such as ACT-R and Soar attempt to provide an integrated account of a range of cognitive theories and empirical findings.

2 An overview of ACT-R

To give you a taste of cognitive modelling, in this chapter we will describe, evaluate and use Anderson's ACT-R cognitive architecture (Anderson and Lebiere, 1998). ACT-R is perhaps the most widely used cognitive architecture in the cognitive modelling community, and reflects a trend towards **hybrid models** that attempt to span Marr's levels of explanation. Although ACT-R is primarily a rule-based cognitive architecture, it has certain characteristics more usually associated with PDP.

2.1 A brief history of ACT-R

ACT (which stands for 'Adaptive Control of Thought') has its roots in Anderson and Bower's (1973) theory of human associative memory, and their model of it, called HAM. A number of different versions of ACT have been developed. The first version of ACT proper, called ACTE, combined elements of HAM's memory representations with rule-based production systems that model control of behaviour and more complex activities like problem solving. In 1983, Anderson revised ACTE producing ACT* (pronounced 'act star'), which revised the underlying memory system to be more plausible biologically, and introduced a mechanism for learning new rules for the first time. ACT* was the first complete theory in the ACT series, and was capable of modelling a wide range of behaviours, from memory to complex problem solving and skill acquisition.

In 1993, ACT-R was developed and since then it has been gradually revised. The 'R' stands for 'rational', and refers to Anderson's (1990) theory of 'rational analysis'. Basically, **rational analysis theory** states that each component of the cognitive system is optimized with respect to demands from the environment, given its computational limitations. ACT-R also shifted the emphasis towards a finer-grained model. Whereas earlier rule-based models tended to use a small number of complex rules, in ACT-R there is a definite shift to a larger number of simple rules. Anderson and Lebiere (1998) in fact argue that the simple chunks of the ACT-R's memory, and the simple rules of its production system, are 'atomic' in the sense that they should not be broken down into further, more fine-grained ACT-R constructs.

2.2   The architecture of ACT-R

The ACT-R cognitive architecture comprises a clear set of components, whose interactions lead to its special behaviour. These components are more or less distinct modules within it. We have shown an overview of the architecture for ACT-R in Figure 3.2.

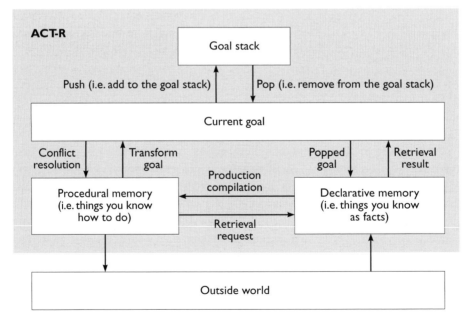

Figure 3.2   An overview of the ACT-R architecture

Source: adapted from Anderson and Lebiere, 1998

The ACT-R architecture makes a strong distinction between two different kinds of memory, **declarative memory** and procedural memory. Put simply, declarative memory is full of things that we just know, for example, that '1 + 3' is '4', that grass is green and that books have pages in. Procedural memory, on the other hand, is full of things that we know how to do. For example, few people would know the answer to '154 + 367' directly, but most would know a procedure that can be used to work out the answer. The steps in this procedure would be stored in procedural memory.

Importantly, declarative memory and procedural memory are not independent, but interrelated. There are two kinds of connection between them. First, a production rule fired in procedural memory may require elements from declarative memory. This route is shown in Figure 3.2 as a 'retrieval request'. Second, new production rules can be created in procedural memory from 'chunks' in declarative memory (this process will be discussed in Section 2.4). This process is known as **production compilation**. The importance of production compilation can be seen in ACT-R models of learning, where new rules are formed as learners become more skilled at solving problems. For example, an intermediate chess player will pick up new rules through experience, not of the rules of the game itself, which they already know, but rules about how to defend against or exploit particular situations on the board (Chase and Simon, 1973).

There is more to the ACT-R architecture than the interplay between declarative and procedural memory, though. There is also a **goal stack** and a **current goal** (see Section 2.5). These are important for models involving lots of rules, as the current goal is a kind of focus of current attention – this represents what ACT-R is currently trying to do. The stack contains other goals; these are goals that are not the immediate focus of attention, but that still need to be dealt with some time later.

As described so far, ACT-R is isolated from the external world. However, it is worth knowing that attempts have been made to encompass and extend ACT-R even further, providing it with a perceptual and motor system, including motor, speech, vision and audition modules. In fact, Salvucci (2001) has used ACT-R to study the effects of using a mobile phone while driving.

This gives you the big picture of ACT-R. Now let's go into each part of the architecture in a little more detail.

2.3 Declarative memory

All of the ACT models, going way back to HAM in 1973, conceived of declarative memory as a collection of **chunks**, or declarative memory elements, which themselves contain a number of elements, usually between two and four. A typical chunk is shown in Figure 3.3.

Chunk1	isa ADDITION-FACT
	Number1 = 1
	Number2 = 3
	Sum = 4

Figure 3.3   An example ACT-R chunk

This chunk encodes the addition fact, '1 + 3 is 4'. Each of the main rows in the chunk holds a value in a different **slot**. Chunks also have the 'isa' slot (pronounced 'is a'), which says what kind of chunk it is (i.e. 'this chunk isa addition fact').

Chunks are not isolated from each other; they are all linked to each other through their values in a kind of network. For example, the chunk shown in Figure 3.3 will be linked to all other chunks that are addition facts or that use the numbers one, three or four. Chunks influence one another through these links by a limited form of spreading activation (discussed in detail in Section 3.3). Put simply, each chunk has a level of **activation**, a kind of energy attached to it. But activation in one chunk tends to leak out and add to all the other chunks it is connected to through its values. For example, increasing the activation of the addition fact '1+3=4' would automatically increase the activation of other addition facts and of chunks which contain '1', '3', or '4' in their slots. Chunks that are both addition facts and that contain '1', '3' or '4' would get even more activation.

Activation is central to many aspects of ACT-R. If a chunk has a lot of activation, it will be easy to find and to retrieve quickly from memory. If a chunk has very low activation, it will be hard to find, and may never be retrieved at all. Highly active chunks, therefore, look a bit like short-term memory, and chunks with less activation look a bit like long-term memory. If a chunk has no activation, it has effectively been forgotten, at least temporarily, until its activation level is increased.

Activation is not constant for a chunk. If nothing happens, a chunk slowly loses activation. But if a chunk is used, it gains activation, and the more it is used, the more it gains. This allows ACT-R to model effects such as priming. For example, if a chunk is retrieved, its activation will increase. If the chunk is then retrieved again shortly after (before the added activation has been lost) it will be retrieved more quickly. So declarative memory in ACT-R is a lot more than a place for storing chunks. It plays an active and essential role in the behaviour of ACT-R itself.

2.4   Procedural memory

The next main component of ACT-R is its procedural memory. This stores procedures in the form of **production rules**, which have a condition (i.e. IF) part, and an action (i.e. THEN) part. Unfortunately, since ACT-R is a computer program, its rules tend to be written in a fairly cryptic form. Figure 3.4 shows a rule, first in an English-like representation, and then in ACT-R form.

Rule in English form

How to add two numbers together

    IF the goal is to find the answer to *number1 + number2* in a column

    and we know that *number1 + number2* is *sum*

    THEN the answer is *sum*

Rule in ACT-R form	Commentary
Add-Numbers	The production rule called Add-numbers fires if...
=goal>	the current goal is...
isa ADD-COLUMN	to add up a column of an addition sum in which ...
first-number =number1	there is a first number (=number1) to be added...
second-number =number2	to a second number (=number2)...
answer nil	and the answer is unknown (nil means it is empty).
=fact>	And also we have a chunk in declarative memory...
isa ADDITION-FACT	and it is an addition fact stating that...
addend1 =number1	the first number (=number1) added to...
addend2 =number2	the second number (=number2) gives...
answer =sum	an answer (=sum).
==>	Then
=goal>	In our current goal we can use...
answer =sum	the answer from the addition fact (=sum) as the answer for the goal

Figure 3.4   An ACT-R production rule in English and in ACT-R form

To give you an idea of the relation between these representations, the condition part of the rule (the IF part) can be found in the rows before the '==>'character, and the action part (the THEN part) appears after it. The bits that begin '=something>'are references to chunks, and each line that follows is a slot name followed by a value. When a word begins with the '='character, it is a **variable**, that is, it can change each time the rule is used. Variables are very important to production rules, as they are what make rules sufficiently general to run with different problems. For example, the rule in Figure 3.4 could be used to add any addition column for which the matching addition fact was stored in declarative memory. Variables and values will be covered in more detail later.

ACT-R uses production rules in the following way. All specified production rules are available to be used depending on the current state. For a production rule to be used, its condition part (the IF part) must match the current goal and use chunks already available in declarative memory. This gives quite subtle control over timing. For example, the greater the activation of a chunk in declarative memory, the faster productions that use that chunk can be fired. ACT-R uses this technique extensively to give reasonably accurate models of human response times (as we shall see in Section 3).

Activation also plays a significant role in procedural memory. Rules have activation too, and if a rule has a very low activation it might be unused even though its conditions match the current state. However, the more a rule is activated, the more likely it is to be retrieved and used again in the future.

Procedural memory is not fixed like a computer program – new rules can be learned through a process called production compilation. **Production compilation** is the name given to the process by which knowledge is transferred from declarative to procedural memory. The process by which production rules are learned in ACT-R has three stages.

1   **Understanding**. The first stage involves understanding instructions and available worked examples. For example, a teacher may provide a child with verbal instructions for multiplying two numbers together. In ACT-R this new knowledge is encoded as chunks in declarative memory.

2   **Production compilation**. In the second stage, we try to solve problems by applying these instructions. By working on a range of problems we start to generalize from our experience. For example, through attempting multiplication problems for themselves a child will start to realize the range of problems to which the multiplication instructions can be applied. In the initial stages, the child may only be able to correctly solve the multiplication problem when it has certain characteristics, such as containing or not containing particular numbers. Through experience the child will come to realize how general instructions can be used to solve a wide range of multiplication problems. In ACT-R this is supported by the process of production compilation. Through application, the declarative representation of the instructions becomes transformed into a production rule. The production rule becomes more general than the declarative chunks as specific values in the chunks become replaced by variables in the production rule. For example, chunks representing the instructions for multiplying 27 by 3, may be generalized into a production rule for multiplying any two digit number by three, and then further generalized for multiplying any two digit number by a one digit number. This process is described in detail in Section 4.1.

3   **Practice**. Through practice we solve problems with increasing speed and accuracy. For example, a child having become more experienced with multiplication problems will deliberate less over the individual steps in the task, and come to solve the problems with relative ease. ACT-R explains this in terms of an increasing use of the production rules and a decreasing use of the declarative instructions. When first developed, the production rules may have a low level of activation, making the retrieval and use of the production rules more difficult. Through use, the activation level of the production rules increases until they take over from the declarative representation of the instructions.

Much of ACT-R's explanatory power comes from the production compilation process, which sets up a continual interplay between the chunks in declarative memory and the rules in procedural memory. Instructions for how to perform a given task start out as chunks in declarative memory, and then as performance improves through practice, these chunks are turned (or compiled) into rules in procedural memory, which do the same thing as the chunks but do it automatically.

To complete the circle, as these rules are used, they may themselves create new chunks in declarative memory. As we shall see in Section 4.2, for example, a child who does not know from memory the answer to '4+2' may use a counting procedure to arrive at the answer. The child may then remember this answer and so subsequently can provide the answer to '4+2' directly from memory. In ACT-R this is modelled by a production rule (e.g. the child's counting procedure) producing a chunk in declarative memory (e.g. a chunk representing '4+2=6') that can later be used to answer the same question without using the original production rule. We will come back to ACT-R's approach to learning in Section 4, where we will look at a model that shows it working in practice.

The idea that memory is divided into declarative and procedural memory is central to the ACT-R theory. One of the sources of evidence for this distinction is the experiment conducted by Rabinowitz and Goldberg (1995), which relies on the fact that declarative encodings of instructions can be reversed more easily than procedural encodings of the same instructions (see Box 3.1).

3.1   Research study

Rabinowitz and Goldberg's (1995) experiment

Rabinowitz and Goldberg's (1995) experiment investigated differences between declarative and procedural encodings of the same instructions. If a declaratively encoded instruction can be reversed more easily than a procedurally encoded one, this lends support to the idea of relatively distinct memory systems.

Participants were given a simple alphabet arithmetic task, with stimuli like 'C + 3 = ?', where the number indicated how many letters the participant should advance along the alphabet. The expected response here would be 'F'. Two participant groups took part in the experiment. The first group was given 12 letter–number combinations in rehearsal, but the second group was given 72 (thereby gaining more practice time). After this practice time, both groups were tested on additive alphabet arithmetic, but also on a transfer task – subtractive arithmetic on the same problems, for example 'F − 3 = ?', with the expected response 'C'.

Participants who received less practice performed better on the transfer task when the problems they had tackled in the first task. For example, they answered more quickly to 'F − 3 = ?' if they had already seen 'C+3=F'. This was not the case for participants that had received more practice.

Participants who received less practice could solve subtraction problems by reversing the addition solutions held in declarative memory. Participants receiving more practice had built a procedure for arithmetic addition within their procedural memory, and this could not be reversed.

2.5   Goals and the goal stack

Production systems like ACT-R's procedural memory are rooted in work on problem solving in the field of artificial intelligence. These systems adopt a goal-directed approach to problem solving. Basically, they take a current goal and a current state, and the system acts either to achieve the goal or add a new goal that needs to be completed first. For example, if someone wishes to have home-made lasagne for their meal, they will probably first set themselves the goal of assembling all the ingredients in their kitchen. This may involve going shopping. Once the initial goal of assembling the ingredients has been met, then he or she can move on to the next stage and make the lasagne using the ingredients.

In ACT-R, while the current goal (e.g. finding the ingredients) is being undertaken, future goals (e.g. cooking the lasagne) are stored on a **goal stack**. The computer science concept of a stack, on which the ACT-R goal stack is based, has been used commonly for many years. A stack is simply a bit of memory where you can put things in and get them out again, but you can only take them out in reverse order (i.e. last in – first out). Computing also has its own terminology for adding and removing items from a stack. Items are said to be 'pushed' to a stack and 'popped' from a stack. This terminology is adopted by ACT-R. Computer stacks can be used to hold a very large number of elements and recall them perfectly. This is also true of the ACT-R goal stack that can store and perfectly recall an arbitrary number of goals. Humans, however, clearly cannot do this – in fact, forgetting a subgoal is a very common 'slip' people make in real life.

Because of this, the ACT-R goal stack can be criticized for its lack of psychological plausibility. Anderson and Lebiere (1998) accept this charge and suggest that this is one area in which future work is needed to refine the architecture. Although the goal stack has these problems, Anderson and Lebiere need to think carefully about how to replace it, as it does have the advantage of making the architecture function in a controlled and serial way as each goal is tried one at a time.

ACT-R exercise 1

The roles of goals, chunks and production rules in the behaviour of an ACT-R model

This exercise gives you the opportunity to view the declarative memory chunks and production rules making up a model of addition. You are able to select different goals and see the process that the model goes through in attempting to satisfy that goal. You are also able to include or exclude different declarative memory chunks or production rules in order to see how this affects the behaviour of the model.

Please consult the Introduction to this book for details of how to access the software to run this exercise.

Summary of Section 2

- ACT-R is a cognitive architecture with three main components: declarative memory, procedural memory and a goal stack.
- Declarative memory is organized as a set of interconnected chunks forming a network, each chunk having a level of activation.
- Procedural memory is comprised of production rules that also have activation levels and that can perform some action if the condition part of the rule is met.
- ACT-R production memory is not fixed, new rules can be learned, modelling skill acquisition through instruction, examples and practice.
- ACT-R rules depend on a current goal and a stack of pending goals, which make a (questionable) assumption of perfect memory, but which do make high-level cognition serial.

3 ACT-R accounts of memory phenomena

As a demonstration of the ability of ACT-R to model human memory, Anderson *et al.* (1998) developed a single model of human performance on list memory tasks.

List memory is an experimental paradigm used in cognitive psychology to investigate how people store and recall items from short-term memory. Typically, participants in an experiment are presented visually with a list of items (such as words or numbers) one after another. They are then asked to recall the presented items, possibly after some delay. A restriction may be placed on the order in which the items should be recalled. The participants may be requested to recall the item in the precise order in which they were presented (termed **forward recall**), the reverse order in which they were presented (termed **backward recall**) or in any order (**free recall**).

The ACT-R model of list memory nicely illustrates many key features of the ACT-R cognitive architecture, and list memory has been an active area of ACT-R research in recent years. Although the list memory task is highly artificial, the precise nature of the task and the wealth of empirical data and theoretical explanations of results (e.g. Baddeley, 1986) provide a lot of information to support the building and evaluation of ACT-R models.

Here we will focus on how ACT-R models human performance of forward recall. The human criteria against which the model will be compared are recall latency (i.e. time taken to recall an item) and recall accuracy. Accuracy and latency data in recall for a nine-element list are shown in Figure 3.5. In the empirical study (Anderson *et al.*, 1998) from which this data was collected, participants were initially presented with a string of empty boxes, one to contain each item in the list. Participants were therefore aware of the list length from the beginning of the study. The items were then presented in their appropriate box, one at a time. As one item appeared, the previous item disappeared, so that only one item was visible at any one time. As the last item disappeared, subjects were instructed either to recall the items in a forward or backward direction. Participants would then enter the items into the boxes in order, and could not return to an earlier box once it had been visited.

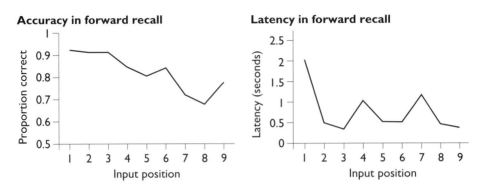

Figure 3.5   Recall accuracy and latency in the forward recall of a nine element list

If we first look at the graph for recall accuracy, two important features should be noted. First, recall accuracy is highest for the first elements in the list. This is called the **primacy effect** and can be explained by assuming that participants rehearse the first elements of the list during the presentation of the later items. Second, accuracy is higher for the last element than the two preceding elements. This is called the **recency effect** and is thought to be due to the last item still being accessible from memory during the recall phase, even though it has not been rehearsed, as its activation level has not decayed. Turning to the graph of recall latency, it should be noted that recall is slower for elements one, four and seven. This is conjectured to be due to the way the items are chunked in declarative memory.

In order to accurately reflect the empirical data, the ACT-R model needs to:

(a) have a representation of how items are chunked in declarative memory,

(b) have production rules for the rehearsal of items and retrieval from memory, and

(c) model activation levels and show how they affect recall accuracy and latency.

These three points will be considered in the following three subsections.

3.1   Declarative representation of lists

Within the ACT-R model of list memory, the list itself is represented in declarative memory as chunks. Chunks are used to represent a list as a set of groups. A **group** can contain as little as two and as many as five or six items.

The way that people mentally group telephone numbers could be represented as ACT-R chunks. Consider for example the main switchboard number for The Open University in Milton Keynes. Written without any spaces to indicate groups the number is 01908274066. Some people, particularly those familiar with the Milton Keynes dialling code, will group the first five items (01908). Individual differences are found in how people tend to group a six digit telephone number, either as two sets of three, or three sets of two. This gives two common groupings of the number, either into three (01908 274 066) or into four (01908 27 40 66) groups.

In a list recall task, participants often organize the list into three groups. This is found to optimize the number of items that can be remembered. For example, the list 581362947 is often grouped as shown in Figure 3.6. To distinguish it from any other lists, we shall refer to it as List1. The three groups are referred to as Group1, 2 and 3. The model of Hitch *et al.* (1996) also represents a list as a set of groups each containing a small number of items.

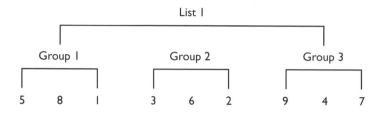

Figure 3.6 Organization of a nine-element list into three groups of three

When grouping lists in declarative memory, one chunk is associated with each group and with each individual item within the group is associated with a chunk. List1, as grouped above, would be encoded using 12 chunks, one chunk for each of the three groups and one chunk for each of the nine elements. A chunk can therefore hold a group of items or just a single item.

ACTIVITY 3.1

How many chunks in total are required to represent a list of 15 elements with

(a) a group size of three and

(b) a group size of five?

COMMENT

(a) Twenty chunks would be required. Five chunks are required for the five groups of three elements. Fifteen chunks are required for the individual elements. (Note that the list itself does not have a chunk. 'List1' appears as a value in each of the 15 chunks.)

(b) Eighteen chunks would be required. Three chunks are required for the three groups of five elements. Fifteen chunks are required for the individual elements.

As mentioned in the previous section, each chunk is represented using **slots** and **values**, however the chunks used to encode groups and individual items have a slightly different set of slots. A chunk associated with individual elements has slots for the group to which it belongs, its position within the group, the overall list to which it belongs and its content (i.e. the list item). The chunk associated with the first item in the list is shown in Figure 3.7. This chunk states that the item in the first position of Group1 of List1 is the value '5'. It is important to note, according to the assumptions of ACT-R, that each individual element has a slot associating the element directly to the list as well as to the group to which it belongs. This allows ACT-R to model some complex memory effects, as we shall see later in Section 3.3.

Chunk1	Position = 1st
	Group = Group1
	List = List1
	Content = 5

Figure 3.7 The chunk associated with the first item of List1

A chunk encoding a group has slots to indicate the list to which it belongs, the number of elements in the group and the position of the group within the list. Each chunk also has a unique name by which it can be referenced. Figure 3.8 represents the chunk associated with the first group of List1. (This group has been given the name Chunk10. While the chunks associated with the nine elements of List1 have been named as Chunks 1 to 9, the chunks associated with the three groups have been named as Chunks 10 to 12.)

Chunk10	list = List1
	Size = 3
	Position = Group1

Figure 3.8 The chunk associated with the first group of List1

ACTIVITY 3.2

(a) Write down the slots and values of the chunk associated with Group3 of List1.

(b) Write down the slots and values of the chunk associated with the last item of Group2 of List1.

COMMENT

(a) According to our numbering scheme, the chunk associated with the third group is Chunk12 and it has a size of three. It also maintains a link to the list. The chunk would therefore look like Figure 3.9:

Chunk12	List = List1
	Size = 3
	Position = Group3

Figure 3.9

(b) The last element of Group2would be Chunk6. As this chunk refers to an individual item, it has a slot for its content. The sixth number in the list is 2. The chunk would therefore look like Figure 3.10:

Chunk6
> Position = 3rd
> Group = Group2
> List = List1
> Content = 2

Figure 3.10

Chunks therefore organize a seemingly flat list of elements into a **hierarchy**, where the list is initially broken down into three groups and the groups broken down into individual elements.

3.2 Production rules for the rehearsal and retrieval of lists

The ACT-R model has to perform a number of procedures in order to simulate performance in the list memory task. The list contents have to be rehearsed in memory and then retrieved, and responses have to be given. These procedures are stored in the form of production rules in procedural memory, as described earlier.

The condition part of the production rule may specify what must be the current goal, and may specify what chunks have to be made available in declarative memory. For example, as was shown in Figure 3.4, the Add-Numbers production rule could only fire if the ADD-COLUMN goal was the current goal and the appropriate ADDITION-FACT chunk was in declarative memory. The action part of the production rule either transforms goals held in memory or performs an action to the world outside the model, such as typing a retrieved word onto a computer screen.

Goal transformations can be of three types. A goal can be modified, created (i.e. 'pushed' on, or placed on top of, the goal stack) or removed (i.e. 'popped' from, or removed from the top of, the goal stack). The ACT-R model of list memory comprises a number of production rules for rehearsing, retrieving and giving responses to the questions or tasks of the experiment. For example, Figure 3.11 represents the English form of the production rule for getting the next item from a group (the ACT-R textual syntax has been removed for clarity). Basically, the rule states that if you can retrieve the item you are trying to recall (i.e. the item at position X in group Y), then set a subgoal to output (i.e. say) the retrieved item and then move on to the next item (i.e. item X+1). The action part of the rule therefore modifies the current goal stack by adding a new goal (output item X) and modifying a goal (now look for item X+1, rather than X).

> Rule in English form
> Get the next item from Group
>
> > **IF** the goal is to get element at position X from group Y
> > and we can retrieve the element Z at position X from group Y
> > **THEN** create a subgoal to output the item
> > and modify the current goal to look for item $X+1$

Figure 3.11   Production for getting the next item from a group

Figure 3.12 shows the production rule used to output an item in a recall task. Here the action part just provides an output and does not transform any goals.

> Rule in English form
> Type out the item
>
> > **IF** the goal is to output item X
> > and we can retrieve a key for X that is found on the keyboard
> > **THEN** output by pressing the key

Figure 3.12   Production for outputting an item via a key press

The production rules shown above contain certain characters written in italics (X, Y and Z). These are variables that act as empty slots and can accept a range of specific values. These are used in order to satisfy the ACT-R assumption that production rules should provide a level of **generalization** and be applicable to a range of specific cases. For example, the 'Get next item from Group' production rule can be used to get any item from a group. Similarly the 'Output the item' production rule can be used

to output any printable character. Goals will be discussed in further depth in Section 4 on arithmetic skills.

3.3   List activation

As we discussed in the previous section, retrieval from declarative memory is performed within the condition part of the production rule. The success of this retrieval process for recall tasks is a function of the activation level of the chunk that matches the condition. The higher the activation level of the chunk the more easily – and faster – it can be retrieved.

Activation is part of the PDP-like nature of the ACT-R architecture. Activation of (artificial neuronal) elements is used within PDP architectures and is itself inspired by our understanding of neurology. The activation level of each chunk in declarative memory is calculated using a set of **activation equations** provided and modifiable within ACT-R.

The activation level of a chunk is calculated as the sum of its base-level activation and associative activation. The **base-level activation** of a chunk depends on the number of times it has been rehearsed in memory and the amount of time that has elapsed since it was last rehearsed. If a chunk has been rehearsed a high number of times and only a small amount of time has elapsed since the last rehearsal, then its base-level activation will be high.

The base-level activation provided by the ACT-R architecture can help to account for primacy and recency effects in list memory. The primacy effect is due to the number of times the item has been rehearsed, increasing its base-level activation. The recency effect is due to the small time lapse since the presentation or last rehearsal of the item, which also means base-level activation will be high.

The **association strength** is the strength of the bond between an item and the required chunk, and influences the flow of activation between chunks. Looking back to Figure 3.6, there will be an association strength between item '5' on the list (the first number on the list) and a chunk that encodes that item, such as Chunk1. The strength of association between an item and a chunk depends on the total number of associations that the item has. An important assumption of the ACT-R architecture is that activation is a limited resource. If an item is only associated with one chunk, then this chunk receives the full associative strength of the item and, therefore, the full effect of any activation. If the item is associated with three chunks, then the association strength is split three ways and less activation will flow to each individual chunk.

The limited capacity of association strength can be used to explain what is known as the fan effect (Anderson, 1974). The **fan effect** is the empirically observed finding that the greater the number of facts related to some concept that a subject has to memorize, the slower the subject will be to recall any one of them. For example, imagine you are asked to memorize three facts about a pretend person called Fred – that he is six foot tall, has a beard and works in a hospital. Your recall will be slower for the fact the Fred is six feet tall because you have been asked to remember other facts about him. If you had been asked to remember just this one fact about Fred, your recall would be quicker. Although the fan effect can be explained in terms of spreading activation, the mechanism within ACT-R is precise and restricted – activation only spreads to the immediate neighbours in the network. However, spreading activation is assumed to encompass a wider region of neurons (or units), than just the immediate neighbours of the activation source.

The fan effect also applies to list memory. In Section 3.1 it was shown that each chunk encoding either a group or an individual item in a list has an association to the list itself, in that case, List1. The association strength for List1 has to be shared out among all the associated chunks. The more chunks that are associated with List1 (either due to a smaller group size or larger list size) the more thinly the association activation has to be spread between the chunks, making it increasingly difficult to (quickly) retrieve any of the associated chunks. Limited association strength therefore offers an account of how list size affects the recall of items from a list. The larger the list the smaller the percentage of items successfully recalled. This is also one of the reasons why the group size is optimally set to three rather than two as this reduces the number of associations with the list concept itself, without overloading any particular group.

In order for a chunk to be retrieved at all, its activation (which is the sum of the baseline activation and the association activation) has to reach a certain level, specified in the ACT-R model. This pre-set level is called the **activation threshold**. A chunk that falls below the activation threshold is unavailable for retrieval by the production rules. The activation level therefore affects recall success. An equation in

ACT-R also specifies the relationship between activation and latency. The weaker the activation, the slower the recall process will be.

However, retrieval is not always 'all or nothing'. It is possible to select a chunk that only partially matches the item sought in the condition part of the production rule. This process called **partial matching** happens if, for example, the partially matching chunk has a high level of activation and a fully matching chunk is either absent or below the activation threshold. Partial matching is also important in modelling certain empirically observed effects. **Positional confusions**, where the participant recalls a correct item but in the wrong position, are common in list recall data. For example, in the case of List1, recalling the number 4 in the seventh position rather than the eighth. Once again, equations in ACT-R determine the likelihood of positional confusion. Items are more likely to be confused if they appear in the same group, and if they appear in adjacent positions in the same group. ACT-R uses this mechanism to successfully model the positional confusions exhibited by human participants.

3.4 Running the model

We have just covered three important features of ACT-R. First, we have seen how lists can be represented in declarative memory. Second, we have seen how production rules can be used to retrieve items from memory. Third, we have seen how ACT-R employs a model of activation that influences recall accuracy and latency. Now we will consider the running of the ACT-R model of list memory to see how these features work. Figure 3.13 shows the performance of the ACT-R model on forward recall superimposed on the empirical data presented in Figure 3.5.

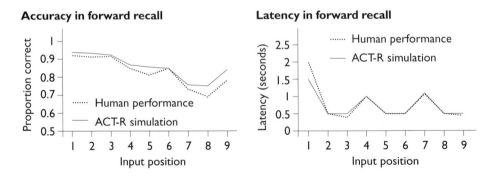

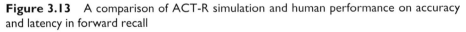

Figure 3.13 A comparison of ACT-R simulation and human performance on accuracy and latency in forward recall

Source: Anderson and Lebiere, 1998

The results for recall accuracy from the empirical study and the running of the ACT-R model are very similar (Figure 3.13, left). Both show a primacy effect, having the highest recall for the first three elements. Both also show a recency effect for the last item in the nine-element list. The simulation closely mirrors the findings but certain parameters had to be set within the ACT-R model in order to fit the results so closely. This included the parameter that affects the likelihood of a positional confusion. The issue of setting parameters in ACT-R and its implications for the validity of the model are considered in Section 3.5.

When examining latency (Figure 3.13, right), data from the empirical study show spikes at intervals of three items that are mirrored in the ACT-R model. In ACT-R, when a production rule is retrieving the next item from a list it takes longer if that item is from the next group rather than from the same group. If the next item is from the same group then the production rule just needs to increment the counter in the current group and retrieve the item. If the next item is from the next group then production rules have to be used to retrieve the next group and then retrieve the first item of that group. So, these data support the assumption that items in declarative memory are grouped, and that groupings of three tend to be used for list recall experiments.

ACT-R exercise 2

The effects of task, grouping and list length on recall accuracy and latency

This exercise invokes an ACT-R model of list memory under different experiment conditions. In the list recall model, there are two sets of controls: 'ACT-R parameters' influence ACT-R's declarative memory; 'Experiment parameters' model the experiment. Pressing the 'Run model' button runs the model with both forward and backwards lists of different length. You should change some of the 'Experiment parameters' and observe the effect on response time and accuracy.

Please consult the Introduction to this book for details of how to access the software to run this exercise.

3.5 Evaluation of the ACT-R approach to modelling memory

ACT-R has been used to develop versions of a model that can explain a range of empirical data related to list memory. The versions however, are not identical in every way. The overall model described above has been used to model data from forward recall, backward recall and also free recall, but in each case the model needs to be customized in certain ways to fit the data.

Certain parameters need to be set, particularly those relating to the activation settings of ACT-R within the model. For example, parameters affecting the likelihood that an item will be recalled and the time delay involved in accessing a new chunk vary across the different versions of the model. Anderson *et al.* (1998) admit this variation and offer explanations, but it is clearly an area of concern requiring further work. If such variation is required to explain different list memory experiments, which use a heavily restricted and artificial task, to what extent can ACT-R hope to provide a unified theory of cognition?

However, ACT-R does impose certain architectural constraints, limiting how the model can work. These include the procedural–declarative distinction and the use of chunks to group items in declarative memory. However, these constraints still allow for some flexibility when modelling empirical data. Decisions on how to deal with this flexibility are called auxiliary assumptions. An **auxiliary assumption** is made on a case by case basis to deal with the peculiarities of a particular experiment. How the rehearsal of previously presented items in a list occurs and how this competes with attention to the presentation of the remaining items in the list is an example of an auxiliary assumption. These can be contrasted with architectural assumptions. An **architectural assumption** (such as the procedural–declarative distinction) makes a general claim as to the nature of human cognition, and is consistent across all cognitive models developed using the architecture. If an architectural assumption of ACT-R made it impossible to model certain empirical data, then this would suggest that the assumption does not reflect a general feature of human cognition, and that the architectural assumption should be rejected or at least modified.

There is ongoing debate as to whether ACT-R (and other cognitive architectures) sufficiently constrain the modelling process. However, one advantage of ACT-R and other cognitive architectures is that at least all assumptions are made explicit, allowing such debates to occur.

ACT-R exercise 3

The effects of ACT-R parameters on model behaviour

This exercise uses the same model as exercise two, but involves changing the settings of the 'ACT-R parameters' to change the behaviour of the model. There are three settings you can change: the amount of activation noise, the threshold (above which things are 'remembered') and the scale factor. These influence which production rules are used: too much 'noise' may cause inappropriate rules to be applied, for example. Try changing these parameters and observe the effect on response time and accuracy.

Please consult the Introduction to this book for details of how to access the software to run this exercise.

Summary of Section 3

- Chunks are used to organize items in declarative memory into groups.
- Chunks have slots and values and are used to encode both groups and individual items.
- Chunks have an activation level comprising baseline activation and association strength.
- ACT-R is used to model the accuracy and latency of forward and backward recall, as well as other list memory experiments.
- Model fitting is used to match the ACT-R model to the empirical results.
- Any model makes associated architectural and auxiliary assumptions that jointly specify the model and how it works.

4 Learning and using arithmetic skills

In the previous section, we saw ACT-R's model of list memory, which focused particularly on how declarative memory items are represented and how their retrieval is affected by levels of activation. In this section, we will focus more on production rules in ACT-R and their role in the modelling of problem-solving behaviour and the learning process as a novice acquires expertise through practice.

4.1 Production compilation

As we discussed in Section 2.4, the ACT-R approach to learning comprises three stages. In the first stage of learning, instructions that the learner has been given are encoded as chunks in declarative memory. A separate chunk is used to represent each step in the instructions. Chunks that represent steps in a process (rather than facts) are called **dependency goal chunks**. A dependency goal chunk is created every time a goal from the goal stack has been successfully completed. For example, if the goal is to find the answer to '3+4', and this is solved by matching the goal with the addition fact '3+4=7', then a dependency chunk would be created. This dependency chunk would in effect say:

> If the goal is to find the answer to 3+4 and there is an addition fact 3+4=7 then the answer is 7

This dependency goal chunk is shown to the left of Figure 3.14. The other chunks that it refers to in declarative memory are shown to the right of the figure. Any dependency chunk represents how an unsolved goal can be turned into a solved goal by using one or more other chunks in memory. The dependency goal chunk in Figure 3.14, which for clarity we have labelled 'How to solve 3+4' states that the unsolved 'Goal1' (3+4=?) was turned into the solved 'Goal2' (3+4=7) using 'Fact34' (3+4=7).

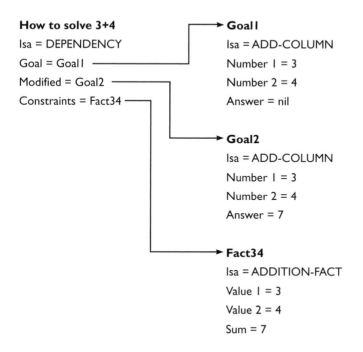

Figure 3.14 An example dependency for adding numbers in arithmeticSource: based on Anderson and Lebiere, 1998

Each dependency goal chunk can be thought of as representing a lesson learned from experience, and the lessons represented in dependency goal chunks are very specific. The dependency goal chunk in Figure 3.14 describes how to solve '3+4' and no other addition sum. Dependency goals become generalized through production compilation. The first step of production compilation turns a specific dependency goal chunk into a specific production rule. The second step turns the specific rule into a general rule. These two steps will be considered in turn.

First, production compilation works by turning the dependency goal chunk into a new production rule. This produces a new rule that has the unsolved goal and the chunks that were used to solve the goal as the IF part of the rule. The solved goal is placed into the THEN part of the rule. If applied to the goal dependency chunk shown in Figure 3.14, the rule in Figure 3.15 would be produced. For illustration, the production rule has been given the name Add-3-to-4.

Rule in ACT-R form	Commentary
Add-3-to-4	The production rule called Add-3-to-4 fires if...
=goal>	the current goal is...
isa ADD-COLUMN	to add up a column of an addition sum...
first-number 3	and the first number is 3...
bottom-number 4	and the second number is 4...
answer nil	and the answer is unknown (nil means it is empty).
=fact>	And also we have a chunk in declarative memory...
isa ADDITION-FACT	and it is an addition fact stating that...
addend1 3	the number 3 added to...
addend2 4	the number 4 gives...
answer 7	an answer 7.
==>	Then
=goal>	in our current goal we can put...
answer 7	the answer as 7.

Figure 3.15 A specific production rule produced from the dependency goal chunk shown in Figure 3.14

So far so good, but this produces a rule that would only work for the problem '3 + 4'. The second part of product compilation involves generalizing the rule so that it can be used to solve a wider range of goals. ACT-R achieves generalization by replacing specific items in the rule by variables. The heuristic used by ACT-R is that if the same item appears in two or more places within the rule then these should be replaced by a variable. For example, in Figure 3.15, the item '3' appears in two places. It appears as the first number in the goal, and as addend1 in the addition fact. Production compilation would replace these with a variable. This means that the items in first-number and addend1 would have to be the same, but not necessarily '3'. A similar transformation would happen to the two occurrences of '4' and the two occurrences of '7'. This would in effect produce a rule that said:

If the goal is to find the answer to X+Y and there is an addition fact X+Y=Z then the answer is Z

The rule that emerges from this process would work just as well for '2 + 2 is 4', and '5 + 2 is 7', as it does for '3 + 4 is 7'. The newly made rule, created by generalizing the rule shown in Figure 3.15 is the one we saw earlier in Figure 3.4. So, ACT-R does not have to be programmed to deal with every eventuality, it can learn new rules to deal with new examples.

Of course, generalizing a rule like this may not always work properly. Although the new rule has become part of procedural memory, its use depends on its activation. If the rule works, it will gain activation and will become an active player in problem-solving actions. On other hand, if it doesn't work, it will gradually lose activation and become less significant, until it is eventually forgotten.

Overall therefore, production compilation transforms a specific 'lesson learned' represented as a dependency goal chunk into a general 'lesson learned' represented as a production rule in procedural memory.

4.2 An example of human problem-solving behaviour: addition by counting

This gives you a pretty good idea of how a single step in problem solving can be learned, but perhaps this is focusing on too small a part of the problem. Now let's look at how this can be extended to learn a more realistic skill, addition by counting. In looking at this, we are turning the clock back a bit from the examples we have shown before, to the point where we have a child who does not yet know that '3 + 4 is 7'. In ACT-R terms, there is no ADDITION-FACT for '3+4=7' in declarative memory.

This introduces a whole new issue: how do children learn these addition facts? One possibility is that they are simply learned by rote – children recite them often enough that they become chunks in declarative memory directly. However, there is a second possibility: that they are developed through a procedure. Basically, given the problem: 'What do you get if you add 3 and 4?' a child starts from '3' and adds '1' to it four times. The result is, of course, '7'. Siegler (1988) provides an account of how children use this counting strategy when learning arithmetic.

The full ACT-R model for this would be a bit hard to read and to understand, so let's look at a formatted version of it (see Figure 3.16). Above each rule is a plain English description of what it does.

These rules may look clumsy but they are enough to model children working out the answer to problems like '3 + 4 is 7', as if by counting on their fingers. Let's look at how these rules work in a little more detail.

First of all, the rules 'Add-numbers' and 'Subgoal-counting' work together. Basically, if the child already knows the answer (for example, the answer is a chunk in declarative memory, as an addition fact, for example) then the child can just say it (that's what 'Add-numbers' does). On the other hand, if the child does not know the answer, they have to begin to work it out. The three rules 'Start-count', 'Add1-count', and 'Stop-count' all work together, once counting is started by the rule 'Subgoal-counting'. 'Start-count' starts the counting process, then 'Add1-count' is used once for each step and 'Stop-count' stops it when it is complete. Then, the rule 'Found-sum' retrieves the answer from the counting process. Finally, there is a rule 'Say' that is used when the child says the answer to the problem. Figure 3.17 shows how a model might trace through these various rules in practice, given the question 'What is the answer to 3 + 4?'

Production rules for addition by counting (in English form)	
This is the rule from Figure 16.8 again. It can answer any addition problem for which it can access the appropriate fact from declarative memory:	
Add-numbers	**IF** goal is to answer a question about the sum of *N1* and *N2* and can retrieve as a fact the sum of *N1* and *N2* **THEN** replace current goal with one to say the sum
If the sum cannot be retrieved because the addition fact is not in declarative memory then this rule will create a subgoal to calculate the answer by counting:	
Subgoal-counting	**IF** goal is to answer a question about the sum of *N1* and *N2* **THEN** create subgoal to calculate the sum of *N1* and *N2* and create subgoal to say the sum
If the goal is to calculate the answer by counting then this rule turns the goal 'Add X to Y' into the goal 'Add 1 to X, Y times':	
Start-count	**IF** goal is to calculate the sum of *N1* and *N2* **THEN** create subgoal to add 1 to *N1*, *N2* times
This can add 1 to the number and create a new goal (for example 'Add 1 to 4, 3 times' can lead to the goal 'Add 1 to 5, 2 times'):	
Add1-count	**IF** goal is to add 1 to *N1*, *N2* times and *New N1* is 1 more than *N1* and *New N2* is 1 less than *N2* **THEN** change goal to add 1 to *New N1*, *New N2* times
This stops the counting process when no more '1's need to be added (for example 'Add 1 to 7, 0 times'):	
Stop-count	**IF** goal to add 1 to a number, zero times **THEN** mark goal as completed
This retrieves the answer from the counting process:	
Found-sum	**IF** goal is to find the sum of *N1* and *N2* and can retrieve the calculated sum of *N1* and *N2* **THEN** mark goal as completed
This prints the answer on the computer screen:	
Say	**IF** goal is to say *N* **THEN** output *N* to the screen and mark current goal as completed

Figure 3.16   Production rules for addition by counting

Source: based on Anderson and Lebiere, 1998

ACT-R trace	Explanation
Cycle 0: Subgoal-counting	Create a subgoal to find the answer to three plus four by counting
Cycle 1: Start-count	Set the goal to add one to three, four times
Cycle 2: Add1-count	Add one to three to make four and change the goal to add one to four, three times
Cycle 3: Add1-count	Add one to four to make five and change the goal to add one to five, two times
Cycle 4: Add1-count	Add one to five to make six and change the goal to add one to six, one time
Cycle 5: Add1-count	Add one to six to make seven and change the goal to add one to seven, zero times
Cycle 6: Stop-count	Goal is add one, zero times, therefore the counting goal is completed
Cycle 7: Found-sum	Calculated answer has been retrieved
Cycle 8: Say	Output the answer to the screen
'Seven'	The outputted answer is seven

Figure 3.17   ACT-R 'trace' for 'What is the answer to 3 + 4?' (first time around)

However, if the same question is put again immediately, you might get a completely different behaviour from ACT-R (as shown in Figure 3.18).

ACT-R trace	Explanation
Cycle 9: Retrieve-sum Cycle 10: Say 'Seven'	Retrieve the answer to three plus four Output the answer to the screen The outputted answer is seven

Figure 3.18   ACT-R 'trace' for 'What is the answer to 3 + 4?' (second time around)

ACTIVITY 3.3

Why do you think ACT-R uses a different process to give the answer second time around?

COMMENT

The second time ACT-R runs, the chunk that records the answer to '3 + 4 is 7' has already been stored in declarative memory, and has a relatively high activation. This means that second time around, the rule 'Add-numbers' can pick up the answer directly.

In practice, this general procedure can work out lots of addition facts, given the ability to count up from one. Over time, this means that chunks corresponding to these addition facts will be stored in declarative memory, and the more they are used (in other, more complex, arithmetic problems, for example) the more they gain activation as chunks in their own right, and the rules may be used less and less. The example shown here, where the answer is retrieved directly after only one trial, is a bit unrealistic – in practice one might want ACT-R to go through the process many times before the new chunk can be retrieved reliably.

Of course, this is not necessarily the only way that children learn these arithmetic facts. Although some children do seem to use this process (Siegler, 1988), others may learn them by rote. Modelling can help to reveal the implications of these strategies in a way that makes it easier to design experiments and use other techniques to study them in more detail. This leads to one of the more interesting features of cognitive models – they correspond more to individuals than to populations, and for this reason we sometimes need to be careful comparing a model's predictions and statistical results from an experiment. In the case of the addition by counting example we have just looked at, we can study differences between individuals in problem solving by looking at the differences between the rules that represent their problem-solving strategies.

ACT-R exercise 4

The creation of new declarative memory chunks during problem solving

Production rules can cause the creation of new chunks in declarative memory. This feature of ACT-R is used to help explain how performance on tasks is affected by practice. Here, using the ACT-R model of addition you should investigate how answering one addition question may affect the time taken by the model to answer a subsequent question.

Please consult the Introduction to this book for details of how to access the software to run this exercise.

4.3   Models of learning and problem solving in practice

In the previous two sections we have seen two complementary parts of the ACT-R approach to learning. In Section 4.1 we considered how the ACT-R production compilation process can be used to create general rules from dependency goal chunks. By contrast, in Section 4.2 we have described how production rules, in this case a model of a counting procedure, can be used to create new facts in the form of chunks in declarative memory. So to what extent does ACT-R provide a general explanation of how humans learn?

Learning is modelled by ACT-R as an incremental process through which new knowledge is acquired declaratively, and performance gradually becomes faster and less error prone though practice. Such an account of learning would seem to accurately reflect how, for example, someone learned to change gears in a manual car. The instructor initially gives verbal instructions (i.e. a declarative account) on how to change gears. Initial attempts by the learner to change gear are slow, deliberate, error prone and rely heavily on the declarative account. Months later the same person will be able to swiftly move through the gears, rarely making errors, and will no longer be using the declarative instructions of how to perform the process. An ACT-R account of this form of learning appears highly satisfactory. Performance gradually becoming faster, less error prone and more automatic can be explained as being due to production compilation.

However, other forms of human learning are harder to explain, as learning may not always be characterized as a gradual increase in performance through experience. For example, children's learning of the past tense verbs in English doesn't quite follow this pattern (Bowerman, 1982). Initially children are very good at forming the past tense correctly. However, over time, and as they learn more words, their performance deteriorates, and they start tending to use the regular verb rule 'add –ed' even when they shouldn't, saying, for example, 'breaked' rather than 'broke'. Of course, over time, they overcome this problem, and the accuracy goes up again – forming a kind of 'U-shaped' pattern.

This pattern can be interpreted as being due to a progression through three ways of performing the task during learning. At first, each problem to be solved (e.g. each past tense verb to be constructed) is dealt with uniquely. The high degree of regularity (e.g. the large number of past tense words that can be created by just adding 'ed') is not reflected in the cognitive mechanism used to generate past tense verbs. Later, a single mechanism is used to solve an (overly) wide range of cases. The child now starts to use 'breaked' rather than 'broke'. Finally, exceptions are correctly handled and the child starts to say 'broke' once again.

A similar U-shaped pattern of performance over time has been found in children's ability to solve certain mathematical puzzles (Richards and Siegler, 1981), and in students' radiological diagnoses (Lesgold et al., 1988). Lesgold et al. found that students roughly three or four years into a course perform worse than more experienced professionals, but also worse than they did the previous year. In terms of performance, it appears that sometimes a skill has to be acquired, lost and then regained. Human learning therefore may be more complex than ACT-R might suggest.

Summary of Section 4

- Complex behaviour can be modelled using production rules, which contain a condition (IF part) and an action (THEN part).
- ACT-R has a production compilation mechanism for learning new production rules from instructions and examples.
- Learning can also involve the creation of new declarative chunks from production rules.

- Learning and problem-solving behaviour in ACT-R, as driven by the production rules, is influenced by levels of activation.
- ACT-R tends to characterize learning as an incremental process through which performance gradually becomes faster and less error prone. Human learning does not always follow this pattern.

5 A comparison of ACT-R and PDP

In the past few sections we have described the ACT-R cognitive architecture. Here we will compare ACT-R as an example of a rule-based cognitive architecture against the PDP cognitive architecture (see Chapter 2).

Children's learning of past tense verbs in English is a good point for comparison, as it has been modelled using both PDP models and rule-based models like ACT-R. The central question is: what is happening to cause the 'U-shaped' pattern effect? One possibility is that there is an area of memory that functions like a PDP network and that can generalize as it learns from examples. Rumelhart and McClelland (1986) proposed a model like this for learning past tenses.

In Rumelhart and McClelland's model, the changes in accuracy are caused by the child learning more new verbs. When there are only a few words, a network can fit in all the words by simply making strong links between individual input and output units. Each past tense verb is therefore dealt with uniquely. There comes a point when this won't work – when there are more words than available units – and then the network needs to build a more generalized association. For a short time the model over-generalizes, as a child does. This over-generalization is corrected in the PDP network through training (see Chapter 2), where the network receives feedback as to the correct answer.

Rumelhart and McClelland's two-layer model was relatively simple – it depended on this forced increase in vocabulary. Plunkett and Marchman (1991) used a three-layer network instead, and found that adding a hidden layer produced a similar 'U-shaped' pattern without needing to increase the vocabulary dramatically at one point in the learning process. They still needed a gradual increase in vocabulary to get the right pattern, however (Plunkett and Marchman, 1996).

In contrast, Taatgen and Anderson (2002) set out to model past tense learning using ACT-R, where there are two parts of memory involved: declarative memory and procedural memory. They suggested that children initially learn past tenses as declarative chunks, and then through a process of production compilation (see Section 4.1) form a slightly unreliable production rule to generate past tenses. Over time, they develop a blocking mechanism that stops the rule from being used when there is an exception stored in declarative memory. The dip in performance is caused by the unreliability of the production rule when initially constructed.

Both the PDP and ACT-R models correspond, more or less, to the observed behaviour, but the underlying explanations differ in a few subtle ways. For example, the PDP model depends on feedback. However, there is a problem with this explanation because children aren't always given feedback, and even when children are corrected, they still tend to use the over-generalized regular verb rule. Conversely, the dip in performance of the ACT-R model is due to the unreliability of the production rule when first formed. This unreliability is responsible for cases of over-generalization, but feedback is not required in order to correct this over-generalization.

The PDP and ACT-R models make different theoretical claims. The PDP model has the assumption that there is one area of memory, and change is driven by change in acquired vocabulary. The ACT-R model has the assumption that there are two areas of memory (declarative and procedural), and change is driven by practice. In principle, these differences can be tested, and experiments used to gather empirical evidence on the matter.

As mentioned in section 1, the key difference between rule-based architectures, such as ACT-R, and the PDP approach is the nature of the representation used in the model. PDP models, being closer to Marr's hardware level, are described as having a sub-symbolic representation. Sub-symbolic models do not contain any explicit representations of symbols such as production rules. Instead, they construct a sub-symbolic neural-like representation that can help support and explain a symbolic account of cognition. Conversely, rule-based systems explicitly use symbolic representations, such as the declarative chunks and production rules we have seen in this chapter.

In terms of their operation, PDP models, as their full name suggests, work in parallel, with signals being passed simultaneously throughout the network of artificial neurons. Symbolic cognitive architectures tend to be serial in operation. In ACT-R only a single production rule fires at any one time. The parallel processing of the network is mimicked in ACT-R by the activation equations that simultaneously update the activation of all elements in declarative memory.

A final important difference between ACT-R and PDP concerns the kinds of cognitive phenomena that they most successfully explain. Sub-symbolic cognitive architectures such as PDP models, although able to emulate rules, are generally stronger at explaining automatic processes (e.g. face recognition). Symbolic cognitive architectures such as ACT-R are stronger at modelling consciously controlled processes such as problem solving.

As we have seen, ACT-R incorporates some features of the PDP approach. However, to what extent is it possible (or desirable) to build a rule-based system fully integrated with a PDP architecture?

This was attempted by Lebiere and Anderson (1993) in the design of ACT-RN, in which aspects of the ACT-R architecture such as chunks and the goal stack were implemented using a PDP network. Although successful to a degree, many features of ACT-R were difficult to model using PDP. This finding led them to actually remove many of these features from ACT-R, on the grounds that they were not neurologically plausible. For example, ACT-R used to allow a slot in a chunk to have a long list of items as its value. This cannot be done in the current version of ACT-R and lists must be represented as described in Section 3.1. The experiment with ACT-RN also led to PDP-like features being incorporated into ACT-R itself.

Partial matching, as introduced in Section 3.3 is one such example. There is therefore reasonable justification to refer to ACT-R as a hybrid architecture that shows both PDP and rule-based characteristics.

It is however still unclear to what extent it is possible to completely integrate symbolic and sub-symbolic architectures. And even if it is possible, it may not always be desirable. The models will necessarily be far more complex, and may inherit the weaknesses rather than the strengths of the symbolic and sub-symbolic approaches. This is one of the reasons why the current version of ACT-R has features motivated by PDP, such as activation, but does not encompass all features of PDP within it.

Summary of Section 5

- Rule-based architectures such as ACT-R provide a symbolic account of human cognition, operate in a largely serial way and are particularly strong at modelling consciously controlled processes such as problem solving.
- PDP architectures provide a sub-symbolic account of human cognition, operate in parallel and are particularly strong at explaining automatic processes such as face recognition.
- Attempts to completely integrate symbolic and sub-symbolic architectures have had limited success, but there appear to be advantages in the translation of certain coarse-grained features from one architecture to the other.

6   When is a model a good model?

Modelling has a long and respectable heritage within psychology, with computers being used to model cognitive behaviour even at the birth of cognitive psychology itself, from 1956. Throughout, there has been a continuing question about how models fit in with experimental psychology. One very big question in cognitive modelling is: given a model, how do you know whether it is a good model or not? In this section we consider three criteria against which a model can be judged, followed by a description of the Newell Test, which constitutes an ambitious agenda for cognitive modelling. The three evaluation criteria we wish to consider are:

- The extent to which the behaviour of the model fits human performance.

- The validity of the model from the viewpoint of psychological theory.

- The parsimony of the model – the extent to which unnecessary complication is avoided.

In Section 1, we defined cognitive modelling as building a model of a cognitive process and comparing the behaviour of the model against human performance. If the model behaves in the same way as humans, then the structure of the model, and the way it works may give some insight into how humans perform the task. Clearly, if the behaviour of the model does not mirror human performance, then there is no support for the hypothesis that the internal workings of the model reflect human cognitive processes. And, of course, this failure of a model to fit the data can itself be an important and useful lesson learned.

However, it should not be assumed that the closer the fit to the empirical data, the better the model (Roberts and Pashler, 2000). Although a good model should at least roughly approximate to the data, the most closely fitting model is not necessarily the best. As described by Pitt and Myung (2002) a cognitive model could actually over-fit the data. A model may be so carefully customized to a specific set of empirical data that the generalizability of the model and its components to similar cognitive processes has been jeopardized. The extent to which the model fits the empirical data is therefore insufficient on its own as a measure of quality.

This leads us to our second criterion. The internal structure of the model, by which it produces behaviour, needs to be defensible in terms of the psychological literature. As described in Section 1.2, one motivating factor in the development of cognitive architectures was to logically separate the cognitive model from the workings of the computer. The features of ACT-R available to the modeller, such as procedural and declarative memory, chunks, production rules and production compilation are the mechanisms by which the model produces its behaviour. Each of these features can be debated and compared against the psychological literature. This clear distinction between the model and its computer implementation has been one of the great successes of work into cognitive architectures.

Our third criterion is parsimony. The law of parsimony or **Ockham's Razor** states that an explanation of a phenomenon should not contain any unnecessary detail. Specifically, and in relation to cognitive modelling, a model should contain only the minimum number of components and so should not contain components that do not impact on the behaviour of the model. Therefore, any component of a model has to provide explanatory significance that justifies the additional complexity that it also brings. Ockham's Razor can also be used to criticise the careful fitting of a model to the empirical data, as this can increase the complexity of the model for little gain.

Despite its increasing maturity, cognitive modelling still lacks a clear method for how models should be evaluated. However the above three criteria can be used to provide a broad evaluation of any cognitive model, whether it be a rule-based or a PDP model.

Other work in the area of model evaluation has aimed to devise and follow an ambitious set of criteria against which individual cognitive models and the progression of the cognitive modelling field as a whole can be tracked. Anderson and Lebiere (2003) elaborate Newell's (1990) 12 criteria for assessing the quality of a model, which they call the **Newell Test**. These are shown in Box 3.2.

3.2

Constraints on a human cognitive architecture (after Anderson and Lebiere, 2003)

A successful model should:

1 Behave as an (almost) arbitrary function of the environment (universality)

2 Operate in real time

3 Exhibit rational (i.e. effective) adaptive behaviour

4 Use vast amounts of knowledge about the environment

5 Behave robustly in the face of error, the unexpected and the unknown

6 Integrate diverse knowledge

7 Use (natural) language

8 Exhibit self-awareness and a sense of self

9 Learn from its environment

10 Acquire capabilities through development

11 Arise through evolution

12 Be realizable within the brain

Anderson and Lebiere give ACT-R a grade for each point and, based on these criteria, there are some areas where ACT-R is strong. It is pretty good at exhibiting rational behaviour, at coping with error, learning, and at modelling real-time behaviour. But there are other areas where ACT-R is much weaker, such as in using natural language, exhibiting self-awareness and being realizable with the brain.

These criteria should however not only be used to highlight the strengths and weaknesses of cognitive architectures such as ACT-R and PDP but also show how researchers working with different architectures can learn from each other. Anderson and Lebiere (2003) claim that the Newell Test could lead PDP researchers to incorporate ideas from ACT-R, similar to the way ACT-R has over recent years incorporated ideas from PDP. These criteria and the cognitive architectures they evaluate can therefore help to provide an overarching account.

As mentioned in Section 1.2, Newell (1973) argued that at that time cognitive psychology was asking lots of small questions, and progressing through small steps, but that the big picture was disjointed because there was little in the way of an overarching framework to glue the work together. He argued that a move to complete theories and models rather than partial ones, to complex composite tasks rather than narrow focused ones, and to models that would cope with many tasks rather than just one or two, would help the science of cognitive psychology to progress more effectively. In many senses, Newell's article laid the foundations for cognitive architectures like ACT-R and Newell's own Soar architecture (Newell, 1990). And the move to using cognitive models in conjunction with empirical studies and the development of cognitive theory, to help connect diverse elements of cognitive psychology, is set to continue.

As a set of points, though, Newell's list of criteria is helpful simply because it is so extensive. It shows just how far there is to travel before cognitive models are capable of explaining cognitive behaviour in an integrated manner. But we should not leave models on this note, as this issue and the list of criteria apply to all cognitive psychological theories not just the kinds of model exemplified by ACT-R. ACT-R may still have a long way to go, but it is one of the best approaches available.

Summary of Section 6

- It is possible to set out many criteria to help judge the usefulness of a model.
- ACT-R performs reasonably well across the board, although it shows weaknesses in the areas of natural language, self-awareness and biological plausibility.
- Models can be useful independently of the quality of their empirical predictions, in that they allow a community of researchers to be brought together to share ideas.

7   Conclusions

The advent of computers was central to the foundations of cognitive psychology. Computers provided both a new set of concepts that could be used to understand human behaviour and a new method that could be used to study it. Symbolic cognitive architectures such as ACT-R, however, are offering something more precise than computer metaphors of the human mind. Rather they assume that the working of the mind is essentially the symbolic representation of knowledge (e.g. in the form of chunks) and the use and transformation of these symbolic representations in order to perform tasks (e.g. actions performed by production rules). These cognitive architectures are emulated on a computer but can be thought of as distinct from the workings of the computer itself. The PDP cognitive architecture is also emulated on a computer, but here the assumption is that cognitive functions can be constructed from artificial neural elements having some similar properties to the human brain. The development of ACT-RN and the incorporation of PDP-like properties into the ACT-R architecture highlights a trend towards a hybrid approach to modelling that aims to combine the benefits of symbolic and sub-symbolic approaches.

Further reading

Anderson, J.R. and Lebiere, C. (1998) *The Atomic Components of Thought*, Mahwah, NJ, Lawrence Erlbaum Associates.

Anderson, J.R. and Lebiere, C. (2003) 'The Newell Test for a theory of mind', *Behavioural and Brain Sciences*, vol.26, pp.587–640.

Taatgen, N.A. and Anderson, J.R. (2002) 'Why do children learn to say "broke"? A model of learning the past tense without feedback', *Cognition*, vol.86, no.2, pp.123–55.

References

Anderson, J.R. (1974) 'Retrieval of prepositional information from long-term memory', *Cognitive Psychology,* vol.6, pp.451–74.

Anderson, J.R. (1990) *The Adaptive Character of Thought*, Hillsdale, NJ, Lawrence Erlbaum.

Anderson, J.R., Bothell, D., Lebiere, C. and Matessa, M. (1998) 'An integrated theory of list memory', *Journal of Memory and Language*, vol.38, pp.341–80.

Anderson, J.R. and Bower, G.H. (1973) *Human Associative Memory*, Washington, Winston and Sons.

Anderson, J.R. and Lebiere, C. (1998) *The Atomic Components of Thought*, Mahwah, NJ, Lawrence Erlbaum Associates.

Anderson, J.R. and Lebiere, C. (2003) 'The Newell Test for a theory of mind', *Behavioural and Brain Sciences,* vol.26, pp.587–640.

Baddeley, A. (1986) *Working Memory*, Oxford, Clarendon Press.

Bowerman, M. (1982) 'Reorganizational processes in lexical and syntactic development' in Wanner, E. and Gleitman, L.R. (eds) *Language Acquisition, The State of the Art*, Cambridge, Cambridge University Press.

Chase, W.G. and Simon, H.A. (1973) 'Perception in chess', *Cognitive Psychology,* vol.4, pp.55–81.

Hitch, G.J., Burgess, N., Towse, J.N. and Culpin, V. (1996) 'Temporal grouping effects in immediate recall: a working memory analysis', *Quarterly Journal of Experimental Psychology*, 49A, pp.116–39.

Lebiere, C. and Anderson, J.R. (1993) 'A connectionist implementation of the ACT-R production system' in *Proceedings of the Fifteenth Annual Meeting of the Cognitive Science Society*, pp.635–40, Hillsdale, NJ, Erlbaum.

Lesgold, A., Rubinson, H., Feltovich, P., Glaser, R., Klopfer, D. and Wang, Y. (1988) 'Expertise in a complex skill: diagnosing X-ray pictures' in Chi, M.T.H., Glaser, R. and Farr, M.J. (eds) *The Nature of Expertise*, Hillsdale, NJ, Erlbaum.

Marr, D. (1982) *Vision: A Computational Investigation into the Human Representation and Processing of Visual Information*, New York, W.H.Freeman.

Newell, A. (1973) 'You can't play 20 questions with Nature and win: projective comments on the papers of this symposium' in Chase, W.G. (ed.) *Visual Information Processing*, pp.283–308, New York, Academic Press.

Newell, A. (1990) *Unified Theories of Cognition*, Cambridge, MA, Harvard University Press.

Pitt, M.A. and Myung, I.J. (2002) 'When a good fit can be bad', *Trends in Cognitive Science*, vol.6, pp.421–5.

Plunkett, K. and Marchman, V. (1991) 'U-shaped learning and frequency effects in a multilayered perceptron: implications for child language acquisition', *Cognition,* vol.38, no.1, pp.43–102.

Plunkett, K. and Marchman, V. (1996) 'Learning from a connectionist model of the acquisition of the English past tense', *Cognition*, vol.61, no.3, pp.299–308.

Rabinowitz, M. and Goldberg, N. (1995) 'Evaluating the structure–process hypothesis' in Weinert, F.E. and Schneider, W. (eds) *Memory Performance and Competencies: Issues in Growth and Development*, Hillsdale, NJ, Lawrence Erlbaum.

Richards, D.D. and Siegler, R.S. (1981) 'U-shaped curves: it's not whether you're right or wrong, it's why' in Strauss, S. and Stavy, R. (eds) *U-shaped Behavioural Growth*, New York, Academic Press.

Roberts, S. and Pashler, H. (2000) 'How persuasive is a good fit? A comment on theory testing', *Psychological Review*, vol.107, pp.358–67.

Rumelhart D.E. and McClelland, J.L. (1986) (eds) *Parallel-Distributed Processing: Explorations in the Microstructure of Cognition*, vol.1, Cambridge, MA, MIT Press.

Salvucci, D.D. (2001) 'Predicting the effects of in-car interface use on driver performance: an integrated model approach', *International Journal of Human-Computer Studies*, vol.55, pp.85–107.

Siegler, R.S. (1988) 'Strategy choice procedures and the development of multiplication skill', *Journal of Experimental Psychology: General*, vol.117, pp.258–75.

Taatgen, N.A. and Anderson, J.R. (2002) 'Why do children learn to say "broke"? A model of learning the past tense without feedback', *Cognition*, vol.86, no.2, pp.123–55.

Neuroimaging: techniques for examining human brain function

Chapter 4

Ingrid S Johnsrude and Olaf Hauk

1 Introduction

Fifty years ago, almost the only way to relate human behaviour and cognition to the function of parts of the brain was to look for specific deficits in patients with damage confined to a particular region of the brain (acquired through, for example, stroke, injury, or surgery for neurological disease). Identifying the location of brain damage would often have to wait until after the patient's death, since the only way to examine brain structure in living people was the **pneumoencephalogram**, a low-resolution, poor-contrast X-ray that was neither painless nor harmless.

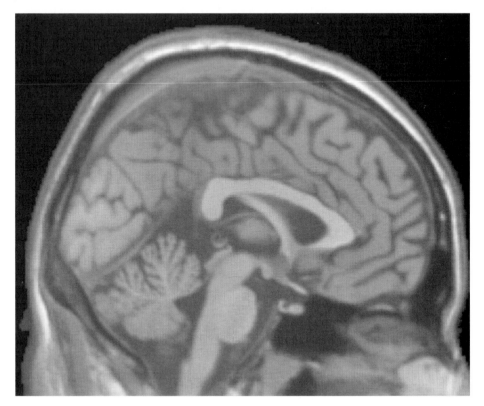

Figure 4.1   A magnetic resonance image of the brain of a neurologically normal individual. With fine spatial resolution, different brain structures can be easily identified: here, the image reveals different tissues such as grey matter (dark grey), white matter (light grey), fat (white) and fluid (black). Similarly, anatomical abnormalities can be identified, delineated, and localized with a high degree of accuracy

Although studies of brain-damaged people (neuropsychology – see Chapter 5) remain extremely valuable, the development of functional imaging techniques has had an enormous impact on the way we assess human cognition. Detailed anatomical images, acquired through techniques such as computerized tomography (CT) and magnetic resonance imaging (MRI), can now be used to identify structure in normal individuals (as shown in Figure 4.1) and localize damage in patients. Furthermore, detailed anatomical images from normal volunteers and patients can be combined with functional information from positron emission tomography (PET), functional magnetic resonance imaging (fMRI), electroencephalography (EEG) and magnetoencephalography (MEG) to explore normal and abnormal brain function.

Most neuroimaging techniques are easy and painless for volunteers. MEG (shown in Figure 4.2(a)) involves sitting in a device that looks rather like an old-fashioned beauty-salon hairdryer. Inside the head piece are sensitive devices for measuring the magnetic fields produced by the brain (see Section 2.1.4). EEG (Figure 4.2(b)) involves putting electrodes, sensitive to the aggregate activity of large numbers of neurons, on the scalp with a conductive gel. Often, as is shown here, the electrodes are incorporated into a cap, which makes setting up the electrode array less time-consuming. Activation PET (Figure 4.2(c)) involves the volunteer lying comfortably on a bed with an IV (intravenous drip) in one arm; a small amount of radioactively labelled water is periodically injected via the IV prior to each scan. In fMRI (Figure 4.2(d) and (e)), as in PET, the volunteer is lying comfortably on a bed which slides into the scanner.

Transcranial magnetic stimulation (TMS), if used within safety limits, can safely and temporarily disrupt function in a specific brain region, essentially producing a temporary 'lesion', in order to evaluate the importance of that area of the brain to performance on a given task. All of these tools are powerful additions to the traditional neuropsychological method of cataloguing deficits in patients, as ways to understand the relationship between brain and behaviour.

Each neuroimaging technique has its own advantages and disadvantages, many of which come under the general heading of **resolution**. The resolution of a technique indicates how far away, in space or time, two events have to be before they can be distinguished as two separate events. For example, EEG and MEG, which measure the electrical (EEG) or magnetic (MEG) fields generated by the activity of groups of neurons, have very good **temporal resolution** (in the order of milliseconds). This means that two events happening very quickly one after the other can be distinguished. However, as will be explained in the next section, the **spatial resolution** of EEG and MEG is only in the range of several centimetres, and the techniques are not equally sensitive over the whole brain. This means that EEG and MEG data cannot be linked to a particular region of the brain with much confidence. PET and fMRI are sensitive to the brain's metabolism (of oxygen in particular) and can be used to localize active tissue with great precision, but their temporal resolution is quite poor (a few hundred milliseconds at best, for the most sophisticated experimental fMRI designs) (see Plate 1 in the colour plates section).

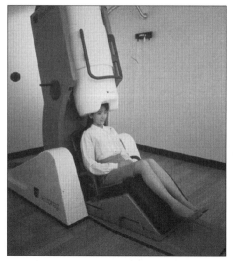
(a)

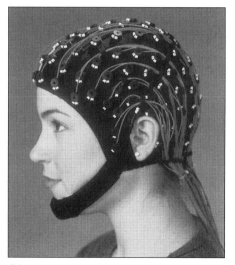
(b)

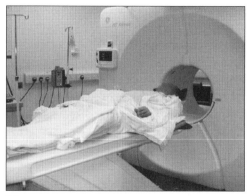
(c)

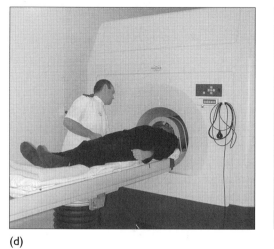
(d)

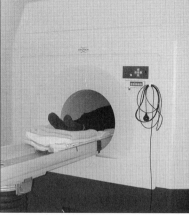
(e)

Figure 4.2 (a) MEG, (b) EEG, (c) Activation PET, (d and e) fMRI

These tools each have their own special place in answering questions about cognition. If a question concerns 'where' in the brain a certain process occurs, then either PET or fMRI would be helpful. Recent fMRI studies, for example, have shown that different parts of the ventral visual processing pathway in the temporal-occipital cortex are specialized for processing different kinds of things such as faces (and other parts of the body), places, and tools. If, however, the question concerns 'when' a process occurs or the order in which different brain areas (identified perhaps using PET or fMRI) become active, then EEG and MEG can be helpful. For example, both EEG and MEG can be used to show that, when a word is heard, frontal and temporal areas known to be important for language become active *after* auditory cortex does. Unlike the other methods, both TMS and the lesion method (the classic neuropsychological method of assessing the cognitive function of patients with focal brain lesions) reveal whether a particular brain area is *necessary* for a particular function, not just whether it is *involved* when a task tapping that function is performed.

This chapter introduces these various techniques, the assumptions underlying the methods, how they work, and what their advantages, disadvantages and limitations are. We review how experiments using these techniques are designed to ask cognitive and neuroscientific questions, how data are analysed, and how results are interpreted. We begin by presenting methods based on measuring the brain's electrical activity (EEG/MEG), then present methods based on brain metabolism (PET/SPECT/fMRI), and then briefly present transcranial magnetic stimulation (TMS) as a tool for inducing 'reversible lesions'. The information presented here should help you to understand papers on topics in cognitive psychology or cognitive neuroscience. It may also help you to begin to think creatively about how particular questions regarding the relationship between brain and behaviour might best be addressed.

2 EEG and MEG: measuring the timing of electrical activity in the brain

The electrical activity of nerve cells (neurons) in the brain produces currents spreading through the head. These currents, representing the integrated activity of many thousands of neurons, also reach the scalp surface. The resulting voltage differences on the scalp can be recorded as the **electroencephalogram (EEG)**. The currents inside the head produce magnetic fields, which can also be measured above the scalp surface as the **magnetoencephalogram (MEG)**. EEG and MEG reflect brain electrical activity with millisecond temporal resolution, and provide the most direct measure correlate of ongoing brain processing that can be obtained non-invasively (without physically entering the body).

2.1 Collecting data

2.1.1 EEG sampling

The **continuous** or **spontaneous EEG** (i.e. voltage fluctuations as a function of time, which can be viewed directly for each electrode during the recording – see Plate 2(a) in the colour plates section) can be clinically very helpful. For example, it can be used to diagnose epilepsy or another seizure disorder, predict seizures, detect abnormal brain states or classify sleep stages.

However, the amplitude of the continuous EEG signal is of the order of several tens of microvolts (μV), i.e. about a million times weaker than that of household batteries. It therefore requires special amplifiers that amplify the signal and convert it to a digital signal that can be stored and processed on a computer. Recordings are taken virtually simultaneously at all recording sites (several tens to several hundreds) and at different time points (usually every few milliseconds). The time difference between sampling points is called the **sampling interval**. The **sampling rate** is given by the number of samples per second, i.e.

$$\frac{1{,}000 \text{ ms}}{(\text{sampling interval in ms})}.$$

In typical EEG or MEG studies, a sampling rate of 200–500 Hertz (Hz) is common (corresponding to sampling intervals of between 5 and 2 ms).

2.1.2 EEG electrodes

Both EEG and MEG are recorded using a system of electrodes or sensors placed on or above the scalp. Electrodes are usually little metal disks that are pasted onto the scalp among the hair. They are either mounted on a cap (e.g. if a large number of electrodes is used), or can be fixed one by one. To assure good data quality, a conductive substance usually has to be inserted between the electrodes and the scalp to improve the contact between the two. A particular advantage of EEG compared to MEG, fMRI and PET is that once the electrodes are fitted the participant is allowed to move the head within certain limits. This makes this technique suitable for infants or for patient groups where head movement cannot be restricted.

To compare results across different studies, electrode locations must be standardized and locations need to be easily determined for individual subjects. Common is the so-called **extended 10/20 system**, where electrode locations are defined with respect to fractions of the distance between **nasion** and **inion** (i.e. root of the nose to 'the little bump on the back of your head', or 'front-back') and the **pre-auricular points** (the little skin lobules in front of your ear canals, or 'left-right'). Electrode labels like 'FPz' or 'PO4' indicate the area of the head ('Fronto-Polar', 'Parieto-Occipital'), odd numbers mark left- and even numbers mark right-hemispheric locations, and the lower the number, the nearer the electrode is to the mid-line ('z' indicates a location on the mid-line). 'TP8' ('Temporo-Parietal') is therefore more to the right than 'TP2', and 'F5' ('Frontal') is more to the left than 'F1'.

2.1.3 Referencing in EEG

Electric potentials are only defined with respect to a reference, i.e. an arbitrarily chosen 'zero level'. The choice of the reference may differ depending on the purpose of the recording. This is similar to measures of height, where the zero level can be at sea level if we refer to the height of mountains, or at ground level if we refer to the height of a building, or floor level for the height of a person.

For each EEG recording, a **reference electrode** has to be selected in advance. Ideally, this electrode would be affected by global voltage changes (e.g. slow voltage shifts due to perspiration) in the same manner as all the other electrodes, such that brain non-specific activity is subtracted out by the referencing. Also, the reference should not pick up signals that are not intended to be recorded, like heart activity, which would be 'subtracted in' by the referencing. Possible locations for reference electrodes are the ear lobes, the tip of the nose, or the mastoids (i.e. the bones behind the ears). With multi-channel recordings (e.g. more than 32 channels), instead of having a single, separate reference electrode, average activity across all channels is used as a reference. In other words, it is common to compute the **average reference**, i.e. to subtract the average across all electrodes from each electrode for each time point. Even if a single reference electrode was used during the recording, it is always possible to reference the data to any of the recording electrodes (or combinations of them, like their average) at a later stage of processing.

2.1.4 MEG recordings

The magnetic field, in contrast to the electric potential, has a direction, usually illustrated by magnetic field lines. The strength of the magnetic fields produced by the human brain is less than a millionth of the earth's magnetic field. Such small field strengths can be measured by so-called **superconducting quantum interference devices** (SQUIDs). Because MEG sensors are so very sensitive, they have to be well shielded against magnetic noise. The shielding of the laboratory and the SQUID technology make an MEG device 10 to 100 times more expensive than an EEG system, and the required permanent helium-cooling (required for the super-conductivity of the detectors) imposes considerable maintenance costs.

A special and important feature of MEG is its sensitivity to the topography of the brain – the details of the structure of its surface. The brain surface is quite dramatically folded, and whether the MEG signal arises in the convex tops of the folds (gyri) or the concave depths of the folds (sulci) affects sensitivity to neuronal current sources (**dipoles**). MEG is particularly insensitive to **radial dipoles**, those directed towards or away from the scalp (like at the top of a gyrus). It mainly 'sees' **tangential dipoles**, which are parallel to the scalp. The full explanation for this characteristic would involve a fair amount of physics and mathematics. A special case of a radial dipole is a dipole located at the centre of a sphere: it must necessarily point away from the centre, and is therefore radial and 'invisible' for MEG. Roughly speaking, the nearer a source is to the centre, 'the more radial' it is. This implies that the deeper a source is in the head, the less visible it is for MEG. This seems to be a disadvantage for MEG, but turns into an advantage if superficial and tangential sources (e.g. in sulci of the cortex) are targeted, since in that case the corresponding MEG signal is less contaminated than EEG by other possibly disturbing sources. Furthermore, it has been shown that superficial and tangential sources can be localized with more accuracy than with EEG, particular in somatosensory and some auditory parts of the brain. MEG has therefore been widely used to study early acoustic and phonetic processing, and the plasticity of the somatosensory and auditory system.

2.2 Computing event-related potentials (ERPs) and event-related fields (ERFs)

Whereas the continuous EEG can be useful clinically, the use of EEG and MEG to investigate more specific perceptual or cognitive processes requires more sophisticated data processing than just recording electrical signals through the arrays of electrodes on the head. Usually, the electrical signals resulting from a particular cognitive event (e.g. hearing a word) are averaged over many trials (see colour Plate 2(b)), a method that assumes the brain response does not markedly change its timing or spatial distribution during the experiment.

Data are divided into time segments (**trials** or **epochs**) of fixed length (e.g. one second), where the time point zero is usually defined as the onset of the stimulus. These time segments can then be averaged either across all stimuli present in the study, or for subgroups of stimuli that are to be compared to each other. Doing so, any random fluctuations should cancel each other out, since they might have positive amplitudes in one segment, but negative amplitudes in another. In contrast, any brain response that is time-locked to the presentation of the stimulus will add up constructively and be reflected in the average activity across trials. These averaged data are usually referred to as the **event-related potential (ERP)** in the case of EEG, and **event-related field** in the case of **MEG**. These have characteristic shapes in time (colour Plate 2(c)) and space (Plate 2(d)), which can be analysed into a series of prototypical deflections or **components** in their time course. The signal at any given time point can be interpolated between channels to give a continuous topographic plot over the whole head.

Different recording sites (electrodes) can be more or less sensitive to these components, so it is important to look at signals at many electrode sites in order to identify components accurately. The components are conventionally labelled according to their **polarity** – P(ositive) or N(egative) – and the typical latency of their occurrence. For example, 'auditory N100' refers to a negative potential at frontal electrode sites, usually observed 100 ms after the onset of an auditory stimulus (e.g. a simple tone, a speech sound, etc.).

The strength and pattern of these components can be measured, and their dependence on task requirements, on stimulus parameters, on degree of attention, etc., can be evaluated. Components known to be related to perceptual processing in the tactile, visual, and auditory domains (known as **evoked potentials**, or **evoked magnetic fields**) can be used by clinicians to check the connections between the peripheral and central nervous systems, much like an electrician might use a voltmeter to diagnose a faulty electrical cable.

For example, the presentation of simple tones is normally succeeded by specific components in the EEG signal. These are classified according to their time of occurrence into **brain-stem responses** (until approximately 20 ms after stimulus onset), **middle latency responses** (20–50 ms approx. after onset), and **slow** or **late responses** (later than 50 ms approx. after onset). It is known that the brain-stem responses originate from parts of the brain stem and/or from a cranial nerve (hence their name), while the late responses are cortical in origin. This information is used in objective **ear testing**, which tests the integrity of the auditory system from brain stem to cortex, and is used to screen for possible congenital deafness in newborns and infants, with whom conventional hearing tests that require a behavioural or verbal response to sound cannot be used, and also in persons who are suspected of faking hearing loss for insurance reasons. By detecting abnormalities in these components of the EEG signal, it can be possible to decide at which stage damage to the auditory system has occurred.

2.2.1 Reduction of noise

The measured signal not only contains the signal of interest, but also noise. For example, during the recording, EEG and MEG signals are undergoing slow shifts over time, such that the mean level might differ considerably across channels, though the smaller and faster signal fluctuations are similar. These signal shifts can be due to slow brain activity, but can also be caused by perspiration (in the case of EEG), muscle tension, or other noise sources. Obviously, one should attempt to remove anything from the data that is not related to the processes of interest. The noise level in the averaged data decreases (only) with the square root of the number of trials. This poses a considerable limitation on the duration of an experiment, and should be carefully considered prior to setting up a study. A usual number of trials per experimental condition in EEG and MEG studies on cognition is approximately 50–100, though in some cases this number can be lower. A low number of trials can be compensated for, in part, by recording data from more subjects. In general, however, the rule is 'the more the better'.

Two other standard procedures for reducing noise are generally applied: filtering and baseline correction.

Filtering is applied to a data set to remove any frequencies that are not part of the signal of interest, i.e. the ERP/ERF components under investigation. In most standard experiments on cognitive brain processes, frequencies above 30 Hz are usually not of interest. Furthermore, the high frequency ranges are most prone to contamination by muscle-related noise activity. Therefore, **low-pass filters** are used to attenuate frequencies above a certain **cut-off frequency** (i.e. they 'let pass' the lower frequencies). Analogously, high-pass filters can remove slow signal shifts. A combination of a low-pass and a high-pass filter is called a **band-pass filter**. A typical band-pass filter for ERP/ERF studies would be 0.1–30 Hz, but this depends largely on the signal of interest and the purpose of the study.

In most ERP and ERF studies, a 'baseline interval' is defined as several tens or hundreds of milliseconds before stimulus onset. For each recording channel, the mean signal over this interval is computed, and subtracted from the signal at all time points. This procedure is usually referred to as **baseline correction**. It is crucial in ERP and ERF experiments to ensure that an observed effect (e.g. an amplitude difference between the components evoked by two sorts of stimuli) is not already present in the signal before the stimuli were presented, since such differences could not possibly reflect stimulus effects and must therefore be artefactual (i.e. a result due not to changes in the independent variable but perhaps to noise or to the way equipment is set up).

2.3 Estimating neuronal sources: the inverse problem

The estimation of the sources in the brain that generate the electrical and magnetic activity recorded by EEG or MEG is usually called the **inverse problem**. What makes this a 'problem' is the fact that we are trying to identify the cause of the EEG or MEG signal from its effect, and that unfortunately many different causes might lead to the same effect. This **inverse problem** is comparable to reconstructing a face from its shadow in profile: only some features (e.g. the shape of the nose and chin) are uniquely determined; other features can only be deduced after additional information is received. Or imagine that you see the shadow of an object on the wall of your room, and you want to know what the object is. If you already know that there are only a few objects possible, the choice might be easy. However, in some cases it may be very hard to know what is casting the shadow (e.g. if you just see a square shadow, is it a wardrobe or a bookshelf?). Furthermore, the more similar the shapes of the objects in question, the more difficult it will be to identify which object causes the shadow in question.

Even if the EEG and MEG signals were measured simultaneously at infinitely many points around the head, the information would still be insufficient to uniquely compute the distribution of currents within the brain that generated these signals (this is known as the **Helmholtz principle**, another expression for the inverse problem).

2.3.1 Approaches to deal with the inverse problem

But all is not lost. Researchers can develop models of the underlying activity of the brain and then compare the EEG and MEG data that these models would produce with the data observed in participants. One can distinguish two broad strategies, depending on whether researchers have additional information about the neuronal generators (perhaps from neuropsychological investigations or other neuroimaging data):

1 Approaches that make specific modelling assumptions, like the number of distinct activated brain regions and their approximate location (for example, that there are two focal sources, one in the left, the other in the right auditory cortex, 80 ms after presentation of a tone).

2 Approaches that make as few assumptions as possible, and focus on rough features of the current distribution (for example, that a language task will result in more left-hemispheric activation compared with a mental rotation task).

Examples of these two approaches, and how the models relate to the neuronal sources, are shown in colour Plate 3. In a simulation, two dipoles were placed, one in the left and one in the right hemisphere. The potential distribution produced by both dipoles together is shown as a contour plot in the left image in Plate 3(c). From mere visual inspection of the potential distribution alone, neither the location of the dipoles nor even the number of sources can be deduced. The right image shows a distributed source solution computed from the same data. It exhibits one peak of activation in each hemisphere, around the true dipole locations. Though the 'blurring' inherent to this method does not allow precise localization of the sources, it can provide information about their number (in our example two) and approximate location (here one source in each hemisphere at roughly symmetrical positions). The images on the left and right represent solutions to the same problem (i.e. the source models produce the same potential distribution over 148 recording channels).

If the number of activated brain regions that generate the recorded signal is assumed to be known, but their locations are still to be determined, so-called **dipole models** can be applied (Plate 3(c), left): the locations and orientations of dipoles are systematically varied until the best fit between the predicted and the measured potential is achieved. If the modelling assumptions fit reality well, the result can be very accurate (in the millimetre range for MEG and in the centimetre range for EEG). These methods are usually applied if perceptual processes and early-evoked components are studied (e.g. somatosensory, auditory and visual processes up to 150–200 ms after stimulus onset).

If there is no information about the number of sources, methods with less restrictive modelling assumptions – so-called **distributed source models** – can be used. A large number of dipoles (hundreds or thousands) is distributed across the brain volume or the brain surface. Their strengths are then estimated such that their summed activity explains the measured signal and an additional criterion is fulfilled, e.g. that the overall source strengths is kept minimal ('minimum norm criterion'). An example for such an estimate is shown on the right of Plate 3(c). At least a 'blurred' version of the real source distribution can often be obtained. Peaks in this estimated current distribution might correspond to centres of activity in the real current distribution. These methods are preferred if modelling assumptions for dipole models cannot be justified, such as in complex cognitive tasks or with noisy data.

There is no 'one fits all' in EEG and MEG source estimation. It requires insight into the modelling assumptions of the method as well as experience to choose the right method for a given purpose.

2.4 Statistical analysis of EEG/MEG data

The statistical analysis of EEG/MEG data is as yet not fully standardized, and the strategies researchers employ can vary considerably depending on their hypotheses. The most frequent approach is 'analysis of variance' or ANOVA (see Chapter 6 on quantitative methods). The signal amplitudes for different electrodes, sensors or dipoles are considered as dependent variables, and recorded for each subject (e.g. just as we might measure mean reaction times or error rates per subject in behavioural experiments).

Imagine a so-called **oddball** experiment (the 'oddball paradigm' is discussed in Section 2.5), in which subjects are presented with two different tones: one tone of 600 Hz, which occurs 90 per cent of the time, and another tone of 1,000 Hz, which occurs only 10 per cent of the time. Subjects are required to press different buttons in response to the frequent and rare tones. Does the maximum amplitude of the ERP in a certain time range change as a function of the probability of the tone? In this case, one would first have to decide which time range to analyse. In this kind of oddball experiment, it is known that rare tones produce a so-called **P300 component**, i.e. a positive deflection of the ERP around centro-parietal electrode sites, which usually reaches its maximum around 300 ms after stimulus onset. It would therefore be reasonable to look for the largest peak around 300 ms at the electrode Pz, and to extract the amplitudes at this electrode and this point in time for all subjects. These values would enter the ANOVA as a dependent variable. 'Probability' would be a single, two-level factor allowing for a comparison between values obtained for the presentation of the rare tones and those obtained for the frequent tones. In general, the result is that the amplitude of the P300 is larger for rare tones.

Does only the amplitude change with the tone's probability of occurrence, or could there also be a change of 'Laterality'? In other words, could the rare tones produce larger amplitudes in either the left or right hemisphere compared with the frequent ones? In this case, one would have to extract amplitude values for at least two electrodes, one in the left and one in the right hemisphere (e.g. P5 and P6, left and right of Pz). The ANOVA now has two factors: Probability (rare and frequent) and Laterality (left and right). If the laterality changes with tone probability, one should obtain an interaction between Probability and Laterality. In the case of simple tones, such an interaction is generally not found, although it might be expected for more complex (e.g. language-related) stimuli.

2.5 The auditory oddball paradigm

The oddball paradigm, in which subjects are exposed to a stream of 'standard' stimuli occasionally interrupted by 'deviant' stimuli, is one of the most widely used paradigms in cognitive electrophysiology. This paradigm is easy to perform even by severely impaired subjects, and the corresponding ERP effects have been studied intensively during the last decades. Two major components are usually observed in ERP and ERF studies using oddball paradigms:

1 The **mismatch negativity** or **MMN**: an early component (between approximately 100 and 200 ms) that is independent of the level of attention, and is generally interpreted as a 'preattentive change detection mechanism'.

2 The P300: a component peaking around 300 ms, generally larger when target stimuli (e.g. deviants) have to be detected in a stream of standards. This component is often interpreted in terms of the 'updating of working memory'.

The data presented in Figure 4.3 are taken from Opitz *et al.* (1999). The same 16 subjects participated in EEG as well as in a functional magnetic resonance imaging (fMRI) experiment. ERPs were recorded from 120 electrode sites. The stimulus set consisted of two 200 ms tones (600 Hz and 1,000 Hz). The experiment was divided into 12 'standard' blocks, in which only the low tone was presented 24 times, and 12 'deviant' blocks, in which 16 low and 8 high tones were presented. This design was chosen in order to run the same experimental paradigm both with EEG and fMRI. In different runs, subjects were either told not to attend to the stimuli, but to watch a cartoon video instead ('unattend' condition), or to silently count the high tones ('attend' condition).

The detection of a change within a sequence of stimuli elicits an MMN shortly after 100 ms, independently of the level of attention. Dipole modelling, where the position of the dipoles is based on the position of activations observed in the companion fMRI experiment, suggests that the sources of this MMN component are localized in left and right superior temporal gyri (STG). The later P300 is elicited when the deviant stimuli are relevant to the performance of a task, and the generators were estimated in left and right transverse temporal gyri (TTG). It should be noted, however, that the relationship between EEG/MEG sources and fMRI/PET activity is still not clearly understood. It is generally not straightforward to constrain EEG/MEG source localization by fMRI/PET results. The development of corresponding methods and their empirical evaluation is currently one of the most exciting areas in the field of neuroimaging.

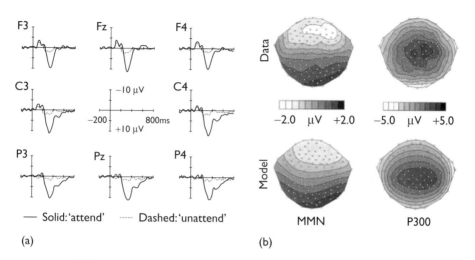

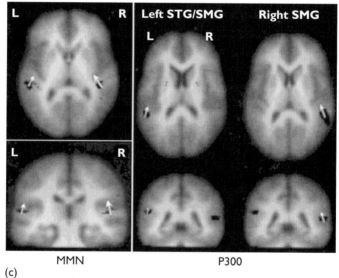

Figure 4.3 The auditory oddball paradigm:

(a) ERP difference waveforms ('standards' (low tones) minus 'deviants' (high tones)) averaged across subjects. Note the early negative deflection at frontal electrode sites (e.g. at Fz around 150 ms) in both conditions (MMN), and the large positive deflection in the 'attend' condition only at posterior electrode sites (P300, e.g. at Pz after 300 ms)

(b) Topography of the MMN (left) and P300 components (right). Both the original data (top) and the prediction of the dipole models (bottom) are shown

(c) Two dipoles fitted to the ERP data explained up to 95 per cent of the data for both the MMN and P300. Dipole locations (as indicated by arrows) were consistent with fMRI activation spots

Source: based on Opitz et al., 1999, Figures 1–5

Summary of Section 2

- EEG and MEG record the electrical activity of the brain millisecond by millisecond, such that they are sensitive to changes in the temporal pattern of cognitive processes.
- They do this only indirectly, which means that the location of corresponding activity in the brain can only be estimated.
- EEG and MEG signals are in principle generated by the same sources inside the brain. However, MEG is less sensitive to deeper and radial sources, but is in turn better in localizing superficial and tangential ones (i.e. those near and approximately parallel to the scalp).
- Data are usually analysed by computing 'event-related potentials/fields' (ERPs/ERFs): data segments are averaged across a large number of trials belonging to the same stimulus category, and then different averages are subtracted from each other to extract the signal specific to a certain cognitive process.

3 Techniques based on metabolism and blood supply

The brain requires a nearly constant supply of oxygen and glucose in order to function properly. Both glucose and oxygen are carried to the brain in the blood supply, via an array of arterial vessels. Although the brain accounts for only about 2 per cent of the body's mass, it consumes about 20 per cent of the body's glucose and oxygen, and receives about 20 per cent of its blood supply. Although the relationship is still not completely understood, activity in neurons is closely linked to glucose consumption, oxygen consumption, and blood flow. Blood in the brain goes to where it is needed: as a local group of neurons becomes active, blood flow in that region increases, as does the amount of oxygen in the blood in that region (**blood oxygenation**). Thus, imaging techniques that are sensitive to blood flow and blood oxygenation can be used to study 'the brain at work'. **Positron emission tomography (PET)**, when used by psychologists, measures how the pattern of blood flow in the brain changes (how it is increased in some areas and decreased in others) as a function of cognitive state. **Functional magnetic resonance imaging (fMRI)** is used by psychologists in a very similar way, to index regional changes in blood oxygenation as a function of cognitive state. We first discuss some of the most common designs used in these neuroimaging experiments, before explaining how the **dependent measure** in these designs (signal, derived from blood flow or blood oxygenation) is obtained in PET and fMRI.

3.1 Experimental design

Neuroimaging experiments are designed to assess relative changes in brain activity (indexed by **regional cerebral blood flow (rCBF)** in the case of PET, or regional changes in blood oxygenation in fMRI) consequent upon changes in stimulus characteristics or task demands. The two most commonly used approaches are subtractive designs and correlational (or parametric) designs.

3.1.1 Subtractive designs

In 1868, the Dutch physiologist Franciscus C. Donders proposed a general method to measure thought processes based on the assumption that tasks can be broken down into component processes (Donders, 1969). One comparison Donders made was between the reaction time to one stimulus presented by itself (simple reaction time) with the reaction time needed to identify a stimulus before responding. Donders believed that the subtraction of the simple reaction time from the identification reaction time would yield the time required for stimulus identification itself. Figure 4.4 gives a similar example in which the time taken to press a key in response (R) to a light coming on (the stimulus S) (Task 1) can be subtracted from the time needed to press the key only when a light of a particular colour is illuminated (Task 2). On the assumption that the identification component in Task 2 can be 'slotted in' between the two components in Task 1, with these other components remaining the same, then the subtraction reveals how long the process of identification takes.

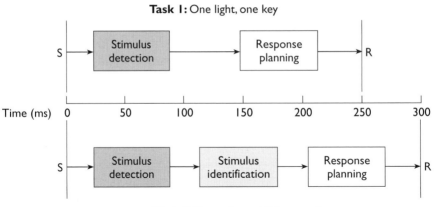

Figure 4.4   Cognitive subtraction. Task 1 involves responding to the detection of a light; Task 2 involves responding to the detection of a light of a particular colour

The same subtractive logic is often used in the design of neuroimaging experiments. That is, if two conditions, *A* and *B*, are identical except that *A* requires a particular cognitive function *f* while *B* does not, then one can identify those cortical regions that are involved in *f* by subtracting the pattern of rCBF observed during *B* from that during *A*. This approach is essentially an extension of Donders's method (Raichle, 1998).

In general, the conditions that are being compared will differ in one of two ways: the stimuli presented during the two conditions may be identical, but the participants may be required to perform different tasks; or the participants may be presented with different kinds of stimuli in each condition, but the task that they are required to perform may be identical. Box 4.1 gives examples of these two approaches.

4.1 — Methods

Subtractive designs

Klein and colleagues (1995) were interested in whether different brain areas are recruited when volunteers use a language they are proficient in but acquired relatively late in life (in this case, French) compared with their native language (English). Participants heard words in English and French, and were asked either to simply repeat what they had heard, or generate synonyms of the words they had heard (in both languages). This latter task, in addition to recruiting areas involved with speech perception and production (as in the repetition tasks) would also recruit areas involved in semantic association and word retrieval and selection (as volunteers 'look for' and select a suitable synonym).

Comparing synonym generation to word repetition, within each language, is an example of the 'same stimuli, different task' approach. In both tasks, subjects heard single words, which they simply repeated in one condition, and to which they generated synonyms in the other. In both English and French, this comparison revealed activation in prefrontal cortex, indicating the importance of this region in the processing of word meaning and in response selection.

Comparing word repetition in the two languages is an example of the 'different stimuli, same task' approach. A small area in the left basal ganglia was observed to be significantly more active when volunteers repeated French compared with English words. This is interesting, since the basal ganglia are known to be involved in skilled motor action, including articulation of words. Perhaps even when English speakers are proficient in French, their motor apparatus has to work 'harder' to pronounce French words.

An elaboration of the idea of cognitive subtraction is the **hierarchical subtractive design**. In studies of this type, conditions are successively 'built up' from cognitive or perceptual components which are assumed to be additive. For example, in a study of speech perception (see Figure 4.5), rest (lying quietly) could be compared with listening to noise bursts, which would activate the auditory system but not the language system. Listening to words and listening to noise bursts would both activate the auditory system, but words would also activate parts of the brain involved in perceiving and understanding language. Repeating words would activate all these regions, and, in addition, regions involved in speech output. Generating synonyms to a heard word, as discussed in Box 4.1, would activate regions involved in semantic search and word retrieval, in addition to areas involved in hearing and repeating words.

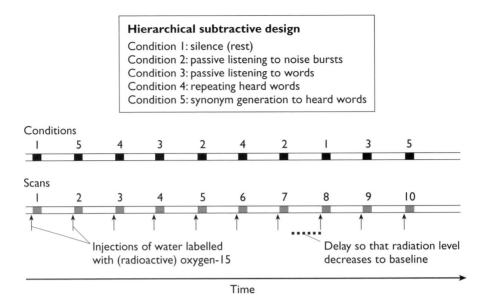

Hierarchical subtractive design
Condition 1: silence (rest)
Condition 2: passive listening to noise bursts
Condition 3: passive listening to words
Condition 4: repeating heard words
Condition 5: synonym generation to heard words

Conditions

Scans

Injections of water labelled
with (radioactive) oxygen-15

Delay so that radiation level
decreases to baseline

Time

Figure 4.5 Example of a PET experiment (a study of verb generation) employing a hierarchical subtractive design. During each 60-second scan, volunteers perform one of the five possible tasks (conditions). Each condition is performed twice in a pseudorandom order, so that each occurs once in the first half of the experiment and once in the last half. Volunteers begin performance of the task just before each injection of radioactively labelled water; then the PET detectors collect data for 60 seconds; then the volunteers stop task performance. A computer reconstructs the data into a whole-brain image showing where radioactively labelled water accumulated during task performance. Scans are separated by a 7–10 minute period in which volunteers lie quietly in the scanner; this is done to permit the radiation level to decline back to a baseline level (see Section 3.2 for more information about the PET method)

Another elaboration of the subtractive approach is the **factorial design**, such as that used in behavioural research. We have already encountered a simple factorial design in the English/French PET study of Klein *et al.* (1995) (see Box 4.1). If we take the two conditions of repetition, and the two conditions of synonym generation, we have described two levels of two factors: Task (Repetition or Generation) and Language (English or French). As in a conventional behavioural experiment with a 2 × 2 factorial design, the data can be analysed to address questions about main effects (What brain areas are active whenever French is used compared with English, across both tasks? What brain areas are more active during synonym generation than repetition, regardless of language?) and interactions (Are there areas in which the activation difference between synonym generation and repetition is greater for French?). Factorial designs are powerful because the experimenter can look at two or more independent variables simultaneously, and also assess whether or not interdependencies exist between these variables.

3.1.2 Correlational/parametric designs

Correlational/parametric designs are used to examine the relationship between a stimulus parameter (such as word presentation rate), or a behavioural response (such as reaction time), and brain activity. Correlational designs are elegant because they avoid many of the complexities of interpretation intrinsic to subtractive designs, including uncertainty about the assumption of additivity of cognitive processes (cf. Friston *et al.*, 1996). Correlation can also be used to assess brain connectivity and how it changes as a function of cognitive state. For example, signal change in one point in the brain can be used to predict activity elsewhere in the brain. If two areas show correlated activity, it is likely that these areas are connected in some way (directly or via another region). As cognitive state changes, so can connections among areas, reflecting recruitment of different functional networks.

We now turn our attention to PET and fMRI techniques themselves – how they work, what their advantages and disadvantages are – before revisiting issues of data processing and analysis in more detail.

3.2 PET: positron emission tomography

3.2.1 How it works

PET cameras are used to measure local concentrations of biologically important compounds (such as glucose, water, neurotransmitters, or drug compounds). Positron-emitting isotopes of oxygen, fluorine, nitrogen, carbon, and other elements are incorporated into glucose, water, or other **neurochemicals** (compounds used by the brain) using chemical reactions, and then these are introduced into the body. (**Positrons** are positively charged electrons that are emitted from the nucleus of unstable (radioactive) isotopes, such as oxygen-15.) The emitted positron combines with an ordinary electron of a nearby atom in an **annihilation reaction**, turning the

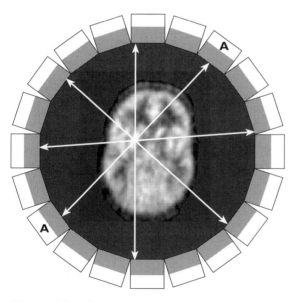

Figure 4.6 Coincidence detection in a PET scanner. When high-energy photons (gamma rays) are detected at opposite detectors (A), positron annihilation must have occurred somewhere along the coincidence line (the straight line connecting the two detectors). The intersection of many successively detected coincidence lines, observed over the course of a scan, pinpoints areas of relative concentration of the radioactive label. A computer uses the data gathered by the detectors to construct two- or three-dimensional images that show where the labelled compound (e.g. water (blood), glucose, or other neurochemical) accumulated in the brain

mass of the two particles into **gamma rays** (high-energy light particles) that are emitted at 180 degrees from each other. These photons easily escape from the human body, and can be recorded by a ring of radiation detectors: the PET scanner (see Figure 4.6). By recording the detection of these photons, it is possible to monitor the distribution of neurochemicals, without disturbing their physiological behaviour, with a temporal resolution ranging from several seconds to several minutes, and with a spatial resolution of several millimetres.

3.2.2 Two kinds of PET study

PET is often used to study **resting metabolism**, that is to say, brain activity in the absence of any particular cognitive task. After being injected with the tracer compound, patients are scanned while lying quietly in the scanner. Such metabolic scans are useful for diagnosing brain disease: in some diseases, affected brain tissue is often less metabolically active than healthy tissue, appearing as 'dark areas' on the resulting images.

When psychologists use PET, however, they are generally interested in knowing where activity increases in the brain as a function of a particular cognitive task. These are called **activation PET** studies. Most activation PET studies use oxygen-15 labelled water as a tracer, since: (a) this isotope decays quickly, and so disappears rapidly from the body; (b) blood is mostly composed of water; and (c) water crosses the blood-brain barrier easily. Labelled water is injected into the blood stream of the volunteer or patient, usually in the arm, and diffuses rapidly throughout the blood supply as the volunteer performs a particular task (listening to a series of words, for example). As brain areas become active (such as auditory cortex, in response to spoken words), blood flow to those areas increases, and this is reflected in an increased concentration of the isotope in that region. Many gamma rays emanate from the region of concentrated isotope and are detected by the PET camera. Thus, activation PET, using labelled water, measures regional cerebral blood flow (rCBF). In most activation PET studies, 8–12 scans are taken, each approximately a minute long, with a 7–10 minute interval between scans; this is long enough for the tracer to disappear from the body before the next injection is given. A single task is performed throughout any given scan. Three to six different tasks (such as listening to words, listening to noise, and resting quietly) are usually tested within a single subject, with approximately 10 subjects in a study (as in Figure 4.5; see Section 3.1.1).

3.2.3 Limitations of PET

The most obvious limitation of activation PET is that blood flow is only an indirect measure of neuronal activity, which is what researchers are really interested in. And changes in blood supply happen several seconds *after* the population of neurons under study has become active. This limitation also applies to functional magnetic resonance imaging and will be discussed in more detail in Section 3.4.1.

Most countries, including the UK, have strict rules regarding the administration of ionizing radiation to ensure the safety of the general public. In the UK, the annual dose to members of the public is limited to 5 milliSieverts (mSv). This overall dose of 5 mSv is comparable to a year of exposure to natural background radiation. All of us are exposed to natural radiation (such as cosmic rays and naturally occurring radon gas) throughout our lives. In the UK, this exposure ranges between 2.5 and

7.8 mSv (in areas with quite high natural concentrations of radon, such as parts of Devon and Cornwall) per year. However, in a typical activation PET study, a participant may experience 8–12 scans, and the total exposure across all of these must not exceed 5 mSv per year. More scans than this are not feasible, since the camera's sensitivity to blood flow depends on the size of dose given in any particular scan. If more scans were taken, then dose per scan would be even smaller. If too little isotope is given, then the camera does not detect gamma rays related to local accumulation of labelled blood.

Regulations in most countries also stipulate that PET cannot be used as a research tool with children or, in the UK, with women of childbearing age. Thus activation PET studies can only be used for research with a subset of the population (men over 18 and postmenopausal women), and only a limited number of experimental conditions can be tested, since only 8–12 scans per volunteer can be taken. Given the limited number of scans, it is difficult to repeat tests with individuals. This limits PET as a tool for investigating processes that occur over a period of time, such as patterns of brain activity before and after learning a skill.

PET is also expensive. In order to create the isotopes that are used as tracers, and to incorporate these into biologically important compounds, an array of sophisticated equipment is required. This equipment is expensive to both operate and maintain, but because most of the isotopes that are used in PET decay quickly, they have to be made in a **cyclotron** adjacent to the camera and as soon as needed. Finally, compared with functional magnetic resonance imaging (fMRI, see Section 3.4), which can answer many of the same kinds of research questions, activation PET studies, in practice, usually have quite poor temporal resolution (often greater than 60 seconds) and poor spatial resolution (the spatial resolution of activation PET depends on a number of factors including the tracer that is used, but is generally in the order of 10 mm or more).

3.2.4 Advantages of PET

PET is a quiet imaging technique, and high-fidelity sound delivery can be easily used with it, making it a valuable tool in auditory research. Unlike fMRI, PET is compatible with the metallic and magnetic components contained in many implants, such as pacemakers and cochlear implants. Furthermore, unlike most fMRI systems, PET permits the researcher to be in close contact with the patient or volunteer: the volunteer is scanned for at most two minutes at a time, preceded and followed by contact with the researcher or radiographer. Also, PET scanners only encircle the head, leaving the body mostly open to the room, and are consequently less likely than MR scanners to provoke claustrophobic reactions.

Most importantly, PET is not restricted to oxygen as a tracer: other radioisotopes can be incorporated into other compounds that are active in the brain (neurochemicals) and that bind specifically to brain receptors of various types. For example, brain receptors for the neurotransmitter dopamine (**neurotransmitters** are chemicals that act as messengers between cells in the brain) are known to play a crucial role in many cognitive processes, in motor function, and in emotion. A compound called **raclopride**, incorporating a radioactive isotope of carbon, binds to a subtype of dopamine receptors. Another compound, **fluorodopa** (labelled with a radioactive isotope of fluorine) mimics a chemical precursor of dopamine. These compounds can be used to study the dopamine system both in normal individuals and in those suffering from disorders that affect it (Parkinson's disease, schizophrenia, depression, addiction). Many other compounds, specialized for study of other neurotransmitter systems, currently exist and more are being developed. This sort of research is not very common because it is very hard to do: complex chemical reactions are required to produce radioactive compounds that are specific to particular brain receptors.

Although tracers other than oxygen are usually used in resting metabolic PET studies, some recent experiments have used such tracers in activation studies. These experiments explore the effects of cognitive state on activity within neurotransmitter systems. For example, in one PET study, raclopride was given to 8 men and they were scanned twice, once while playing a video game with a monetary reward, and once while staring at a blank screen (the control task). The results showed that playing the game was more associated with dopamine release and binding with dopamine receptors in a part of the brain (the **ventral striatum**) that is known from animal research to be involved in the appreciation of reward. Furthermore, this increase in dopamine release and binding correlated with level of performance achieved on the video game (Koepp *et al.*, 1998). Thus PET is a unique tool with considerable potential for mapping and studying neurotransmitter systems and neurochemically specific processes in both healthy volunteers and in patient groups.

3.3 SPECT: single photon emission computerized tomography

In SPECT, as in PET, a small amount of a radioactive compound is injected into the body. The compounds that are used generally mimic the action of one of the brain's neurochemicals, and so accumulate in the brain in areas where the metabolic process involving the compound of interest typically occurs. As with PET, gamma rays are emitted from the compound, and these are detected by a **gamma camera**. A computer is used to reconstruct the brain image in three dimensions. Like PET, this imaging technique is used to measure metabolism throughout the brain. Generally, SPECT tracers are more limited than PET tracers in the kinds of brain activity they can monitor. SPECT tracers also deteriorate more slowly than many PET tracers, which means that SPECT scans usually last longer than PET scans do, and much more time must elapse between scans to ensure that radiation levels fall to baseline. However, because SPECT tracers are longer lasting, compounds can be synthesized in centralized laboratories and then shipped to facilities where SPECT is used, so SPECT requires much less specialized technical equipment and staff than PET. While PET is more versatile than SPECT and produces more detailed images with a higher degree of resolution, particularly of deeper brain structures, SPECT is much less expensive.

3.4 fMRI: functional magnetic resonance imaging

The last few years has seen a rapid shift of emphasis in functional imaging away from PET activation studies towards functional MRI. Not only is MRI more widely available than PET, but with no associated radiation load it has quickly become an attractive alternative for cognitive studies in healthy volunteers. PET radiation limits mean that few observations can be obtained per volunteer; many more scans can be acquired using fMRI. This results in much stronger signals, making it possible to study brain activity in individual volunteers (not just in groups), so that studies of individual differences are possible. Not only has this development reduced the need for group 'averaging' within studies, but it also allows studies to be repeated in individual volunteers. One consequence is that many longer-term dynamic cognitive processes, such as learning, can be examined effectively. However, it is probably the superior spatial and temporal resolution of fMRI over PET that most clearly established fMRI as a major tool for the study of human cognition.

MRI is the general name for a broad class of techniques that use magnetic fields and radio waves to image the structure, organization, and function of biological systems without injecting radioactive tracers. Two of these techniques are used commonly in psychology and cognitive neuroscience. Structural MRI reveals the anatomical structure of the brain (see Figure 4.1), whereas functional MRI (fMRI) measures regional levels of blood oxygenation, which are assumed to reflect the volunteer's cognitive state.

3.4.1 How MRI works

If you have ever played with magnets, you will know that magnetic fields are not stopped by materials that are electrically insulating. For example, a magnet under a thin wooden table will move a paperclip on its surface; similarly, magnetic fields pass easily through the skull. A large cylindrical magnet around a volunteer's head and upper body creates a strong magnetic field, with a direction that is parallel to the volunteer's body. Other magnets are applied so that the strength of this field changes systematically across the head. Various atomic nuclei, particularly the proton

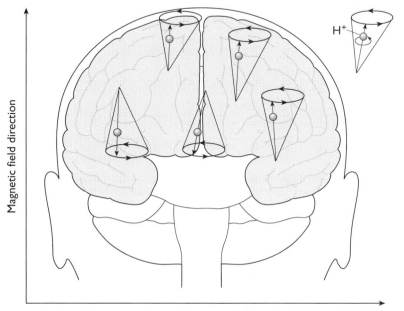

Figure 4.7 Hydrogen nuclei (protons) aligning in a strong magnetic field in the head of a volunteer. Each proton spins about an axis; in turn, the axis also wobbles or precesses around the axis of the magnetic field

nucleus of the hydrogen atom (which is very common in the brain, since there are two atoms of hydrogen in every water molecule and the brain is mostly water), align themselves with the magnetic field. These hydrogen protons, which spin anyway, precess (like the wobble of spinning tops) about the axis of the applied magnetic field at a characteristic frequency that depends on the strength of the field that they are in (See Figure 4.7). Initially, the protons precess (wobble) out of synchrony with each other. When radiofrequency energy is applied, the protons suddenly become synchronized in their movements, but, because they all precess at different rates, they drift out of synchrony again quite soon. However, as this happens they release energy. The frequency of the energy they release depends on the field strength they experience; that is, their position in the head. Sensors just outside the head detect the frequency of these energies, and a computer can be used to reconstruct an image of the distribution of protons, and with it, different tissues (e.g. grey matter, white matter, blood, cerebrospinal fluid) of the brain. This tissue contrast is coded in greyscale in the images.

Functional MRI (fMRI) relies on the different magnetic properties of oxygenated and deoxygenated blood, and allows scientists to observe how the relative concentrations of oxygenated and deoxygenated blood change with cognitive state. Oxygen is carried to the brain in haemoglobin molecules in red blood cells. The bright red blood in the arterial supply relinquishes its oxygen to brain tissue in capillary beds (where oxyhaemoglobin is converted into deoxyhaemoglobin). Purplish deoxygenated blood flows away from capillary beds in the draining venules and veins. As neural activity increases in a part of the brain, more oxygen is extracted from the blood, but blood flow and blood volume in that part also increase. The blood volume increases more than is necessary – it overcompensates for the increase in oxygen consumption. (Imagine every fire engine in London arriving on the doorstep of a chip-pan fire in Notting Hill!) More oxygenated blood is supplied than is needed, which has the effect of decreasing the concentration of deoxyhaemoglobin in the system of venules and veins draining the patch of active tissue (see Figure 4.8(a)). Since deoxyhaemoglobin and oxyhaemoglobin have different magnetic properties, this change in concentration alters the magnetic field strength in the region, which is reflected in the patterns of energy released by protons during scanning. This effect is known as **blood oxygen level dependent (BOLD) contrast**. Thus the fMRI signal is only a secondary consequence of neural activity and does not measure neural activity directly. The **haemodynamic response**, which is the change in BOLD that occurs with a change in neural activity in a particular brain region, happens much more slowly than activity in neurons does. It takes 4–5 seconds to develop after neural activity increases, and takes as long again to decay after neural activity stops (see Figure 4.8(b)). Thus, when the experimental condition changes, BOLD response takes 4–5 seconds to change also. This is called the **haemodynamic lag**. This sluggish response limits our ability to know exactly when a bit of brain tissue actually became active after stimulus presentation, but since the lag is relatively constant, the timing of two or more events relative to each other can be measured with greater precision; potentially within a few hundreds of milliseconds (Menon and Kim, 1999).

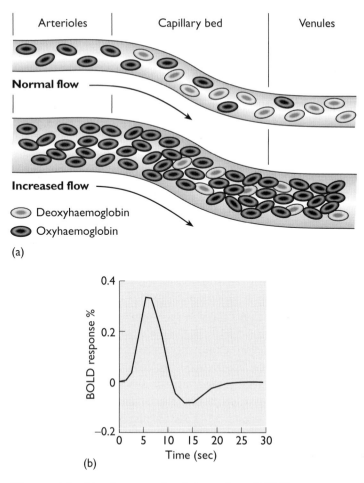

Figure 4.8 Blood oxygen level dependent (BOLD) contrast and the haemodynamic response function:

(a) Functional MRI scans are exquisitely sensitive to subtle fluctuations in magnetic field strength. Oxyhaemoglobin, found in arterial blood, and deoxyhaemoglobin, found in venous blood, have different magnetic properties and when their relative proportions in the blood change, as happens when a patch of neural tissue becomes active, the resulting change in the local magnetic field can be detected

(b) The metabolic change described in (a) is not instantaneous: it takes several seconds to develop (haemodynamic lag), and equally long to settle back to baseline. The example here sketches, for a point in auditory cortex, what the percentage change in BOLD (from a resting level) might be as a function of time since hearing someone snap their fingers (at time 0). This is called the haemodynamic response function (HRF)

Source: (a) adapted from P Jezzard, http://www.fmrib.ox.ac.uk/fmri_intro/brief.html

The spatial resolution of fMRI is mostly limited by the strength of the magnet used to generate the main magnetic field: the stronger the magnet, the finer the potential resolution. This is for two closely related reasons. First, stronger magnets are just more sensitive, so small signal changes (small areas of activated tissue) can be detected more easily, and two such small regions of activation can be more easily distinguished. Second, more sensitivity means that instead of picking up signal in veins (which produce large signal changes), signal in small venules and in the capillary bed can be detected. Since venules and capillaries are much closer to the active neural tissue than veins are – veins can be several millimetres away from actually active tissue – spatial resolution is improved. The fact that signal in veins can be mistaken for signal in brain tissue, unless precautions are taken, is one limitation of fMRI. Further limitations and advantages are detailed in the next sections.

3.4.2 Limitations

As with PET, fMRI is sensitive to changes in the local blood supply when a population of neurons becomes active. It is only an indirect measure of neural activity, and since changes in blood supply happen slowly, temporal resolution is limited, and is not as good as with EEG and MEG.

We have already explained how, since large BOLD changes can occur in veins, apparent activation can be located at some distance 'downstream' from brain tissue that is actually active. Without knowing where veins are located in each subject (like brain anatomy, the organization of blood vessels, particularly on the venous side, can be very different from person to person), venous activation can be mistaken for tissue activation. This obviously makes it difficult to infer confidently that the tissue in a region of significant signal change is actually involved in the cognitive process being studied (the real activated tissue may be up to a centimetre or more 'upstream'). There are several ways of getting around this problem. First, more powerful magnets, or different imaging protocols, can be used to improve signal strength in venules and capillaries. Second, MRI can also be used to make maps of blood vessel distribution (**angiograms**) in each individual: these maps can be compared to patterns of activation to identify and eliminate activation in vessels.

Several other limitations of the fMRI technique are based on the physics of the BOLD signal. BOLD is a special case of a subtle fluctuation in local magnetic field strength, which can be detected with specialized imaging protocols. Such imaging protocols are necessarily sensitive to all subtle changes in local field strength, including those caused by the brain's structure itself, not just by the state of the local blood supply. For example, air-filled pockets in the head (like the sinuses) have a very different effect on local magnetic field strength than do brain tissues: thus the magnetic field changes quite dramatically at the front of the head where the sinuses are. Because fMRI actually requires a quite uniform magnetic field, these relatively dramatic changes in field strength produce decreased signal (sometimes no signal at all) in affected regions. For this reason, inferior frontal and temporal cortex, close to such air pockets, can be hard to image. Unfortunately these regions are interesting to psychologists since they are implicated in decision-making behaviour and smell (orbitofrontal cortex), emotion (amygdala), memory (hippocampus) and language (lateral temporal cortex). An inability to 'see' these areas properly using fMRI makes it difficult (but not impossible – again, strategies to minimize this problem are in quite common use) to use as a research tool in these areas.

Fluctuations in field strength (**field inhomogeneities**) can also produce geometric distortion in images, apparently 'stretching' some parts and 'squashing' others, resulting in an image that is quite a different shape from the real brain. A popular way to 'correct' images for this problem is to map the magnetic field inhomogeneities for each volunteer.

Other limitations of MR are purely practical. First, the strong magnetic field means that volunteers with ferromagnetic implants (such as pacemakers, or pins to repair broken bones, or most types of cochlear implant) cannot be scanned safely. It also makes for a difficult experimental situation, since totally magnet-compatible stimulus-delivery systems (video projectors, headphones, response boxes) must be used. However, most fMRI systems are now equipped with a video projector which can present a picture (usually the screen of the computer controlling the stimulus delivery), headphones through which sounds can be presented, and response devices such as a buttonbox or joystick.

When the scanner is acquiring data it is very noisy – noise levels up to 130 dB are common. This is loud enough to damage unprotected ears. This noise is unpleasant, and even when partially blocked with earplugs can be distracting. Given this high level of background noise, special care must be taken when designing studies using sound. The most common approach is to scan intermittently, not continuously, alternating several seconds of sound presentation with 1 or 2 seconds of scanning. In this way, sounds are presented in a quiet background, and the delay in the haemodynamic response (see Figure 4.8(b)) means that a scan taken 4–6 seconds after stimulus presentation will optimally detect elevated signal due to that stimulus.

The data quality of fMRI is seriously compromised by subject movement, so subjects must stay perfectly still during scanning. This also means that they cannot speak, so a task requiring speech or other movements of the head is not practical. Most fMRI tasks involve either keypress or joystick responses. The restriction on movement means that patient groups with movement disorders can be difficult to scan. Finally, some subjects cannot tolerate the confined space of the MRI scanner.

3.4.3 Advantages

fMRI can be repeated within subjects, so it can be used to study processes that change over time, for example as a function of development, or as an individual recovers from injury or stroke, or acquires a new skill. It has quite good temporal and spatial resolution, and these both continue to improve as techniques are refined.

An fMRI scan can produce an image of BOLD signal, covering most or all of the brain, as fast as every second. If an experiment is targeted at a particular brain area (the auditory cortex, for example), then a small brain volume consisting mostly of the area of interest can be scanned, and **acquisition time** (the time required to take one scan) can be reduced even further. In principle, fMRI can produce an image that distinguishes structures less than a millimetre apart, and this potential is being realized. (For example, in visual cortex, cells that respond preferentially to lines of a given orientation are arranged into columns, which in the cat are half a millimetre wide and approximately 1 mm apart. Kim and colleagues (2000) were able to use fMRI to map such orientation columns in the visual cortex of the cat.)

In summary, fMRI is an increasingly common tool that psychologists use to determine how different parts of the brain are specialized for different cognitive processes. Although there are several limitations to the technique, it is a field that is growing and developing rapidly. We shall now discuss how imaging data must be processed before they can be analysed. In general, these stages of processing apply to both PET and fMRI. Exceptions will be clearly noted.

3.5   Image processing and analysis

The analysis of imaging data is a multistage process (see colour Plate 4). First, the scans must be **reconstructed**. The raw data that is collected in PET, SPECT and fMRI does not resemble an image. A mathematical transform, such as Fourier analysis, is required to turn the data into a set of images: **the image time series** (the sequence of images acquired over time). Additional steps are then often required for fMRI data to correct for artefact and distortion. We now review the most important processing steps required for reconstructed images to be prepared for the stage of processing that is closest to the researcher's heart – the statistical analysis that reveals where significant activation related to experimental variables occurred.

First, although movement of the head is generally restrained in some way (by lying in a moulded helmet, or with a headpiece), some movement is nevertheless inevitable over the course of a scanning session (several minutes to a few hours). Any movement means that the position of the brain within the images will vary over time. Thus, the images need to be **realigned**, bringing them all back into registration, correcting for head movement.

One concept that is almost universally used in functional imaging is that of a **standard space** – a standard space provides a way to locate positions in the head (in three dimensions) and allows comparison among different brains (see colour Plate 5). First, an imaginary line is drawn between the **anterior commissure (AC)** and the **posterior commissure (PC)** – two small brain structures that are in very similar positions from person to person. This is the y-axis, and defines front–back (see Plate 5(a) and (b)). Another axis (x) is perpendicular to y, also goes through the AC, and defines left–right (Plate 5(b)). A final axis, z, is perpendicular to the first two, also intersects the AC, and defines up–down (Plate 5(a) and (b)). All three axes intersect, or pass through the origin, at the AC. These axes define the **standardized stereotaxic coordinate system**, sometimes called the **Talairach coordinate system** after an influential brain atlas (Talairach and Tournoux, 1988). Any location in the brain can be indexed by values of these three coordinates, using units that are approximately a millimetre (Plate 5(c)).

Spatial normalization (see colour Plate 4) refers to the process by which brain volumes are changed in shape, size, and orientation so they approximately match that of a **template**, in standard space. A template is usually an average of many representative individual brain volumes. This is done so brains of different subjects (who will have brains of different shapes and sizes) can be easily compared, and so data can be averaged across subjects. It also allows a researcher to match up low-resolution functional data with a high-resolution anatomical image, so activations can be precisely located with respect to brain cortical anatomy. **Anatomical landmarks**, such as the **anterior commissure**, the **Sylvian fissure**, and the **interhemispheric fissure**, will be in an (almost) identical position in all normalized brains. (Brains are all very different, however, and even after spatial normalization some anatomical variability remains.)

When brains are spatially normalized, a particular set of stereotaxic coordinates refers to the same brain region in everyone (see Plate 5(c)). This permits the researcher to use **reference atlases** which are in the same space as the template, and which give, for each set of x, y, z coordinates, detailed information about the brain at that point: for instance, atlases can provide information about the likely tissue type, anatomical structure, and what other brain regions might be connected.

It should be noted that sometimes researchers are interested in knowing more about what is different in the anatomy and pattern of activation across individuals, and are not so interested in what is common. In such cases, spatial normalization will be removing some of the differences that interest the researcher.

After normalization, data are usually **spatially smoothed**, meaning that the activation at each point is replaced by a weighted average of the activation measured not just at that point, but at all neighbouring points. This has three benefits. First, it improves power, making activations easier to detect. Second, it ensures that the data conform to the assumptions of the statistical model that will be used to determine the significance of the activations. Third, it compensates for the fact that the same activation might be in slightly different places across individuals, since structural and functional anatomy will not be identical even after spatial normalization.

The disadvantage of spatial smoothing is that it reduces spatial resolution, since the signal is 'smeared out' over adjacent regions. This effect is generally greater in PET data than in fMRI data: in PET data, two activations up to 2 cm apart can be smeared together to appear as one, whereas in fMRI, once activations are more than one centimetre apart, they usually appear as separate. The experimenter can change the amount of smoothing in order to examine whether what is apparently a single blob after smoothing might actually arise from two or more discrete but neighbouring locations.

The final step before data analysis is **temporal filtering**. As with EEG and MEG data (see Section 2.2.1), noise in fMRI data can be removed by filtering. For example, it is common to use a high-pass filter in order to remove slowly varying components in the time series which may be due to physiological effects or to scanner-related drifts in baseline signal. Once this is done, the data are (finally!) ready for statistical analysis.

3.6 Data analysis

3.6.1 Predicting how signal will change over time, and testing such models

The most common way to analyse imaging data is to set up a model that predicts how the signal in the brain will change over scans if it is related to stimulus presentation or task performance. For the PET example in Figure 4.5, regions of the brain that are uniquely involved in synonym generation would be expected to show greater signal in scans 2 and 10 (when subjects were performing the synonym generation task) than in scans 3 and 6 (when they were repeating words, a condition that is closely matched in its other cognitive demands to synonym generation). Each point in the brain is tested separately; that is, at each point in the brain, paired t-tests (over subjects) would indicate whether the signal is higher during synonym generation than during word repetition.

In fMRI, since scans are taken much more often, the haemodynamic response function (HRF) (see Section 3.4.1) must be taken into account when predicting how measured activation will change over time, as a function of stimulus or task. The **data analysis** stage in colour Plate 4 shows a block design in which sound alternates between being 'on' for several seconds and 'off' for an equal period of time. Because of the HRF, the BOLD signal that would be predicted from this design would not increase until a few seconds into the 'on' periods, and then would stay elevated for a few seconds after the sound has been turned off. At each point in the brain, regression equations (see Chapter 6 on quantitative methods) are used to test how well the model fits the observed signal change over scans. The goodness of fit is indexed by **parameter estimates**. The larger the parameter estimate at a given point in the brain, the better the model fits at that point.

3.6.2 Correction for multiple comparisons

Statistical tests are carried out at each of several thousand points in the brain, independently (200,000 points would not be unusual). If we set the significance threshold to 0.05, which is conventional for single statistical tests, then it will be practically guaranteed that one of the tests will reach significance by chance alone (i.e. it will generate a false positive or Type I error – see Chapter 6 on quantitative methods). Indeed, with so many tests, there are likely to be many Type I errors. How can we distinguish between these false positives, and those comparisons where the signal was truly elevated for experimental reasons? We must correct for the fact that so many tests are being carried out: we need a **multiple-comparisons correction**. This can be done in several ways, but such **statistical thresholding** always has the effect of increasing the statistical threshold at which something is judged to be significant. The **activation image** (see Plate 4) shows which points in the brain are activated at a particular (specified) level of significance, usually $p < 0.05$ corrected for multiple comparisons.

Sometimes, researchers have predictions about where in the brain they are expecting to find activation. In such cases, they do not need to correct for tests conducted over the whole brain, just for the tests conducted in the region in which they are interested. The statistical criterion for significance is therefore lower than if a correction had been applied based on tests over the whole brain. The smaller the region they are interested in, based on their hypotheses and on previous work, the smaller the correction needs to be. It is usually helpful in imaging studies to have **anatomical hypotheses**, based on existing literature, about where activation is likely to be observed when perceiving a particular kind of stimulus or performing a particular task.

Summary of Section 3

- PET and fMRI are sensitive to changes in regional blood flow and blood oxygenation: these are indirect measures of neural activity.
- PET requires the administration of a small dose of radiation. Only a limited number of scans can be taken, and it cannot be used as a research tool with children or with women of childbearing age.

- PET can also be used to examine activity within specific neurochemical pathways in the brain, so that neurochemically specific changes as a function of cognitive state can be assessed.
- SPECT is very similar to PET in the way that it works. It has generally poorer spatial and temporal resolution, but is much cheaper to use.
- Imaging data must be extensively processed before they can be analysed. Data processing steps include realignment, spatial normalization, spatial smoothing, and temporal filtering.
- Data analysis is usually conducted independently at every point in the brain. Models that predict signal change over scans are tested against observed values. If all points in the brain are tested, significance thresholds must be adjusted to control for Type I errors (or false positives). Alternatively, researchers can restrict their analyses to the part of the brain they are interested in, thereby reducing the multiple-comparisons problem and permitting use of lower statistical thresholds.

4   Transcranial magnetic stimulation (TMS)

In TMS, a brief current is induced in brain tissue through the scalp and skull, using a brief magnetic pulse delivered via a coil (about the size of a hairdryer) placed over the head (see colour Plate 6). The magnetic field, which is quite strong although very brief, passes through the scalp and skull and into the brain. The shape of the coil determines the properties and size of the field: a **figure-8 coil**, which produces a very strong and focused field at the brain location that is deep relative to the crossing in the '8', is the most popular. The induced current in the brain then renders the local tissue more or less active, depending on the TMS technique that is employed. TMS is non-invasive, is apparently free of serious side effects (if used properly; see BioMag Laboratory, 2001), and has considerable potential as a research, diagnostic, and even therapeutic tool.

As a research tool for exploring the mapping of cognitive functions in the brain (to which we will restrict our discussion), TMS is used to temporarily and reversibly disrupt normal brain function in healthy subjects. This approach is conceptually similar to classic neuropsychology, in which patients with focal brain damage are carefully assessed for evidence of cognitive deficits. Any impaired cognitive function is assumed to rely on the damaged bit of brain. In TMS, activity in an area thought to be necessary for the performance of a particular function can be temporarily interrupted, and then performance on tasks relevant to that function can be assessed. Normal function resumes quickly after actual stimulation has stopped, and so tests are usually administered at the same time as the TMS pulses.

Because the field is created on the surface of the head, there is a trade-off between the size of the brain area that is stimulated and the depth to which the stimulation can reach. Even the strongest and most focused fields cannot penetrate very much further than the surface of the cortex, so that only surface locations (including motor cortex and other frontal areas) are suitable for study. Also, the temporalis muscle, which lies between the scalp and the skull over the temporal lobe, can be caused to contract quite painfully with TMS stimulation, and so TMS is not often used over the temporal lobe.

TMS, like neuropsychology, provides information about what parts of the brain are critical for particular cognitive functions. This is unlike fMRI and PET, which cannot differentiate between areas showing activity that is merely correlated with a particular cognitive function, and areas that are essential to the function.

Summary of Section 4

- TMS can be used to disrupt brain function temporarily. When used properly, it is a safe way to induce a 'reversible lesion' in a particular region of the brain, to determine whether that region is critically involved in the performance of a given task.
- It is only suitable for use with regions on the surface of the brain, and cannot easily be used to study function in the temporal lobe.

5   Choosing a technique

In general, choosing which neuroimaging technique to use for a particular purpose requires researchers to consider a number of different factors. Try the following activity.

ACTIVITY 4.1

There is a theory that states that speech perception is not purely auditory. The hypothesis is that when people hear speech, it automatically activates motor regions involved in pronouncing speech sounds. Colour Plate 7 shows where motor areas related to speech production are likely to be. Try to think of ways in which you could use two different techniques you have learned about to evaluate this theory. Note down the reasons for your choice of technique (why you chose the ones you did, and why you didn't choose the others). How might you set up an experiment to evaluate the theory? What kind of volunteers would you recruit? What kind of experimental design would you use? What would you measure? How would you establish whether you had a significant effect? Note down your answers to these questions. Would the results reveal what areas might be involved in speech perception versus those absolutely necessary for speech perception?

COMMENT

The most appropriate techniques, given the question, are TMS and fMRI. MEG/EEG aren't useful since the question is about *where* in the brain activation is observed, and fine temporal resolution isn't really necessary. PET and SPECT both have a radiation load, and, since this experiment can be performed in normal volunteers (without metallic implants), fMRI is most suitable. An argument could be made that PET is better since this would necessarily be an auditory study and fMRI is noisy, but fMRI can be used for auditory studies as long as they are designed properly. Specifically, the fMRI study should use intermittent (sparse) imaging, where stimulus presentation is alternated with scan acquisition. Experimental design could either be parametric (possibly varying rate or amount of speech) or subtractive. If subtractive, then the experimental conditions should involve listening to speech (either isolated sounds, single words, or sentences). Control conditions should include one that uses non-speech sounds matched to the speech sounds on duration (as in the hierarchical subtraction PET example, Figure 4.5). The analysis would either look for regions that correlated with the parametric factor (in the case of a parametric design) or regions in which activation during experimental conditions was higher than during control conditions. Since a region of interest is included in the hypothesis, the problem of multiple comparisons can be lessened, and the significance threshold used can be more liberal than if tests were conducted over the whole brain.

A TMS experiment would involve delivering TMS over the inferior motor region while the volunteer hears speech, and then testing perception or comprehension for the stimulus. This could be compared to TMS over other regions of the brain (not expected to be involved in speech perception) while the volunteer hears speech. Any stimulus recall, recognition or comprehension test, administered after the speech stimulus (and TMS pulse), could be the dependent measure. Changes in performance on the task would be examined as a function of brain area stimulated: if the inferior motor region is necessary for speech perception, performance will be impaired after TMS stimulation there. If the motor region is either involved but not critical or is not involved at all, task performance will not change as a function of stimulation site.

6 Summary and conclusions

This chapter has introduced you to several methods for the study of normal brain function in healthy volunteers. These are summarized in Table 4.1. Most of these techniques are also popular for use with patients, to examine brain function in people with specific diseases or mental disorders. EEG and MEG give excellent temporal resolution and are sensitive to neuronal activity directly, although they reflect aggregate activity over large groups of neurons. It is hard, without knowing exactly how many groups of neurons are active, to locate EEG and MEG activity with any precision. PET, SPECT and fMRI are sensitive to local changes in brain metabolism, particularly blood flow and the oxygenation state of blood. These are indirectly related to neuronal activity and happen much more slowly, so temporal resolution is not very good. However, these metabolic changes happen in or very close to active neural tissue, and so sources of activation can be located with confidence. PET and SPECT can also be used to study the relationship between specific neurotransmitter systems and cognitive function. Finally, TMS can be used to temporarily inactivate neural tissue close to the skull, in order to determine the importance of that region of the brain for particular cognitive functions.

Table 4.1 A summary of methods used to study the relationship between brain and behaviour in normal volunteers

Technique	Spatial resolution	Temporal resolution	Physiological basis
EEG	>10 mm*	1 ms or less	Summed electrical activity over large groups of neurons
MEG	>5 mm*	1 ms or less	Summed magnetic fields produced by large groups of active neurons
PET	5–20 mm[†]	10 sec.– minutes[†]	Radioactive decay occurring where labelled compound (water in blood, neurochemical) has accumulated
SPECT	20 mm	minutes	Radioactive decay occurring where labelled compound (neurochemical) has accumulated
fMRI	< 5 mm	200 ms–1 sec.[‡]	Magnetic field fluctuations produced by local changes in the proportions of oxyhaemoglobin and deoxyhaemoglobin in blood
TMS	5–10 mm	< ½ sec.	Strong focal magnetic field transiently disrupts activity in large group of neurons

* A general reliable figure cannot be given, since for both EEG and MEG spatial resolution depends on several factors such as modelling assumptions, number of sensors, or signal-to-noise ratio

[†] Spatial and temporal resolution in PET depends on the compound that is used: compounds that act specifically within particular neurotransmitter systems can take longer to accumulate detectable signal but can be localized with greater precision (since we know where these neurotransmitter systems are found) than labelled water.

[‡] The lower bound of this range refers specifically to when the timings of two events are measured relative to each other within the same brain area of the same subject.

Each of these techniques has its unique advantages and disadvantages. As technology progresses, we can expect the temporal and spatial resolution of all of these tools to improve somewhat, although we are near the practical limits of what is possible already. A major challenge for the coming years will be to combine data from these different methods in order to overcome the limitations of any individual technique. For example, combining EEG and fMRI would give us the excellent temporal resolution of EEG combined with the excellent spatial resolution of fMRI. Combining data across these tools will provide pictures of the functional organization of the brain that are unprecedented in their detail and richness.

Further reading

Cabeza, R. and Kingstone, A. (2001) *Handbook of Functional Neuroimaging of Cognition*, Cambridge, MA, MIT Press/Triliteral.

Kertesz, A. (1994) *Localization and Neuroimaging in Neuropsychology*, New York, Academic Press.

Toga, A.W. and Mazziotta, J.C. (2000) *Brain Mapping: The Methods*, New York, Academic Press.

References

BioMag Laboratory, Helsinki University Central Hospital (2001) *Safety of TMS*, www.biomag.hus.fi/tms/safety.html (accessed 4 June, 2004).

Churchland, P.S. and Sejnowski, T.J. (1988) 'Perspectives on cognitive neuroscience', *Science*, vol.242, pp.741–5.

Cohen, M.S. and Bookheimer, S.Y. (1994) 'Localization of brain function using magnetic resonance imaging', *Trends in Neurosciences*, vol.17, pp.268–77.

Donders, F. (1969) 'On the speed of mental processes', in Koster, W.G. (ed.) *Acta Psychologica, Attention and Performance II*, Amsterdam, North-Holland Publishing.

Friston, K.J., Price, C.J., Fletcher, P., Moore, C., Frackowiak, R.S. and Dolan, R.J. (1996) 'The trouble with cognitive subtraction', *Neuroimage*, vol.4, pp.97–104.

George, M.S. (2003) 'Stimulating the brain', *Scientific American*, vol.289, no.3, pp.67–73.

Kim, D.S., Duong, T.Q. and Kim, S.G. (2000) 'High-resolution mapping of iso-orientation columns by fMRI', *Nature Neuroscience*, vol.3, pp.164–9.

Klein, D., Milner, B., Zatorre, R.J., Meyer, E. and Evans, A.C. (1995) 'The neural substrates underlying word generation: a bilingual functional-imaging study', *Proceedings of the National Academy of Sciences of the USA*, vol.92, pp.2899–903.

Koepp, M.J., Gunn, R.N., Lawrence, A.D., Cunningham, V.J., Dagher, A., Jones, T., Brooks, D.J., Bench, C.J. and Grasby, P.M. (1998) 'Evidence for striatal dopamine release during a video game', *Nature*, vol.393, pp.266–8.

Menon, R.S. and Kim, S.G. (1999) 'Spatial and temporal limits in cognitive neuroimaging with fMR', *Trends in Cognitive Sciences*, vol.3, pp.207–16.

Opitz, B., Mecklinger, A., Von Cramon, D.Y. and Kruggel, F. (1999) 'Combining electrophysiological and hemodynamic measures of the auditory oddball', *Psychophysiology*, vol.36, pp.142–7.

Raichle, M.E. (1998) 'Behind the scenes of functional brain imaging: a historical and physiological perspective', *Proceedings of the National Academy of Sciences of the USA*, vol.95, pp.765–72.

Talairach, J. and Tournoux, P. (1988) *Co-planar Stereotaxic Atlas of the Human Brain. 3-Dimensional Proportional System: An Approach to Cerebral Imaging*, New York, Thieme.

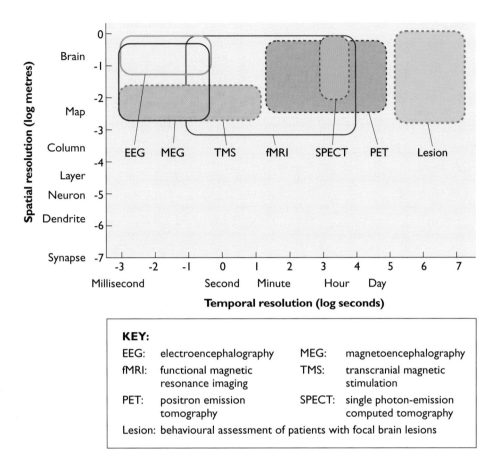

Plate I The ranges of temporal and spatial resolution of methods used to study human brain function, based on performance with typical hardware and commonly used experimental protocols. Shading indicates invasive techniques. The vertical axis includes references to 'maps' (e.g. visual or motor maps of space and the body); 'columns' (which are functionally specialized regions within a particular brain region – e.g. orientation columns in the visual cortex contain neurons which all fire when viewing a line that is angled a particular way); and 'layers' (the cortex of the brain is composed of six layers)

Source: adapted from Cohen and Bookheimer, 1994; Churchland and Sejnowski, 1988

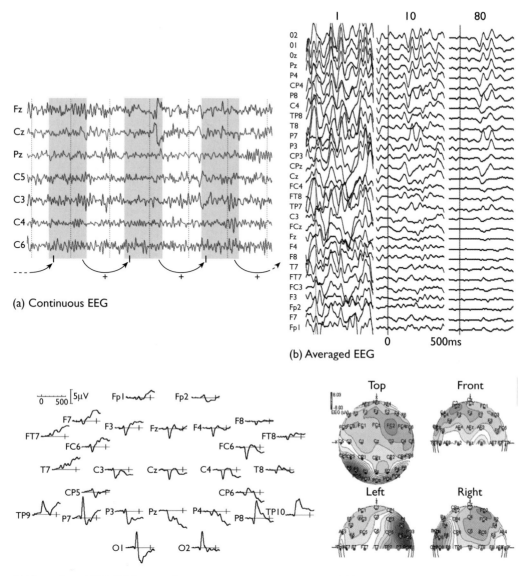

(a) Continuous EEG

(b) Averaged EEG

(c) Time plot of ERP ('ERP curves')

(d) Topography of ERP at 90 ms

Plate 2 Data pre-processing of event-related EEG and MEG data:
(a) Illustration of the averaging procedure used in standard ERP analysis
(b) Averages consisting of 1, 10 and 80 time segments, respectively. Note that the pre-stimulus interval ('baseline') flattens with increasing number of segments, while the event-related response becomes less distorted by noise, i.e. the 'signal-to-noise ratio' (SNR) increases
(c) The averaged curves can be plotted for each electrode or sensor location separately. Channels are plotted according to their relative position on the head
(d) A continuous topographic plot over the head. Red colour indicates positive and blue colour negative signals. The picture shows the event-related potential topography 90 ms after visual presentation of a word, with two distinct positive peaks over left and right occipital scalp areas, presumably reflecting processing of visual stimulus features

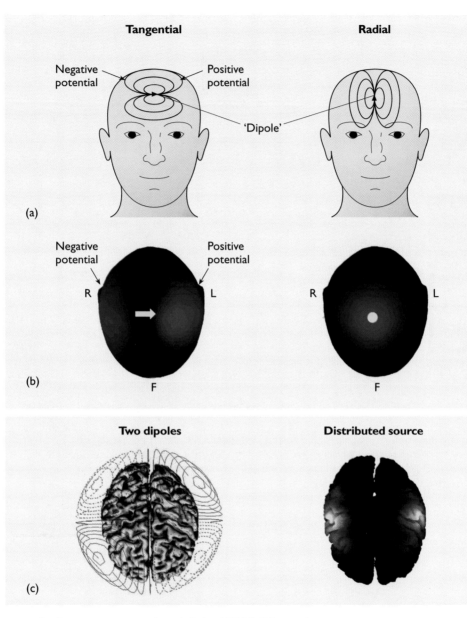

Plate 3 The generation and modelling of EEG/MEG signals:
(a) The summed electrical activity within a small area of cortex can be described by a so-called 'dipole'. This dipole describes the strength and direction of the current flow within this area. Each dipole has a positive scalp potential in the direction in which it points, and a negative potential in the opposite direction
(b) (*left*) Potential distribution for a tangential dipole (pointing right-to-left), and (*right*) potential distribution for a radial dipole (pointing downwards). The magnetic field of a tangential dipole is roughly perpendicular to its potential distribution (not shown)
(c) Illustration of the 'inverse problem' in EEG/MEG analysis: the images both represent different ways in which the same surface electrical and magnetic activity could be produced

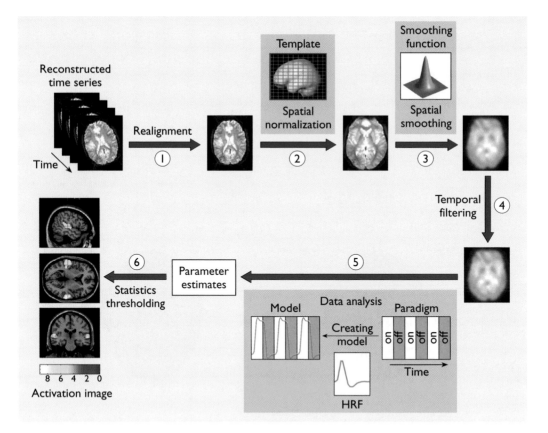

Plate 4 Typical steps of image processing and analysis of fMRI data. Processing of PET and SPECT data is very similar up to the analysis stage. Because images are not acquired as quickly with PET and SPECT as with fMRI, the analysis of such data does not need to take the haemodynamic response function (see Section 3.4.1) into account

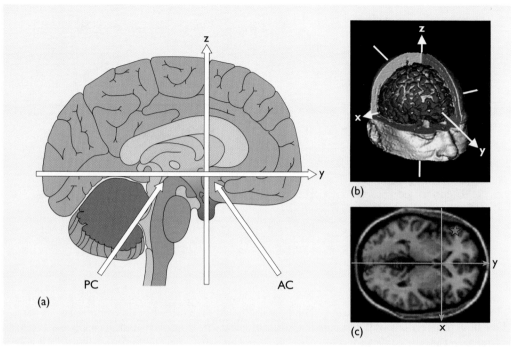

Plate 5 Standardized stereotaxic coordinate system, with perpendicular x-, y- and z-axes (see (a) and (b)). The star in (c) is in the location (x,y,z) −45, +15, +10. This is approximately 4.5 cm left of the midline, 1.5 cm in front of the anterior commissure, and 1 cm above the AC–PC line. This point always falls in the left inferior frontal gyrus in normalized brains

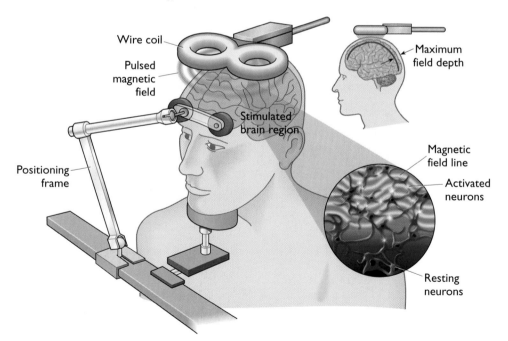

Plate 6 Transcranial magnetic stimulation (TMS). With the head fixed in position, a wire coil is placed over the scalp and skull. A strong magnetic field is induced by current flowing in the coil, and this field penetrates into a focal area of cortex. This causes a disruption of neural activity in the affected region

Source: George, 2003, p.69

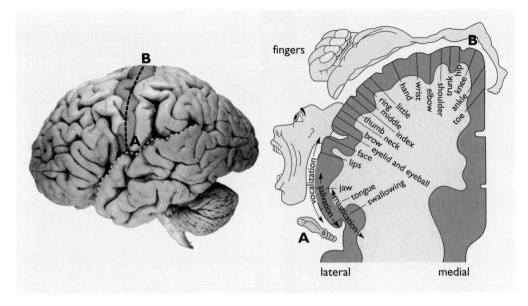

Plate 7 The 'motor homunculus'. The primary motor region (A–B) represents different parts of the body in an orderly way. The part of the motor cortex involved in mouth and tongue movements (and so in speech production) is found at the lower end, near the Sylvian fissure (blue dotted line)

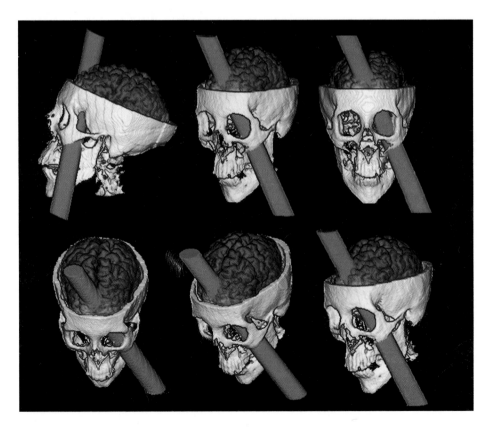

Plate 8 This computerized image of Phineas Gage's skull shows the path that the tamping iron followed through his skull

Source: Damasio et al., 1994

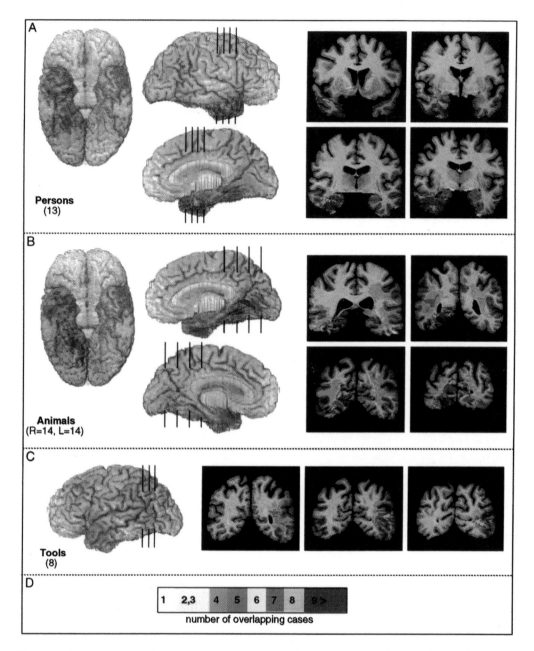

Plate 9 Lesion location for participants with impaired recognition for different kinds of category: (A) Impaired recognition of unique persons. The surface overlap (left half of panel) is shown in the inferior view (leftmost), and in the right lateral (upper) and mesial views (lower) of the normal brain. The lines on the lateral and mesial views indicate the position of the four coronal slices seen in the right half of the panel. In the coronal cuts, the extent of lesion overlap into white matter can be appreciated (B) Impaired recognition of animals. In the left half of the panel, the surface overlap can be seen in the inferior and mesial views of the right and left hemispheres. The four coronal slices in the right half of the panel show the depth overlap

(C) Impaired recognition of tools. The surface overlap is shown in the lateral view of the left hemisphere, and the depth overlap is shown in the three coronal slices

(D) Colour bar indicating the number of participants contributing to the overlaps

Source: Tranel *et al.*, 1997

Cognitive neuropsychology

Chapter 5

Ashok Jansari

1   Introduction: why study damaged brains?

If one of the main goals of cognitive psychology is to understand normal human behaviour, then why do cognitive neuropsychologists study damaged brains? Craik puts it succinctly:

> In any well-made machine one is ignorant of the working of most of the parts – the better they work the less we are conscious of them ... it is only a fault which draws attention to the existence of a mechanism at all.
>
> *Craik, 1943*

The human cognitive system is so finely tuned, having evolved over millions of years, that whereas we may be conscious of some aspects of how and why we do things (for example, how we plan the steps to do a load of laundry so that colours don't run between clothes), details of our most striking abilities (e.g. how you manage to translate the patterns of black ink on this page into an understanding of what I am trying to say), are not available to conscious report. Cognitive psychology is predicated on the assumption that details of such cognitive mechanisms can be inferred through the careful and imaginative use of experimentation with normal human participants. Cognitive neuropsychology is predicated on the somewhat different belief that only when the intact system malfunctions is it possible to get a real sense of the complexity of the mechanisms involved.

As an analogy, imagine the workings of my broken-down car. Cars are highly complex systems whose detailed design is known to engineers and mechanics but not to me: my car might break down for a number of reasons that only a mechanic or engineer could clarify. I could ask them what caused the breakdown; e.g. ask them to explain how the broken part(s), such as the fan belt, works. Such an explanation would reveal that the car is made up of functionally distinct components and the contribution that the faulty part normally makes to the car's functioning. If I was particularly unfortunate, my car might break down again. This time suppose the mechanic points out that the gear box is at fault, and explains how that normally works. If my bad luck continued, I could ultimately learn how every part works. The point is, of course, that looking at the car when it works perfectly gives me very few clues about its internal intricacy. The faulty system gives us clues as to its normal functioning.

Of course, the car is an artefact that has been designed for specific purposes and so we can imagine how someone could come to know how each part works. The human brain and cognitive system are much more complex and it is only through research that we can work out their internal, cognitive processes. Nevertheless, it is in the same sense of looking at a damaged system that cognitive neuropsychologists study the full range of complex cognitive processes such as object recognition, reading, memory, problem solving, and so on. They have two broad and interlinked aims. The first is to explain the behaviour of brain-damaged patients in terms of damage to a previously normally functioning system. The second aim is to use information gained from studying brain-damaged patients to infer characteristics of normal cognition. So, a damaged system (e.g. impaired memory as in amnesia) can be used to create or support models of the fully-functioning system (such as Atkinson and Shiffrin's, 1968, modal model), and then these models can be used to explain the patterns of deficits seen in patients (for example why people with amnesia have an inability to transfer information from short-term to long-term memory). However, intact cognition and the brain-damaged system go hand in hand and it is because of this that the two major goals are so closely linked.

This chapter provides a historical perspective of the field of cognitive neuropsychology and a context to the development of its use as a method within cognitive psychology. The historical evolution of knowledge and technology (such as the invention of ever-more accurate ways of looking at the brain) has itself resulted in a branching of the goals of neuropsychology. Whereas initially, perhaps for clinical reasons, simply understanding a patient's deficit was the primary aim, now studying patients has become a vital tool in the kit of the cognitive psychologist, whose aim is the explanation of cognition. This evolution of goals has itself been paralleled by more and more sophisticated methods of research, and it is these to which we shall turn in Section 4. Just as there is a range of different goals within the discipline, there are a number of different methods available, the choice of which depends on the aims of the particular neuropsychologist. To effectively conduct research they need to be aware of a range of issues and that these issues can have an impact on the choice of methods used, on the type of patient studied and on the interpretation that is feasible. Section 6 covers these issues. The chapter concludes with a brief overview of a development within the field in the 1990s, cognitive rehabilitation, which shows how information gained from research can sometimes be fed back into the rehabilitation of some aspects of a patient's condition.

2   A historical perspective

The very earliest roots of cognitive neuropsychology lie in the work of the phrenologists such as Gall and Spurzheim (1970). The **phrenologists** believed that mental 'faculties' or abilities were located in different parts of the brain, and that contours on the surface of the skull revealed the extent of an individual's abilities (see Figure 5.1). Another phrenologist, Fowler, inscribed the following on the backs of the phrenology heads that his company produced: "For thirty years I have studied Crania and living heads from all parts of the world, and have found in every instance that there is a perfect correspondence between the conformation of the healthy skull of an individual and his known characteristics."

For instance, Fowler believed that the 'literary, observing and knowing faculties' were situated above the right eye, that selfish properties resided under the skull above the right ear and that 'marriage, conjugality, constancy' was found near the base of the skull at the back of the head, slightly to the left of centre.

Of course, phrenology was soon discredited, but its suggestion that abilities could be functionally separated into components, and that these might be localized in different parts of the brain, is strikingly contemporary. Indeed, such suggestions are remarkably similar to the idea that cognition is modular.

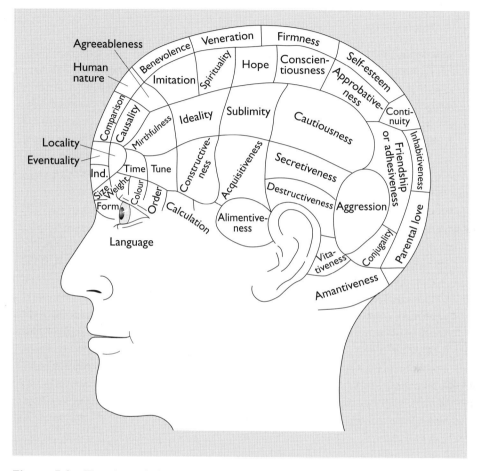

Figure 5.1   The classical phrenological head with the locations of the different mental 'faculties'

The assumption of some kind of modular organization was supported by a pivotal event in neuropsychology whose true importance was realized only many years later. In 1848, during a bizarre incident at the construction site of a Canadian railroad, Phineas Gage, one of the workers, accidentally set off an explosion that resulted in a tamping iron shooting up through his lower cheek and out of the top of his head, flying 20ft in the air before landing. Amazingly, the heat of the bar cauterized and therefore sealed the hole that it made in Gage's head. Not only did he survive, he was able to walk away from the scene and talk quite easily! Initially, it seemed that this accident had had no major harmful effects. However, with time, this previously amiable and reliable man became quite unreliable, made very bad judgments (e.g. he managed to ruin himself financially) and seemed to lose social skills. A neurologist, Harlow (1868) suggested that the damage to Phineas Gage's brain had disrupted his abilities to plan and to maintain socially accepted behaviour.

At the time, it was not possible for Harlow to investigate his ideas but, curiously, almost a hundred and fifty years later it became possible to confirm Harlow's preliminary evaluation (see Box 5.1).

5.1 ──────────────────────── **Research study**

Phineas Gage

About 150 years after Phineas Gage's accident, a patient, EVR, underwent surgery to remove a tumour from an area in the frontal lobes just above the left eye. Because neurosurgery unavoidably involves intrusive procedures, a certain amount of brain damage is caused if the tumour is not on the surface of the brain. EVR's tumour was very deep in his frontal lobes and he was left with brain damage at the base of his left frontal lobe. Following recovery, the neurologists working with him noticed an identical change in behaviour to that seen in Phineas Gage: EVR totally immersed himself in mundane tasks, entered into risky business ventures, bankrupted himself and ultimately lost his job (Damasio, 1994).

Seeing the similarity between EVR and how Phineas Gage had been described, Hanna Damasio tried to recreate the damage that must have occurred to Phineas Gage's brain. Using Phineas Gage's skull and the original iron bar (both kept in the Harvard Medical Museum in Boston) she recreated the original shape of his brain prior to the accident. Then using a sophisticated brain-imaging system, computer simulations 'shot' the iron bar through Phineas Gage's simulated brain to determine what exact parts had been damaged in the accident (see colour Plate 8). The findings showed that the damage Phineas Gage had sustained was in the same location as EVR's. Thus, by studying EVR, it became possible to confirm Harlow's evaluation of Phineas Gage's cognitive deficits (Damasio et al., 1994). Although the main import of this study is historical, it also shows how behavioural description of individuals can combine with clinical, experimental and brain imaging work to help create models of cognitive functioning.

Although Harlow had identified one of the first neuropsychological patients to be documented, his work did not receive substantial attention. Instead, the true roots of contemporary neuropsychology are to be found in the work of the French neurologist Paul Broca. In 1861 he treated a man who became known as 'Tan' (Broca, 1861/1965). Following a stroke (the bursting of a blood vessel in the brain), Tan had great difficulty making intelligible utterances. At most, he could produce only a few syllables at any one time, and nothing that sounded like real connected language. (He became known as Tan because of the sound of one of the syllables that he could make.) In spite of his profound inability to produce intelligible language – his aphasia – Tan was able to understand fully what was said to him. Broca proposed that a part of Tan's brain was damaged that was responsible for co-ordinating the muscle movements required for speech. Damage to this area, in spite of the vocal apparatus in the throat and mouth remaining intact, would result in the pattern of behaviour found in Tan. Post-mortem analysis of Tan's brain revealed what Broca had suspected – that damage to Tan's brain was localized to a particular area (since known as Broca's area) with the rest of his brain remaining relatively intact (Broca, 1861/1965).

In 1874, just a decade after Broca's seminal work, another neurologist, Karl Wernicke, was working with patients that exhibited the reverse of Tan's pattern of behavioural problems (Wernicke, 1874). Thus, they appeared to be able to speak fluently. They produced whole words in continuous speech that sounded superficially at least like full sentences – but had difficulties in understanding what was said to them. Although, on the surface, their speech seemed fluent, on closer examination it was found to contain many errors (such as neologisms) and was very difficult to comprehend. You can get a sense of this from a more recent example where a patient is describing a picture known as 'the cookie theft picture' (part of a diagnostic battery of tests for assessing language problems, see Figure 5.2). The patient describes it as 'Well, this is ... mother is away here working her work out o' here to get her better, but when she's looking, the two boys looking in the other part. One their small tile into her time here. She's working another time because she's getting to. So two boys working together and one is sneakin' around here, making his work an' his further funnas his time he had' (Goodglass and Kaplan, 1972, p.81). 'Funnas' is a new word or neologism.

Figure 5.2   The cookie theft picture

Source: Goodglass and Kaplan, 1972

Wernicke proposed that his patients had sustained damage to an area responsible for storing the sound patterns of words, resulting in their difficulties in comprehending speech. Post-mortem examination of one of his patients, as with Broca's patient, showed a clear specific area of damage, in the temporal lobe and slightly further back in the brain than Broca's area. Historically, this area is now known as Wernicke's area (see Figure 5.3). Although Wernicke's suggestion explained poor comprehension it didn't account for his patients' difficulties in producing fluent speech, and this issue is still not fully understood, c.f. Butterworth, (1979).

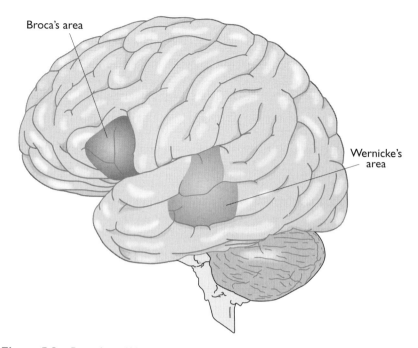

Figure 5.3 Broca's and Wernicke's areas of the brain, the locations of speech production and comprehension, respectively (a lateral view of the left side of the brain)

Although both Broca and Wernicke were neurologists (medical doctors who treated patients with brain damage), they are regarded as the fathers of modern day neuropsychology.

Broca and Wernicke were known as 'localizationalists' because they believed that certain functions were firmly localized in particular areas of the brain, i.e. speech production in Broca's area and comprehension in Wernicke's area. The result of this trend towards localizing functions anatomically was that eventually others, such as Lichteim (1885), started attempting to create models of cognitive processes, such as the production of spoken language. Due to the way these early neuropsychologists relied on visual means of describing their models in terms of boxes, representing stages, and arrows, representing information flow between them (box and arrow diagrams), they became known as the 'diagram makers'. Initially, this approach received considerable support but, over time, it attracted criticism because the models lacked clarity as to the processes involved. For example, it was postulated that there were centres that held the meanings of words and others that enabled the vocal system to produce words; however, neither centre was clearly defined. Critics of the approach have described it as 'black boxology' (since the centres are likened to black boxes that cannot be looked into). A particularly damning formulation of this criticism comes from Sutherland who defined the approach as 'the construction and ostentatious display of meaningless flow charts by psychologists as a substitute for thought' (Sutherland, 1989, p.58). As a consequence of criticism like this (levelled at the localizationalist approach since the beginning of the twentieth century) the diagram makers' approach fell into disrepute.

Although neurologists continued working with patients, it was not until the rise of the 'information processing approach' and the birth of cognitive psychology that the ideas of the early diagram makers regained popularity. Cognitive psychology gave researchers something to put inside the black boxes that had been the diagram makers' downfall. Whereas Lichteim may have said that there was a centre for word recognition that, if damaged, would result in difficulties in understanding language, armed with ideas about information processing, computation and representation, cognitive psychologists could now attempt to describe what might happen in such centres.

Another important factor in the evolution of cognitive neuropsychology has been the development of more and more sophisticated techniques for imaging the brain's activity (such as PET, MRI and fMRI – see Chapter 4). Whereas Broca and others had to wait until their patients' deaths to be able to look at their brains, it is now possible to image the living brain. This has had a significant impact for a number of reasons. First, before the development of these techniques, researchers had to rely on simple paper and pencil tests, and then draw inferences as to the nature of the underlying brain damage (e.g. bad performance on certain subtests in an aphasia 'test' battery would imply damage in Broca's area). Now, however, it is possible to obtain images of damage in the living brain. This has a significant impact on being able to treat patients – should surgery be necessary, imaging techniques can provide surgeons with detailed anatomical pictures. Second, information concerning which parts of the brain are damaged in particular patients allows psychologists to develop more accurate models of the behaviour that they are trying to explain. Techniques such as fMRI make it possible to look at what parts of the brain are particularly active when normal healthy participants carry out tasks. This allows cognitive neuropsychologists to integrate data concerning both healthy and damaged brains (see Section 4).

Summary

- Historically, neuropsychology developed in the middle of the nineteenth century through neurologists' observations of consistent patterns of impairment in their patients.
- Early researchers were known as localizationalists because they believed that particular mental functions were situated in specific locations in the brain.
- The diagram makers, building on the ideas of the localizationalists, formulated models of mental processing in terms of 'box and arrow' diagrams.
- The demise of the diagram makers' approach gave way to renewed interest in the field of neuropsychology with the advent of cognitive psychology and the information processing approach during the twentieth century.
- The development of more advanced techniques, such as standardized research methods and brain-imaging technology, further developed the field towards the end of the twentieth century.

3   Goals

Throughout the historical development of neuropsychology, the goals of those studying brain damage have evolved and branched. Over a century ago, neurologists were studying patients with brain damage mainly for treatment purposes. However, as the work of people like Broca and Wernicke developed, their hypotheses about what patterns of damage tell us about intact cognition were brought together by the diagram makers for the purposes of explaining mental processes. Indeed contemporary cognitive neuropsychology has a number of diverse goals, all of which depend on the type of work that the neuropsychologist is conducting. For example, a clinical neuropsychologist, who is working with a patient after they have suffered brain damage, will be interested in trying to get a good overall profile of the patient's problems and strengths, perhaps with a view to providing them with appropriate support in their day-to-day life. Someone working in rehabilitation will be interested in using a patient's preserved abilities to help them to acquire strategies for coping with impairment(s). A research neuropsychologist aims to discover what patients' problems tell us about the cognitive functions affected by brain damage, what they tell us about the normal system and what might be done to aid individual patients. In this way, the researcher would be feeding into the knowledge base of the other types of neuropsychologists. Broadly speaking, there are four main goals that define the field of neuropsychology, with different combinations of these being reflected in different kinds of neuropsychological work. These are:

- lesion localization;
- assessment of a patient's deficit;
- building models of normal cognition; and
- localization of different cognitive functions within the brain.

Neuropsychologists may need to achieve multiple goals, so that, for example, a researcher might need to assess patients before trying to build a cognitive model, and a clinician might conduct an assessment in order to determine the likely location of brain damage.

The disparity of goals illustrates the breadth of neuropsychology, but cognitive neuropsychology is just a part of a much larger field of research known as neuroscience. Neuroscience is a multidisciplinary approach that brings together a number of diverse ways of looking at the brain and cognition. These include cell anatomy, pathology, neurology, electrophysiology, neuroimaging and connectionist modelling. The difference between the approaches lies primarily in the level of neural or cognitive functioning being analyzed and the research methods employed. For example, cell anatomy is concerned with the structure and interconnections of individual cells, and neurology focuses on how the symptoms of abnormal function point towards a specific diagnosis and prognosis (e.g. stroke, degenerative illness or epilepsy); connectionist modelling on the other hand involves creating computational models of how particular systems work (such as face recognition for example).

3.1 Lesion localization

Before the advent of brain-imaging techniques, a neuropsychologist had to build up a picture of the site of brain damage in a patient using tests known to involve specific areas of the brain. These tests are largely 'paper and pencil' ones, designed to detect known patterns of brain damage. For instance, the Wisconsin Card Sorting Test (Grant and Berg, 1948) was designed to assess the ability to change behaviour as a result of external feedback. The test uses a pack of cards that differ in a number of dimensions, namely shape, colour and number of objects each card depicts. The participant's task is to sort the cards according to dimensions that are chosen by the experimenter but not made explicit to the participant. The experimenter gives feedback on the sorting produced by the participant, but this may simply involve the experimenter saying whether the participant is sorting correctly or incorrectly. For example, the experimenter's initial rule may require sorting the cards by shape but then, after a number of trials, the experimenter may change the rule (e.g. to 'sort by colour') and his or her feedback would change accordingly, for example, by responding 'incorrect' to a sort determined by shape. All being well, by trial and error, the participant infers what the new dimension is on the basis of the feedback given after each trial. After the new dimension (e.g. colour) has been discovered, following a number of correct trials, the rule is changed again, perhaps to sorting by number. It is known that patients who have damage to the frontal lobes can have particular difficulties with the WCST, for example they might continue to sort according to a certain dimension, such as shape, even though the feedback implies that shape is now irrelevant to the rule. Consequently, a patient's poor performance on this task (defined relative to strict criteria for normal and abnormal performance), can be taken as evidence that they may have damage to the frontal lobes.

Today, localization of lesions using standardized paper and pencil tests is somewhat redundant. Neuroimaging techniques such as MRI provide accurate pictures of brain damage. However, these techniques can be costly and so if the clinician is content with a general profile of a patient's abilities (and therefore *likely* brain damage), without needing to know the precise location of lesions, then the use of paper and pencil tests may be sufficient.

Moreover, in some cases, a technique such as MRI may show no gross damage despite the patient having very clear problems. PG is a patient with very clear memory problems– a few weeks after an event he has largely forgotten it. By February, for example, he will have forgotten what he did at Christmas. Although MRI scans showed no noticeable brain damage, detailed testing involving tests specifically designed to investigate his problems, revealed a marked impairment in laying down and holding onto memories for more than a few weeks (Jansari et al., 2003).

In conclusion, localization of lesions by the use of standardized tests is not as prevalent within neuropsychology as it once was. However, it remains an extremely valuable technique.

3.2 Assessment of deficit

A *clinical* neuropsychologist's main aim is to assess a patient's problem(s) by the use of whichever techniques are available, be they interviews, specific clinical tests or brain scans. Following this, if necessary, they can make a recommendation as to what types of support the patient may need.

A growing need for accurate assessment comes from the development of rehabilitation programs. Most of these attempt to circumvent a patient's main problems (e.g. an inability to lay down new long-term memories) and instead use their preserved abilities, such as preserved procedural memories (see Section 7).

3.3   Model building

Lesion localization and assessment were once the most important goals within neuropsychology, but this changed dramatically with the advent of cognitive psychology. As Selnes puts it:

> The purpose of the investigation was no longer to localize or quantify the nature of the deficit, but rather to treat the cognitive impairment as an experimental condition (induced by nature) suitable for probing specific hypotheses ...
>
> *Selnes, 2001, p.38*

In this sense, the main goal became to create and test models of cognition in order to help us understand and explain complex cognitive processes, such as reading, for example.

Cognitive neuropsychology can sometimes work simply to support models that have already been developed on the basis of cognitive psychological investigations with normal participants. For example, in the 1960s mounting evidence suggested there was a difference between retaining information in memory for a few minutes and retaining it for a longer period. This sort of observation ultimately led Atkinson and Schiffrin (1968) to propose the 'modal' or 'multi-store' model of human memory in which there were different memory stores, one for short-term memory (STM) and one for long-term memory (LTM). This model was then further supported by neuropsychological evidence from the contrasting cases of patients HM and KF with a deficient LTM and a deficient STM respectively (see Section 5). (Of course, there are number of complications with this simple picture – for example, see **Rutherford, 2005**).

In other cases, neuropsychology can help to develop a model by providing novel insights into the nature of a psychological process. An example is the study of individuals who, following specific brain damage, develop an object-recognition difficulty or **agnosia**. This is a complex disorder, famously described in Oliver Sacks's *The Man Who Mistook His Wife For A Hat* (1985). The patient, whilst having normal vision, could not correctly identify objects. For example, when shown a glove, the patient's best attempt to name it was 'It could be a change purse ... for coins of five sizes' (Sacks, 1985).

Detailed research into patients with agnosia allowed the emergence of an understanding of how the disorder relates to normal object recognition. In a detailed case study, Humphreys and Riddoch (1987) tested a stroke patient, HJA. Although able to copy line drawings of objects, HJA was unable to *name* the same line drawings. Following a fine-grained analysis of HJA's visual recognition and drawing abilities, Humphreys and Riddoch (1987) suggested that there is a stage in the object recognition process at which visual information is 'integrated' into one coherent representation. Their suggestion is that HJA cannot do this integration and so whilst able to copy line drawings, the visual information required for this did not allow him to recognize the object. Another patient JF was also unable to name objects that he could draw perfectly well but in JF's case, he didn't have any difficulty in miming the use of the object (Lhermitte and Beauvois, 1973). This led to the conclusion that it is possible to access semantic information concerning an object and yet still be unable to name it. Without these neuropsychological findings (concerning integration of visual information and access to semantic information being part of a long chain of processes required to name an object), it would be extremely difficult to identify these different processing stages.

A further example of a novel finding that helps to explain normal cognitive processes is provided by the rare **split brain syndrome**. This arises from a drastic surgical procedure, pioneered in 1965 by Bogen and Vogel, to alleviate intractable epilepsy (Bogen and Vogel, 1965). The procedure, which is carried out only in extreme circumstances, aims to prevent epilepsy spreading from one cerebral hemisphere to another. It involves severing the tract of fibres, known as the corpus callosum (see Figure 5.4), which connects the two hemispheres, with the result that they then operate in relative isolation from one another. Because the procedure (called a commissurotomy) is carried out so rarely, there are only about fifty split brain patients in the world.

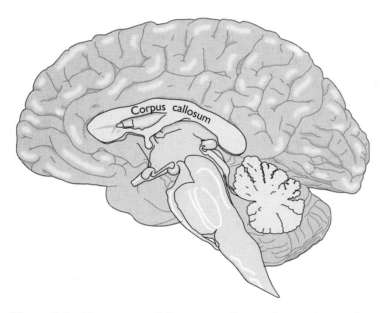

Figure 5.4   The position of the corpus callosum. A sagittal view of the brain

Due to the pioneering work of researchers such as Sperry and Gazzaniga (e.g. Gazzaniga *et al.*, 1962; Sperry and Gazzaniga, 1967) we now know that a patient with a split brain shows a number of characteristics that together form a syndrome of problems. A classic one is known as **astereognosis**, which manifests itself as an inability to identify an object that is held in the left hand without being able to look at it. This can be demonstrated using an experiment in which the subject can only feel a range of objects but is prevented from seeing them (see Figure 5.5 overleaf).

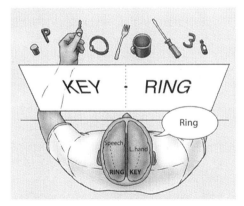

Figure 5.5 In this Gazzaniga *et al.* experiment, a split-brain patient is prevented from seeing what is held in the left hand and, because the connection between the speech-oriented left hemisphere and the somatosensory cortex of the right hemisphere is cut, the subject is unable to identify the object

Source: Gazzaniga *et al.*, 1998, p.331

This work has allowed scientists to confirm the idea that information from the left hand about what an object feels like, its size, texture, etc., is processed initially by the right hemisphere and that information from the right hand is processed by the left hemisphere. That is, for motor control and processing of tactile information, the brain's organization is **contralateral** – each of the hemispheres is in control of, or processes information from, the *opposite* side of the body. As a result, information deriving from the left hand about a small hard object that has a big cavity in it as well as a section on the side for holding it (such as a cup) will firstly be processed by the somatosensory cortex in the right hemisphere. Although this hemisphere can represent the object in terms of how it feels, its name is thought to be inaccessible because this linguistic information is represented in the left hemisphere. That is, ordinarily, sensory information about the cup needs to be passed to the left hemisphere, via the corpus callosum, for the name to be accessed. Since this tract of connections has been cut in split brain patients, such transmission of information is not possible – sensory information is 'trapped' in the right hemisphere and the patient cannot name the object! However, as soon as the cup is put in the right hand, the patient can access its name because information from this hand goes to the somatosensory cortex in the left hemisphere. This representation of the physical feel of the object can then be used to access its name, since the linguistic information is also in the left hemisphere. Curiously, then, when a split brain patient cannot see an object, his or her right hand can 'name' it even though their left hand cannot! This sort of neuropsychological finding helped to support existing theories of specialization of the two hemispheres for which scientists already had some evidence. Therefore, it is now known that motor control of one part of the body is controlled by the contralateral hemisphere, that the left hemisphere is specialized for linguistic processing whilst the right specializes in spatial thought and that most of the information flow between these areas happens cortically through the corpus callosum.

Other work on split brain patients has provided novel findings. For example Luck *et al.* have looked at whether attentional processes are split between the two hemispheres or whether each hemisphere has its own attentional system; their findings suggest the latter (Luck *et al.*, 1994). Ramachandran *et al.* have looked at which types of cognitive information are transferred between the cerebral cortices via the corpus callosum and which types are transferred subcortically via other pathways that are spared in the commissurotomy procedure (Ramachandran *et al.*,1986). Their work has suggested that 'lower order' cognitive information such as shape and motion can be transferred subcortically, whereas 'higher order' information such as language and meaning is transferred cortically. Without information gained from split brain patients, this kind of insight into normal cognitive processing would be difficult to obtain. Specifically, the findings from split brain patients provide valuable information concerning the extent of hemispheric specialization and the cortical and sub-cortical flow of information between the hemispheres. In summary, neuropsychology as a whole can provide a vital link in the chain involved in building models of normal cognition.

3.4 Localization of function

Although the early workers in the field such as Broca, Wernicke and Lichteim were attempting to identify specific areas of the brain as being involved in certain processes, this is just one possible goal of cognitive neuropsychology. Indeed, many other researchers feel that the need to explain the nature of cognitive processes is more pressing than the question of where in the brain they occur. And still others acknowledge the issue of function localization but separate this from the question of the cognitive processing involved. For example, although there exist complex neuropsychological models of face- and object-recognition, the emphasis in many of the models is on the types of representations involved and the flow of information processing, rather than on the role of specific locations in the brain (e.g. Bruce and Young, 1986; Humphreys *et al.*, 1988).

Finally cognitive neuroscientists who use neuropsychology as one of their range of methods are concerned with trying to work out *how* a cognitive process works as well as *where* in the brain it primarily occurs and use data from patients, normal controls, animal studies, molecular studies, etc. It should be noted that whereas the early localizationalists such as Broca and Wernicke may have believed that certain areas were solely involved in particular functions, cognitive function is now known generally to involve many areas of the brain working *together* (much like the earlier example of the car working as a whole). Cognitive neuroscientists simply suggest that there are certain areas that are at the *end-point* of a long, processing pathway for particular functions. So for example, the whole of the visual system needs to be functioning well to recognize people's faces but Damasio *et al.*, suggest that the **right temporal pole** (an area of the brain just below the right temple) is the most critical component (Damasio *et al.*, 1996). Similarly, work in the field of memory, is now attempting to work out the exact role of the (left) temporal lobe and in particular, a specific area within it known as the perirhinal cortex, in the formation of memories. This work attempts to address both the types of representation involved at different points in cognitive processing and also where the various stages of processing occur (e.g. Aggleton and Brown, 1999). Figure 5.6 shows a preliminary understanding of the critical areas for a range of cognitive functions.

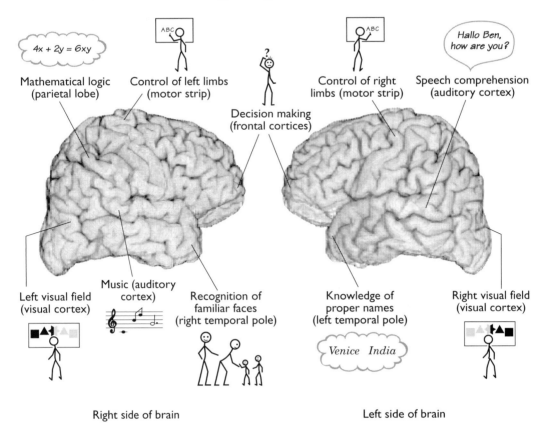

Figure 5.6 The different areas of specialization in the left and right hemispheres of the brain

In spite of the variety of positions researchers take with regard to function localization, it could be said to be an *ultimate* aim of neuropsychology since, as well as giving an understanding of how and where different cognitive information is processed, localization would allow us to make predictions about the consequences of brain damage. For instance, neurosurgeons wanting to remove a tumour or the focus of epileptic seizures need to know that their invasive surgery will have minimal detrimental effects. Knowing that language processing generally, but not always takes place in the left hemisphere now means that a pre-operative test (known as an amytal abreaction) is conducted on patients who are about to undergo surgery. If the test confirms the processing of language in the left hemisphere, the surgeon(s) will attempt to spare the language areas of the left hemisphere as much as possible.

Summary

- There are four main goals of cognitive neuropsychology: identification of localization of a lesion; assessment of the deficits suffered by a patient; creation of cognitive models; and finally identification of localization of function.
- The goals of neuropsychology depend on the role of the neuropsychologist – workers in the clinical, research and rehabilitation fields all have slightly different goals.
- Localization of a lesion was one of the earliest goals of neuropsychology since knowing where a patient has brain damage has an important impact on understanding their deficits.
- Assessment of deficit is important for gaining a profile of the impaired and intact abilities following brain damage and is the main goal of clinical neuropsychology.
- The building of cognitive models is the main goal of researchers who utilize information gained from studying damaged systems to propose accounts of cognitive processing.
- Localization of function is related to the early localizationalist approach but is now an advanced goal where the information gained from a number of related disciplines within neuroscience can help identify where in the brain different aspects of processing occur.

4   Techniques used for assessing and studying brain damage

Reflecting the fact that different neuropsychologists pursue slightly different goals, these are a variety of methods in use within neuropsychology.

4.1   Standardized testing

Clinicians tend to draw on an extensive range of 'standardized' tests that have been carefully constructed to tap very specific functions. For instance, there are tests that assess memory functioning (e.g. the Wechsler Memory Scale-III, or WMS-III), general intellectual functioning (e.g. the Wechsler Adult Intelligence Scale, or WAIS) and visuo-spatial abilities (e.g. the Birmingham Object Recognition Battery, or BORB). These may be short single tests or involve a large number of subtests aimed at tapping different subcomponents of the particular cognitive function being investigated.

One of the most important and useful aspects of standardized clinical tests is that they will have been created with graded difficulty and the performance for a large range of participants is published with each test. These published 'norms' can be analysed separately by whatever demographic variables are thought to be important in the performance of the task. For example, if age is thought to affect scores, then norms will be published for different age groups and a patient's performance can be compared with those from the same age group. Some tests (e.g. the Visual Object and Space Perception test, or VOSP) also provide data for the performance of large groups of people with particular kinds of brain damage, allowing the clinician to see immediately if a patient's score falls within the range typical of one of these groups. The clinical neuropsychologist may then use the information from standardized tests in reporting to other health care professionals involved in the patient's welfare, on the basis of which treatment or rehabilitation regimes may be devised.

4.2   Experimental neuropsychology

As mentioned above, the experimental neuropsychologist assesses patients in order to probe particular theories of cognition: the patient becomes a test-bed for ideas. There are five main methods that are available for this purpose. These are:

- the use of standardized tests (as above)

- employing paradigms already used in cognitive psychology

- designing new techniques aimed at looking at specific issues in a patient or group of patients

- neuroimaging (see Chapter 4) and

- connectionist modelling (see Chapter 2).

As we will see these are not mutually exclusive – it is possible to use a variety of methods in combination. However, some methods may not be available for a number of reasons.

Patients are often initially assessed using whatever standardized tests are available. This allows the neuropsychologist to build up a picture of the patient's impairments and their intact abilities. Following this initial assessment, paradigms that are already used in cognitive psychology can be used to probe particular issues. A classic example involves the identification of separate short-term and long-term memory processes. Normal healthy participants, when asked to remember a list of words and then tested for immediate recall, will generate a classic U-shaped curve known as the 'serial position curve' (SPC). The curve shows the probability of someone recalling a word as a function of its position in the list, and has three main portions: very good recall of the first few items (known as 'primacy'), very good recall of the last few items (known as 'recency') and intermediate to lower recall of the items not at the extremes (known as the 'asymptote').

It has been suggested that primacy arises because early items in the list have been successfully transferred to LTM whilst recency reflects the fact that items are still being held in STM. Mid-list items are poorly recalled because they are less likely to have been successfully transferred to LTM (because of concentration on the early items) and will have been displaced from STM by later items. If this explanation is correct, then it would be predicted that patients unable to transfer information from STM to LTM would not show all three portions of the curve. This is exactly what was found by Baddeley and Warrington (1970) – their participants with amnesia showed a SPC in which there was little evidence of primacy, whilst the amount of recency was indistinguishable from that of non-brain-damaged controls (see Figure 5.7). This robust neuropsychological finding helped to support an influential cognitive theory of the separation of different memory stores (Atkinson and Shiffrin, 1968) (though for further discussion, for example, see **Rutherford, 2005**).

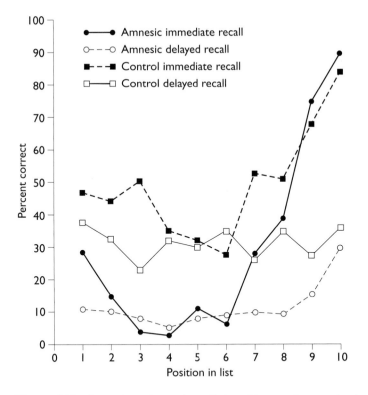

Figure 5.7 Amnesic patients show little evidence of remembering early items in a list (primacy) but their recall of more recent items is identical to that of normal patients

Source: Baddeley and Warrington, 1970

As well as using tasks such as the free recall paradigm described above, an important task of the neuropsychological experimenter is to be able to create tasks that are specific to the patient under investigation. By the very nature of investigative work, new issues are being explored and therefore the use of standardized clinical tests and already existing experimental tests will not always be appropriate. For example, Jansari *et al.* tested an epileptic patient PG who complained of memory problems (Jansari *et al.*, 2003). His SPC was normal, however, as was his performance on standardized clinical memory tests. This apparently normal clinical profile in the face of complaints of memory problems led to a detailed case study of his LTM. It is thought that in the normally functioning brain, a neurobiological consolidation process within LTM gradually strengthens memory traces of past events, allowing them to be later recalled. It was felt that PG's epilepsy might be disrupting this consolidation. The standardized clinical tests were designed to assess the *transfer* of information from STM to LTM but not the strength of the resulting long-term memories. Now it is well known that repeated recall of a particular piece of information (a memory) strengthens its representation in LTM. If PG's memory problems arose because information in his LTM was represented less strongly than normal, then repeated recall should reduce the problem. After having been presented with stories for later recall, his recall was poor for stories he was only ever allowed to recall once (ranging from a day to four weeks after initial presentation). However, for stories he was allowed to recall more often, his recall matched that of normal healthy controls (see Figure 5.8).

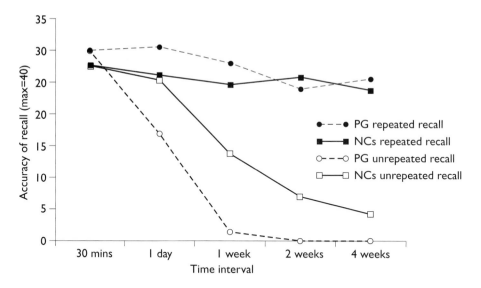

Figure 5.8 By repeatedly recalling stories, PG was able to improve his recall of the story to the level of normal subjects

Source: Jansari et al., 2003

Experimental neuropsychologists will often, if possible, use some sort of brain-imaging technique (such as CAT or MRI scans). These techniques yield images of the structure of the brain and can reveal any gross lesions (or areas of damage). More sophisticated techniques (such as PET, fMRI and SPECT) can image the brain while it is performing cognitive tasks to see which parts are utilized for different tasks (see Chapter 4). For example, in two studies, Damasio and colleagues used a number of functional brain-imaging techniques to identify which parts of the brain were most active when normal controls were answering questions on different types of information. They found specific areas associated with knowledge for people, animals and tools. They then divided a group of brain-damaged patients with object-recognition difficulties into three sub-groups, depending on which of the same three classes of objects they had most difficulty recognizing. Finally, they tried to identify areas of brain damage that were common within each group of patients. They found that the patients had lesions in the same areas that were most active when normal controls viewed the same objects (see colour Plate 9). Damage to each of these areas therefore resulted in the differing behavioural patterns in recognition found in the patients (Damasio et al., 1996; Tranel et al., 1997).

Although brain-imaging can be a powerful and useful technique, it does have limitations. It is expensive and not readily available to all researchers. Moreover, with some patients, such as PG mentioned earlier, some scanning techniques reveal no physical or functional problems despite the patient exhibiting a behavioural impairment. Finally, it is even possible to question the usefulness of brain-imaging for clarifying cognitive processes; however, it is beyond the scope of this chapter to go into such debates.

A further method that has gained much momentum within the field is that of cognitive modelling (of which connectionist modelling is one approach). The basic aim of cognitive modelling is to build models (using computer programs) that behave in the same way as humans (see Chapter 3). Having developed an account of say, face recognition, perhaps drawing on a combination of all the other available methods, a cognitive modeller will then seek to program its various aspects in a cognitive model. The model can then be tested by providing it with input and comparing the output it produces to normal human performance. If the system successfully mimics human behaviour (in that it provides correct answers when humans do, and incorrect answers when humans also make errors), then there is some justification for believing that normal cognitive processes are similar. Of course, there is no guarantee that the model actually functions in the same way as the normal human system (Coltheart, 2001); cognitive modelling simply suggests plausible mechanisms and processes.

One of the reasons this method has become popular in neuropsychology is that, with some models, it is possible to 'lesion' the model by damaging some of its components. In effect, this creates an analogue to the brain damage that disrupts parts of a patient's normally functioning system. The lesioned model can now be tested by comparing it to the performance of neuropsychological patients. This method has proved very successful in certain parts of cognition. For example, Farah and McClelland (1991) created a model of the problems experienced by certain patients with agnosia (object-recognition difficulty) such as their having more difficulty in naming living things (e.g. animals) than non-living things (e.g. types of furniture), a finding first documented by Warrington and Shallice (1984). Similarly, Coltheart (2001) has tried to recreate in a model the reading errors exhibited by patients with different forms of acquired dyslexia (see below).

In summary, therefore, there is a wide range of methods available to the experimental neuropsychologist. The choice will depend on a large number of factors, including the type of patient being studied, the specificity of their deficit, the range of models already in existence that might explain (parts of) their behaviour and the availability of techniques such as neuroimaging and cognitive modelling.

An important point here is that just as the different neuropsychological methods are not in competition with one another, the same argument holds for the choice of a neuropsychological approach as opposed to other approaches to studying cognition. Neuropsychology is a method that *complements* and works together with other methods rather than being an *alternative*. A classic example of how different approaches can complement one another is found in the development of models of face processing. Early studies using introspective diary methods gave an insight into the general stages of face processing resulting in Young *et al*. functional model of face processing (Young *et al*., 1985). Experimental work, first on normal and then brain-damaged individuals, then led to the components of this model being expanded and clarified in the Bruce and Young (1986) model. Finally, problems with this latter model led to Burton *et al*. creating IAC, a connectionist model able to account for most of the findings to date (Burton *et al*., 1990). For further information see **Pike and Brace** (2005).

Summary

- The techniques used by neuropsychologists depend on their particular goal in working with a patient.
- Assessment is carried out using standardized tests for which published data on the performance of a variety of participant groups is available. This allows the clinician to evaluate the extent of problems with different areas of cognition.
- Experimental research involves a range of techniques including both established tasks and new paradigms specially created for working with particular patients or patient groups.
- Neuroimaging has already established itself as a vital tool in research, though there may be some cases where it is unable to shed light on deficits in patients that are manifest behaviourally.
- A further method of research involves implementing proposed models using connectionist architectures, which allow the plausibility of the models to be tested.

5 Dissociations and double dissociations

Having used various techniques to evaluate a patient's intact abilities and deficits, the next task of the neuropsychologist is to make inferences from the evidence gained. How do neuropsychologists infer the existence of separate cognitive functions within the brain (e.g. language being separate from memory)? How can they infer that each function is composed of separate processes (e.g. within face processing, different paths for recognition of faces and recognition of the emotion in the face)? Neuropsychologists look to see which cognitive problems tend to occur together and, more importantly, which ones can occur in the absence of other problems. For example, it has been repeatedly observed that certain patients retain an ability to remember items for a few minutes but lose their ability to remember the same information for longer periods (e.g. patient HM reported by Scoville and Milner, 1957). The conclusion is that two types of memory are involved and that in these patients, the two kinds of memory **dissociate** from one another – it is possible to lose one whilst retaining the other intact. This sort of **dissociation** was used to support early models of memory such as the modal model proposed by Atkinson and Schiffrin (1968) which has separate STM and LTM components.

However, it can be argued that a single dissociation does not entitle us to postulate independent processes. There could be a simpler explanation. For instance, suppose there were just one memory system, and that in that system the more effort you put into remembering information, the more likely it was that you would retain it for longer periods. That is, more 'effort' is required to retain information for a few hours than it is to do so for just a few minutes (see Figure 5.9a). Now if brain damage reduced the cognitive effort a person was able to make, this might have little impact on the ability to retain information for short periods but a large impact on retention over longer periods (see Figure 5.9b). The situation would be similar to having had a heavy illness for a few weeks, resulting in easy exercise such as walking being possible but more strenuous activities such as running or swimming proving more challenging. The pattern of memory loss would be as in HM and other amnesic persons but this would not be evidence for separate STM and LTM stores or processes.

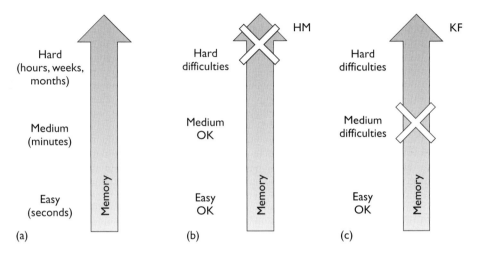

Figure 5.9 (a) In a hypothetical 'unitary' memory system, more 'effort' is required to retain information over longer periods; (b) Damage to the hypothetical unitary system is most likely to affect performance on more difficult memory tasks. This could explain cases such as HM who have an inability to remember events that happened more than a few minutes ago; (c) If the hypothetical unitary system is more severely damaged resulting in problems with memory for information heard a few minutes ago, it is impossible to explain how a patient such as KF can still be able to remember what happened an hour, a week or many months ago

Is this explanation in terms of 'difficulty' to be preferred to one that invokes (at least) two separate processes? What if a patient was found who has no problems with remembering information from a few weeks ago but cannot repeat back a list of six single digit numbers after ten seconds? This type of performance could not be explained in terms of 'difficulty' because if someone can do the 'difficult' task of remembering from weeks ago, then they should be able to do the 'easy' task (Figure 5.9c). However, such a patient has been reported. Following an injury, KF has had problems with certain aspects of STM but his LTM is normal (Shallice and Warrington, 1970). These contrasting patterns of impairment shown by HM and KF, where HM has impaired LTM but intact STM whilst KF has impaired STM but intact LTM, is known as a **double dissociation**. This type of finding is extremely useful for neuropsychologists since it seems strongly to imply the existence of two separate systems either of which can be damaged. Such a double dissociation allows researchers to say that (at least to some degree) STM and LTM are separate processes. The existence of further double dissociations then allows for further fractionation of memory (Figure 5.10 overleaf).

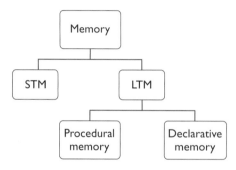

Figure 5.10 Conceptual 'memory tree' that can be created from evidence of dissociations and double dissociations

Other clear examples of double dissociation occur in face processing, between recognition of someone's identity and recognition of the emotion on their face (e.g. Adolphs *et al.*, 1994), and in reading, between phonological and surface dyslexia (e.g. Coltheart, 1987). It should be noted that, although double dissociations are usually found *between* patients, they can also be found *within* the processing of one patient. For example, a patient DB has a condition known as **blindsight** – there are areas of his vision in which he is effectively blind, yet he processes at least some visual information from that area, albeit without awareness; a case of 'seeing but not being aware of it' (Weiskrantz, 1986, 1987). In a complex experiment comparing this area of blindness with areas of intact processing, a double dissociation was found between his ability to make judgements about low-level visual processing and his ability to accurately detect shapes (a higher-level visual task). Within-subject double dissociations have also been reported in patients with neglect (Beschin *et al.*, 2000; Pisella *et al.*, 2002).

Generally speaking, double dissociations are extremely useful in the development of cognitive models of normal functions. However, there are some who advise caution when interpreting such findings. For example, Young *et al.* (1993) list a number of problems including:

1 Patients who show double dissociations are often studied in different laboratories and with methods that are not standardized. So different stimuli may have been used to demonstrate their problems. For example, in the field of object recognition some researchers (e.g. Warrington and Shallice, 1984) have reported patients who have much greater problems recognizing living things than non-living things whilst others (e.g. Sacchett and Humphreys, 1992) have reported the reverse case. This has led many (e.g. McCarthy and Warrington, 1990) to argue that the semantic system is split along categorical lines with a major subdivision between living and non-living objects. However, critics (e.g. Gaffan and Heywood, 1993) have argued that the double dissociation may be an artefact of the different studies having used different materials for testing. As a counter to this possibility, Hillis and Caramazza (1991) have shown a clear double dissociation between two patients, tested at similar times, in the same laboratory and on the same material.

2   How a deficit or dissociation in a patient is judged can be a highly subjective matter. For example, imagine a person who performs *below normal* on two tasks but better on task A than on task B. If a second patient is found, who is also below normal on both tasks but shows the reverse pattern (i.e. better performance on task B than on A), can these two patterns be interpreted as a double dissociation? Some argue that it is necessary for at least one of the two functions to be relatively intact in each patient to justify the use of the data from the two patients to claim a double dissociation. In this hypothetical example, since neither patient shows intact performance on either of the two tasks, it can be suggested that the evidence is not strong enough to prove a double dissociation.

3   'Normal' performance on a task does not necessarily mean normal cognitive functioning since a person may be using a compensatory strategy not found in people with an intact cognitive system (see later section). For example, Humphreys and Riddoch's (1987) patient HJA seemed to be able to copy line drawings well, implying an intact ability to perceive the drawings properly. However, closer inspection showed that his drawing strategy was very laborious and piece-meal with different parts of the object being selectively reproduced, rather than what one might expect if HJA perceived the object as a complete whole. It is therefore important to ensure that a patient is tested in a variety of ways to ensure that seemingly normal performance is being produced in a normal fashion.

Moreover, researchers have questioned the extent to which a double dissociation does imply the existence of separate systems. Glymour (1994), for example, argues that a double dissociation could arise from a single process containing distinct stages that can sustain damage independently from one another. Juola and Plunkett (1998) describe the results of damaging a connectionist model, which they argue implements a 'single route, single mechanism'. Damage nevertheless gave rise to the appearance of a double dissociation. Again, the implication is that double dissociations cannot be taken to necessarily imply the existence of separate processing systems.

Clearly it is important to observe caution when interpreting dissociations and double dissociations. Since these interpretations can have major theoretical implications, it is also important that patients are tested as rigorously as possible. As Ellis and Young (1988) say, it 'would be unwise to regard the search for double dissociations as some sort of royal road to understanding the structure of the mind' (1988, p.5).

Summary

- If one cognitive ability is impaired in a patient (e.g. language) whilst leaving another intact (e.g. memory), these two abilities are said to **dissociate** and to possibly constitute separate cognitive processes.
- It is possible to explain some cases of single dissociation in terms of a unitary system rather than having to invoke two separate processes. In this simpler

system, the more effortful aspects of processing (e.g. remembering events from many years ago) can be impaired whilst leaving more basic aspects (e.g. retaining five digits in memory for a minute) intact. If such an explanation is possible, researchers should adopt it on grounds of simplicity.

- However, if two patients are found, one of whom is impaired on task A (e.g. ability to recognize emotion shown in a face) but has no problems with task B (e.g. ability to recognize faces) whilst another patient shows the reverse pattern (impaired on B but intact on A), these two abilities are said to show a **double dissociation**. A finding like this can be strong evidence for the existence of separate cognitive processes.
- Nevertheless, there are many caveats to be borne in mind concerning the interpretation of double dissociations.

6 Important issues for cognitive neuropsychological research

Whatever the main aim of the neuropsychologist, be it conducting a clinical assessment or empirical research, he or she needs to be aware of a number of issues when working with patients with brain damage. If the patient is being assessed for research purposes, it will be necessary to consider how representative they are of the normal population, since the aim of research is to generalize to intact cognitive processes. Similarly, in trying to compare patients, the extent to which it is possible to compare individuals with different brains and whose brain damage could differ either only subtly or greatly, needs to be given careful thought. The assumptions made in drawing inferences from the nature of damaged systems to normal intact processing need to be made carefully. Similarly, the appreciation that the brain may show some changes in recovering from damage needs to be considered. An important question when conducting empirical research concerns the choice and number of patients in a study – is it better to conduct a fine-grained analysis of one patient or to study a group of patients that appear to have a common deficit? Finally, brain damage early in life, when the brain is still forming, can have different consequences from damage that occurs to a fully formed brain. So, it is important to consider the period of the patient's life during which they suffered brain damage, as this can significantly alter the interpretation placed on findings.

6.1 The Martian among us

A central assumption of neuropsychology is that, before brain damage the patient's cognitive system worked in essentially the same way as any other person's. If this is the case, then it may be possible to infer from the patient's damaged system how the normal intact system functions. However, what if the assumption proves unfounded and even before brain damage the patient had an unusual cognitive system, quite unlike the rest of the population? This is what Caramazza (1986) describes as the problem of the 'Martian among us.' If the patient has an abnormal cognitive system to begin with, then any inferences drawn from their damaged system to the nature of the normal cognitive system would be unsound. As a result, one of the principal goals of neuropsychology, to investigate the functioning of the normal intact system, would be undermined. This, of course, is a serious issue, especially since it is not possible to go back and check that the patient's intact system was indeed normal prior to brain damage. It is for this reason that single case studies need to be extremely detailed and rigorous and are usually followed up by investigating other patients.

6.2 Comparing brains

One way in which scientific research moves forward is through the replication and extension of studies that are deemed important. In the case of cognitive neuropsychology, one could test out theories suggested by the study of one patient on another patient with similar problems. However, even if two patients were to show similar behavioural profiles, would that mean that their brains were similar, with the same size and extent of brain lesions? Even small differences in the size of lesions can produce subtle behavioural differences that may impact significantly on task performance.

However, even the brains of healthy identical twins show differences in structure, so caution should be applied when comparing the brains of patients (see Figure 5.11 overleaf). One need not be a specialist in brain anatomy to see that the two brains in Figure 5.11 look similar but are far from *identical*. If this is the case for genetically identical individuals, then the brains of patients who are unrelated to one another are likely to have differed prior to damage.

Even if two brains were identical, nature or even neurosurgery does not result in 'clean lesions' restricted to distinct well-defined regions. A blood vessel bursting may result in widespread damage affecting a number of different areas. For example, researchers may be interested in production of spoken language which, as described above, involves Broca's area in the frontal lobes. They might therefore wish to study a patient who has suffered stroke damage in this area. However, the patient may also have experienced damage to adjacent cortical areas. The result is that as well as difficulty in producing coherent speech, the patient may have other cognitive problems as well. Therefore, the patient's speech problems could arise solely because of damage to Broca's area, or solely because of damage to neighbouring areas (perhaps, because that interrupts the flow of information to Broca's area) or because of a combination of both types of damage. If this sort of issue can cause complications when studying one damaged brain, it is therefore not surprising that comparing two patients who may both have differing damage that extends beyond Broca's area can greatly compound the problem. As a result, neuropsychologists need to carefully consider all of the damage suffered by a patient rather than just the ones of interest for their research. Again, this requires thorough analysis of the patient's intact and impaired abilities.

6.3 Subtractivity

An important assumption of cognitive neuropsychology is that a damaged system is just the same as a normal one but with certain modules or processing systems removed or damaged. This assumption of **subtractivity** then makes it possible to conceptually 'fractionate' the cognitive system, as shown in Box 5.2 on page 165.

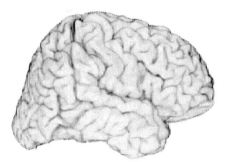
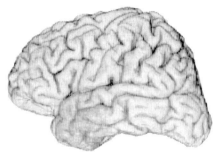
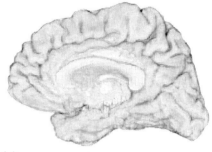
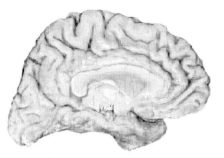

(a)

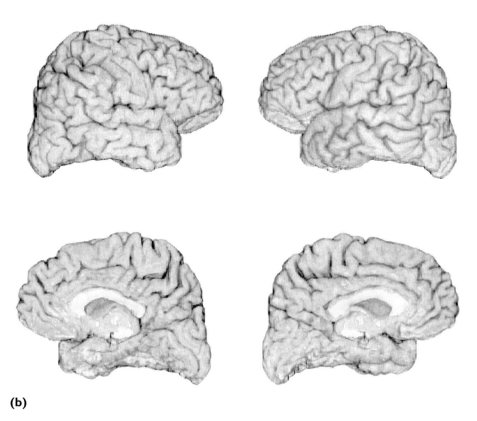

(b)

Figure 5.11 Scans of the brains of identical twins (a) and (b)

A simplified example of the fractionation of cognition

Assume, for sake of argument that, by the use of double dissociations and the study of many patients, it has been possible to infer the existence of five main components of the cognitive system. You could imagine that these five are problem solving, reading, object recognition, face recognition and memory, but such details are not necessary – the example is only illustrative. If cognition had been seen intuitively as one big system, it would then be subdivided, conceptually, into five modules (Figure 5.12). (Of course, there have been many detailed and complex arguments concerning the subdivision or fractionation of cognition – for present purposes we need only imagine that these have resulted in the five subdivisions shown.)

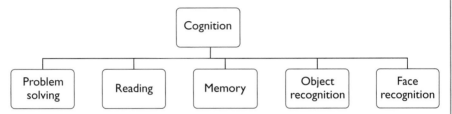

Figure 5.12 A hypothetical subdivision of the cognitive system into five major components

Researchers working with patients with memory problems have repeatedly found that, following brain damage, some patients can hold onto information for a few seconds but cannot retain it for longer. Similarly, as mentioned previously, there are some (very rare) patients who cannot remember a short string of digits for a few seconds but nonetheless have a perfectly normal ability to lay down long-term memories. If we ignore complications (such as discussed in **Rutherford, 2005**) then the double dissociation can be taken as evidence for a further sub-division of the memory component into STM and LTM (Figure 5.13).

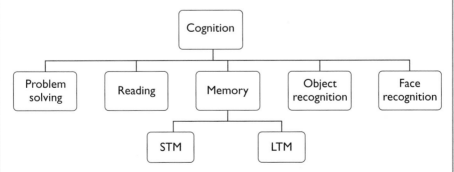

Figure 5.13 Double dissociations could provide evidence for the further sub-division of memory into two stores, STM and LTM

Further research on patient HM showed that he could learn to perform tasks such as the Tower of Hanoi puzzle without becoming aware of having done the task before. Since learning the task might span weeks or months, knowledge of how to perform the task has clearly become part of LTM. Indeed, researchers such as Cohen and Squire (1980) proposed that LTM consists of two general types of memory, memory for facts and events, known as **declarative** memory and memory for skills, known as **procedural** memory (see Figure 5.14). Work with amnesic patients such as HM suggests they have experienced damage to their declarative memory, but not their procedural memory.

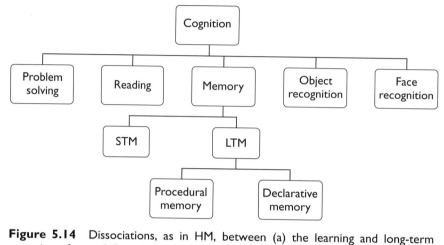

Figure 5.14 Dissociations, as in HM, between (a) the learning and long-term retention of new skills and (b) conscious knowledge of learning those skills, allows LTM to be further sub-divided into procedural and declarative memory

By careful observation of double dissociations, it is possible to reason that cognition is fractionated into many different functional components. However, note that at each step, the assumption of subtractivity is made. That is, a patient may be interpreted as having experienced damage to one or more processing systems, but it is assumed that other systems are undamaged and that the remainder of the system operates normally.

By studying a variety of patients, it is possible to infer further subdivisions. For example, Baddeley and colleagues (e.g. Baddeley *et al.*, 1975; Baddeley and Hitch, 1977) have shown how it is possible to replace what was previously thought of as STM with a more complex model of working memory, which contains a number of different subsystems (for example, see **Hitch, 2005**). In this way, by working meticulously on different patients with different types of problem and assuming that, with each one, one or more aspect of the overall cognitive system has been damaged, a model of the entire system can be created. This then meets one of the goals of neuropsychology, which is to use information from brain-damaged patients to infer the structure of the normal intact system. At the same time, deficits seen subsequently in patients can be used to evaluate the inferred system by seeing if their particular pattern of deficit can be explained via the subtraction of particular components. Finally, when it is discovered that not all aspects of the system have been damaged – for example, that in people with amnesia procedural memory is intact – it is possible to try to use these undamaged processing systems in rehabilitation (a point to which we return later).

6.4 Plasticity

Through applying the assumption of subtractivity, successful and complex models of normal cognition have been developed. However, it is important to note that the assumption may not always be strictly valid because of the plasticity of the brain. **Plasticity** refers to the ability of the brain to repair itself both at the neuronal and cognitive level. As Rose and Johnson (1996) state:

> Far from being fixed, unchangeable and static, we now know that the brain is a dynamic and interactive organ, constantly changing in terms of cellular activity, neural circuitry and transmitter chemistry in response to demands placed upon it.

For example, it is known from work on animal brains that neurons lost in lesions can be replaced. Also, under certain circumstances, the normal function of an area of the brain that has been damaged can 'move' to another undamaged area. For example, babies that suffer severe strokes in their left hemisphere (where language is *normally* processed) can nevertheless sometimes develop language processing in their right hemisphere (Bates, 1998).

In the adult brain, this nearly complete switch of language from the left to the right hemisphere is not found. However, if even *some* cognitive functions can move to another intact part of the brain, then the assumption of subtractivity does not strictly apply, and so inferences from patients to the normal cognitive system are not strictly valid.

Consider the following use of subtractivity. Imagine that, by studying normal control participants and patients with different types of dyslexia, each having suffered damage to their left hemisphere, researchers have identified six sub-components to the reading system that we can label A through F (see Figure 5.15). Furthermore, imagine it is claimed that, following extensive damage to this system (which we can illustrate in Figure 5.16 as affecting E and F), some aspects of reading begin to utilize an entirely different processing system. We can depict this 'new' system as sub-component X in Figure 5.16.

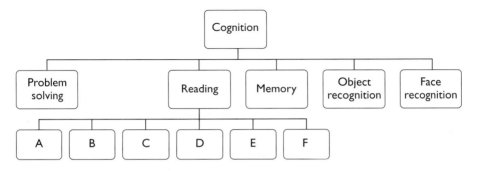

Figure 5.15 Imagine that researchers have identified six sub-components to the reading system (A–F)

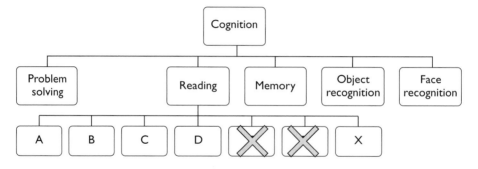

Figure 5.16   Imagine that, following damage to the hypothetical sub-components E and F, the individual's brain begins to use a different processing system for some aspects of reading (X)

In fact, in the case of deep dyslexia, just this kind of claim has been made. In particular, it has been argued that, subsequent to brain damage, some aspects of reading begin to occur using a processing system that plays no part in the normal reading system (Coltheart, 1987). It is beyond the scope of this chapter to give a full account of the theory, but it is claimed that there is a complex interaction between this 'new' right hemisphere processing system and those aspects of reading that are still intact in the left hemisphere. This interaction is thought to be suboptimal resulting in a cluster of consistent reading errors in deep dyslexic patients that include semantic errors (e.g. reading the word 'SWORD' as 'dagger'), visual errors (e.g. reading 'WHILE' as 'white') and difficulties in reading words of low imageability (e.g. having more problems reading 'JUSTICE' than 'TABLE'). This theory of deep dyslexia involving a right hemisphere processing system is one that is still under debate.

For present purposes, however, it is important to note that the theory illustrates a difficulty for the assumption of subtractivity. Notice that this 'new' processing system (akin to process X in Figure 5.16) is not representative of the normal reading system (which, in Figure 5.16, comprises modules A to F). Hence, deep dyslexia might not reflect the operation of a normal system with certain components damaged, but the operation of a non-normal system. To date, there is very little evidence that the right hemisphere becomes involved in normal intact reading. As a result, because of the possibility of this kind of plasticity, researchers need to apply caution when assuming subtractivity.

6.5   Single-case versus group studies

Conventionally, experimental psychology proceeds by measuring differences and subjecting these to statistical analysis. Such analyses indicate the likelihood of obtaining such differences by chance, through sampling. Often, a large number of participants are studied in order to ensure generalizability. However, in neuropsychological research, it may be impossible to find more than a few patients with a rare condition, so preventing the use of group designs. Even if it were possible to find a group of such patients, problems can arise due to the heterogeneity of brain damage in the group. The result is that the neuropsychologist is often faced with a decision as to whether to study a single patient in depth or to try to use a group of patients all with the same cognitive deficit. Let us look first at some of the difficulties associated with each approach, and then consider the criteria that a researcher might use in arriving at their decision.

Difficulties with single-case studies

- As discussed above, the possibility that a patient had unusual brain architecture prior to brain damage raises the question of the legitimacy of trying to generalize from a single individual with brain damage to the nature of normal cognition. For example, the brains of split brain patients may have developed non-conventionally due to their epilepsy, and the patients may have created compensatory strategies that do not reflect normal cognition.

- Single-case studies cannot address theories that imply relationships between two variables (e.g. brain size and intelligence) since correlational designs need more than one subject.

- Sometimes the possibility that performance may vary over time is not taken into consideration – this is important since patients can vary from the acute to the chronic phase of brain damage. Therefore, if brain damage has been recent, it is important to study a single patient at a number of points in time in case their functioning is still stabilizing.

- Researchers may unwittingly fall into the trap of selecting a single patient because they appear to confirm a particular theory, while not seeking patients that might disconfirm the theory. As a result, it can sometimes be difficult to replicate findings from different laboratories.

Difficulties with group studies

- Grouping of subjects is legitimate in conventional experimental research since it assumes a certain degree of homogeneity within each group of participants. However, a group of neuropsychological patients is unlikely to show the same homogeneity in terms of brain damage – as discussed above, there is likely to be variability in the types and extent of lesions.

- Grouping subjects according to *syndromes* (a cluster of symptoms), such as Broca's or Wernicke's aphasia, will introduce variability since although the patients will share symptoms, there also tend to be many other behavioural differences (often overlooked).

- Subtle differences between subjects in their performance on a task can be masked when averaging data across groups.

- Why study groups of subjects when one compelling case study can be the exception that proves the rule? On the assumption that 'the architecture of cognition is constant across people' (Coltheart, 2001, p.18) (that is, the patient is *not* a 'Martian among us'), generalizing from the single case should be legitimate.

With such a diversity of issues, how should a neuropsychologist decide which methodology to choose? Perhaps the first consideration should be the resources available. Some research institutions (for example hospitals with a large focus on research) have access to large groups of patients whilst others can access only limited numbers. A second consideration is the particular field of research because patients with some types of deficit are extremely rare while other kinds of deficit occur more frequently. For example, Capgras Syndrome – in which a patient feels that his or her family have been replaced by impostors (e.g. Alexander *et al.*, 1979; see also **Pike and Brace, 2005**) – is so rare that it would be difficult to find two patients to study at the same time. Wernicke-Korsakoff Syndrome, which is a cluster of deficits (the hallmark symptom being classical amnesia), is much more common and so group studies are possible (e.g. Albert *et al.*, 1979; Kopelman, 1989). Finally, the rigour with which researchers address methodological concerns is of relevance – if all the caveats of studying single cases are borne in mind, and a patient is tested thoroughly, then a single-case study can be highly informative.

6.6 Developmental versus acquired neuropsychological disorders

Brain damage can occur at any time in someone's life – it could happen pre-natally, in the womb, post-natally as a result of complications or due to a premature birth, during childhood accidents, or during adulthood. To further complicate matters, the cognitive system may have problems not due to brain damage but because of a genetically inherited disorder.

A developmental disorder is a condition that appears in childhood and is associated with a delay in the development of a psychological ability. Of course, the disorder may arise for different reasons, including a possible genetic basis. A disorder that arises because of physical brain damage is referred to as an 'acquired' one. So a child who had always had a reading problem, without experiencing brain damage, would be classified as having developmental dyslexia. Someone who could read but then has a reading impairment following a stroke would be classed as having acquired dyslexia. These two major groups themselves subdivide depending on the types of problems seen in patients. For example, in the field of acquired dyslexia, there exist a number of different forms such as 'surface dyslexia' (e.g. Marshall and Newcombe, 1973) and 'phonological dyslexia' (e.g. Beauvois and Dérousné, 1979).

For a number of reasons, more research has been carried out on acquired disorders than developmental ones. One reason is that with the former the assumption of subtractivity may be more legitimate – in inferring how the normal system works it may be more useful to look at one that used to work normally but has now been damaged, rather than one that never seemed to work normally. Since the reading system of a person with developmental dyslexia may not have formed normally, it may not be sound to draw conclusions about how the normal adult reading system works. However, the study of developmental disorders can still be extremely useful for understanding the problems that certain groups of young children and adolescents face in an attempt to find ways to help them. In recent years for example, dyslexia has been taken much more seriously in the school system, which now allows the children who suffer from it to gain the support they need. As knowledge grows about how to study such groups, this area will develop greatly.

Due to the issue of plasticity mentioned above *when*, in an individual's life, they suffer from brain damage has important implications both theoretically and clinically. If damage occurs very early in life, then some level of neuronal repair and/ or a certain amount of reorganization may be possible. This is unlikely if damage occurs later in life. Hence, the same type of brain damage in childhood and adulthood can have very different consequences in terms of the permanent problems that remain with the patient.

For example, some babies who are born very prematurely and whose lungs are not yet strong enough to circulate blood around the body sufficiently, suffer damage to the brain because it is starved of oxygen for a brief but crucial period of time. In one such baby, the only damage caused was in a very discrete but important part of the **hippocampus** an area that is vital for memory (Vargha-Khadem *et al.*, 1997). Despite this, the baby grew up relatively normally and it was only at around the age of six that it was noticed that he had significant memory problems. Although he has quite severe problems with his memory, he is still able to hold down a job and look after himself to a certain degree. Adults who suffer the same brain damage to the hippocampus, however, have much greater difficulty in learning to cope because it is impossible for the brain to 'rewire' at that age and difficult to develop new coping strategies. For example, two very well documented patients with severe amnesia HM (Corkin, 2002) in North America and CW (Wilson and Wearing, 1995) in Britain both have to live in care homes because of the impossibility of them living independent lives.

Summary

- Researchers need to be aware of the possibility that a patient may *not* be representative of the general population and that replication is therefore vital to support conclusions about normal cognition.
- Due to physical differences between any two brains and the fact that brain damage can often be diffuse rather than neatly localized, it is important to compare data from patients systematically both at the behavioural and neurological level.
- The assumption of subtractivity centres around the idea that what is observed in a patient is the effect of a whole cognitive system that has had certain modules impaired or removed whilst leaving the rest of the system intact. By applying this assumption systematically and with care, neuropsychologists aim to construct an understanding of the normal intact system.
- Researchers need to be aware of the possibility of plasticity both neurally (regrowth of brain tissue if damage occurs *very* early in life) and cognitively ('movement' or adaptation of a function) following brain trauma.
- Whether researchers should study single individuals or groups of patients is an important research question. There is no correct answer and there are many factors that determine the choice of method.
- It is necessary to distinguish between developmental disorders and those that are acquired following trauma. The application of methods and interpretation of results will depend on whether the behavioural problem is developmental or acquired.

7   Cognitive neuropsychological rehabilitation

As we have seen, cognitive neuropsychologists are trying to develop an understanding of normal intact cognition as well as a particular patient's deficits. Additionally, accurate assessment allows the clinician to see what problems a patient faces, and also what abilities are still preserved. As the understanding of the workings of the brain and cognition increase, so does the clinician's ability to devise techniques for helping and rehabilitating patients by capitalizing on the abilities that are known to be preserved and that can still allow some level of normal functioning.

Suppose a memory-impaired patient exhibits the pattern shown in Figure 5.17, i.e. a normally functioning STM and procedural memory with an impaired declarative memory.

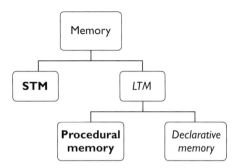

Figure 5.17   Diagram of preserved and impaired abilities in amnesia – italics represents impaired forms of memory and bold represents intact forms

HM, for example, has been taught a mirror-drawing task in which he has to trace a line between two stars, one inside the other but he can only see the reflection of his hand in a mirror. It is possible to see if HM learns this by seeing how many errors (counted as the number of times he crosses the lines) he makes on successive trials (see Figure 5.18). Despite not being able to remember having done the task before, HM's error rate reduces greatly to the point of showing perfect performance (see Figure 5.19). A more practical example is provided by Hunkin *et al*. (1998) who showed how it was possible to teach a person with amnesia to use a computer for word processing (see Figure 5.20). This sort of skill can allow someone with memory impairment to have a degree of independence that would not have been possible previously.

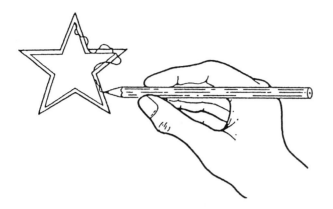

Figure 5.18 HM's mirror-drawing task in which he can only see what his hand is drawing in the reflection of a mirror

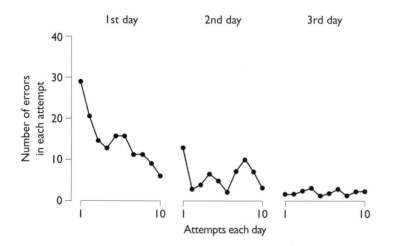

Figure 5.19 HM's mirror-drawing abilities improved with repeated attempts despite an impaired LTM since the number of his errors reduced over time

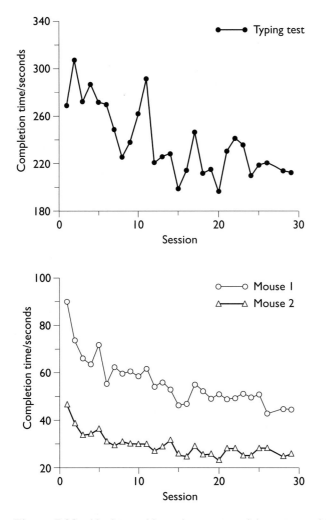

Figure 5.20 Hunkin *et al.* have demonstrated that it is possible to teach computer skills to a person with amnesia since completion times for the task reduce over time

With the knowledge that research studies like this have been successful in adding to the skill-base of a patient, neuropsychologists have been able to develop rehabilitation programs that do not require a normal LTM or conscious memory for previous learning. This is still a relatively new field in neuropsychology since researchers need to understand damaged and intact processes in patients before effective techniques can be devised. However, Wilson and colleagues (see, for example, Wilson *et al.*, 2001) have developed rehabilitation techniques, such as NeuroPage, a memory paging aid. Patients are taught the skill of checking the pager regularly over the course of a day, so that he or she can be reminded to do things that otherwise would be forgotten. See Box 5.3 for a remarkable case of a patient who has been taught to lead an independent life as a result of rehabilitation work.

5.3 — Research study

Rehabilitation of memory: the case of JC

Wilson *et al.* (1997) present the case of a patient (JC) who, while studying at university, suffered a brain haemorrhage that left him with damage to the left hemisphere. Whereas JC's STM was left intact, he had severe problems in transferring information to LTM. As a result, he was unable to continue with his studies. Over a period of time he was taught rehabilitation techniques that involved the use of external aids (such as writing things down in a notebook and keeping information on a databank wristwatch), mnemonics, rehearsal strategies and chaining (breaking a task into steps and learning them one step at a time). The remarkable result was that JC was able to go to technical college to learn a craft, furniture making, using his intact procedural memory. As JC said, 'When away from home, I used my coat as a base. I used my Dictaphone to plan my course work and found it was best to do the planning at the end of each session' (Wilson *et al.*, 1997, p.184). As a result of the success of this rehabilitation regime, JC was able to run a small business from home, buy a flat and even go on holiday on his own – all in a patient with a pure amnesia that prevents him from effectively transferring information from STM to LTM!

Wilson *et al.* suggest three predictors for the successful use of compensatory strategies:

1   The earlier the brain damage, the more chance there is of developing compensatory strategies.

2   Lack of other cognitive deficits.

3   A low score on the Rivermead Behavioural Memory Test (a test of everyday memory), a low score predicting a better ability to hold on to new information in a real-life setting.

It is fortunate that JC meets these criteria. Other patients may not do so, for example, if they were older when brain damage occurred or they have other difficulties such as language problems. However, the fact that cognitive neuropsychological research has helped devise ways of tapping the intact abilities of patients with brain damage in order to improve their standard of life shows how powerful neuropsychological methods can be. A continuing aim of neuropsychology is, by careful research, to understand as much as possible about the intact and damaged cognitive system to eventually help as many individuals as possible.

Summary

- As understanding of normal cognition and the effects of brain damage grow, clinicians are better placed to develop techniques for some aspects of rehabilitation.
- These often involve capitalizing on the abilities that aren't compromised by brain damage (e.g. procedural and implicit memory in a memory-impaired patient).
- There are a number of predictors that are thought to determine the extent and success of rehabilitation and these include how early in life brain damage occurred and the lack or presence of deficits other than the central deficit.

8 Conclusion

This chapter has provided an overview of cognitive neuropsychology. A historical perspective is especially important since neuropsychology is a relatively new field that has shown substantial evolution. The goals of neuropsychology have developed from mere assessment of patients and understanding of what could be wrong with them (as in Broca's time) to the use of neuropsychology to reveal the nature of normal cognition. The goals evolved partly because of the availability of better techniques for assessing patients (e.g. standardized tests) and then better research paradigms that arrived as a consequence of the advent of cognitive psychology. Consonant with the development of goals, it has become clearer that there are numerous methodological issues that researchers need to take into consideration when studying patients and interpreting data. Finally, the chapter concluded with a description of one of the newest goals of neuropsychology – rehabilitation – which aims to apply some of the lessons learnt from studying damaged brains towards improving the lives of patients themselves.

Of course, neuropsychology is not a *stand alone* method, nor does it pretend to be the 'best' one. It should be used in conjunction with other methods wherever appropriate. As a result, neuropsychology has informed many areas of cognition such as memory, the work on different forms of dyslexia (which has allowed sophisticated models of reading to be created); work on aphasia (which has allowed researchers and clinicians to understand the complexities of the production and comprehension of language); the work on problems faced by patients with object and face agnosia, also known as prosopagnosia (which has allowed an under-standing of visual recognition processes). Through the continued application of neuropsychological techniques, in conjunction with other methods, our under-standing of normal cognition will develop still further.

Further reading

Andrewes, D.G. (2001) *Neuropsychology: From Theory to Practice*, Hove, Psychology Press. An excellent undergraduate level text book, with good coverage of all major areas of neuropsychology.

Ramachandran, V.S. and Blakeslee, S. (1998) *Phantoms in the Brain: Probing the Mysteries of the Human Mind*, New York, William Morrow. A book written specifically for the layperson. It provides a fascinating introduction to the investigation of brain damage with each chapter focusing on a patient with an intriguing neurological problem.

Rapp, B. (2001) *Handbook of Cognitive Neuropsychology*, Hove, Psychology Press. An advanced level book covering more complex issues within neuropsychology. It should not be read as an introduction.

References

Adolphs, R., Tranel, E., Damasio, H. and Damasio, A.R. (1994) 'Impaired recognition of emotion in facial expressions following bilateral damage to the human amygdale', *Nature*, vol.372, pp.669–72.

Aggleton, J.P. and Brown, M.W. (1999) 'Episodic memory, amnesia, and the hippocampal-anterior thalamic axis', *Behavioral and Brain Sciences*, vol.22, pp.425–89.

Albert, M.S., Butters, N. and Levin, J. (1979) 'Temporal gradients in retrograde amnesia of patients with alcoholic Korsakoff's disease', *Archives of Neurology (Chicago)*, vol.36, pp.546–9.

Alexander, M.P., Stuss, D.T. and Benson, D.F. (1979) 'Capgrass syndrome: a reduplicative phenomenon', *Neurology*, vol.29, pp.334–9.

Atkinson, R.C. and Shiffrin, R.M. (1968) 'Human memory: a proposed system and its control processes' in Spence, K.W. and Spence, J.T. (eds) *The Psychology of Learning and Motivation: Advances in Research and Theory*, pp.90–195, New York, Academic Press.

Baddeley, A.D. and Warrington, E.K. (1970) 'Amnesia and the distinction between long and short-term memory', *Journal of Verbal Learning and Verbal Behavior*, vol.9, pp.176–89.

Baddeley, A.D., Thomson, N. and Buchanan, M. (1975) 'Word length and the structure of short-term memory', *Journal of Verbal Learning and Verbal Behavior,* vol.14, pp.575–89.

Baddeley, A.D. and Hitch, G.J. (1977) 'Working memory' in Bower, G.A. (ed.) *Recent Advances in Learning and Motivation*, New York, Academic Press.

Bates, E. (1998) '"Recovery and development after trauma". Review of Broman, S. and Michel, M.E. "Traumatic head injury in children"', *Contemporary Psychology*, vol.43, pp.39–40.

Beauvois, M.F. and Dérousné, J. (1979) 'Phonological alexia: three discussions', *Journal of Neurology, Neurosurgery and Psychiatry*, vol.42, pp.1115–24.

Beschin, N., Basso, A. and Della Sala, S. (2000) 'Perceiving left and imagining right: dissociation in neglect', *Cortex*, vol.36, pp.401–14.

Bogen, J.E. and Vogel, P.J. (1965) 'Neurological status in the long term following cerebral commissurotomy' in Michel F. and Schott B. (eds) *Les Syndromes de Disconnexion Calleuse Chez L' Homme*, Lyon, Hospital Neurologique.

Broca, P. (1861/1965) 'Remarques sur le siège de la faculté du langage articulé suivies d'une observation d'aphémie' in Herrnstein, R. and Boring E.G. (eds) (1965) *A Source Book in the History of Psychology*, Cambridge, MA, Havard University Press.

Bruce, V. and Young, A. (1986) 'Understanding face recognition', *British Journal of Psychology*, vol.77, pp.305–27.

Burton, M., Bruce, V. and Johnson, R. (1990) 'Understanding face recognition with an interactive activation model', *British Journal of Psychology*, vol.81, pp.361–80.

Butterworth, B. (1979) 'Hesitation and the production of verbal paraphasias and neologism in jargon aphasia', *Brain and Language*, vol.8, pp.133–61.

Caramazza, A. (1986) 'On drawing inferences about the structure of normal cognitive systems from the analysis of patterns of impaired performance: the case for single-patient studies', *Brain and Cognition,* vol.5, pp.41–66.

Cohen, N.J. and Squire, L.R. (1980) 'Preserved learning and retention of pattern analyzing skill in amnesia: dissociation of knowing how and knowing that', *Science*, vol.210, pp.207–10.

Coltheart, M. (1987) 'Reading, phonological recoding, and deep dyslexia' in Coltheart, M., Patterson, K.E. and Marshall, J.C. (eds) *Deep Dyslexia*, London, Routledge/Kegan Paul.

Coltheart, M. (2001) 'Assumptions and methods in cognitive neuropsychology' in Rapp, B. (ed.) *Handbook of Cognitive Neuropsychology*, Hove, Psychology Press.

Corkin, S. (2002) 'What's new with the amnesic patient H.M?' *Nature Reviews*, *Neuroscience*, vol.3, pp.153–60.

Craik, K. (1943) *The Nature of Explanation*, Cambridge, Cambridge University Press.

Damasio, A.R. (1994) *Descartes' Error: Emotion, Reason and the Human Brain*, New York, Grosset/Putnam.

Damasio, H., Grabowski, T., Frank, R., Galaburda, A.M. and Damasio, A.R. (1994) 'The return of Phineas Gage: clues about brain from skull of famous patient', *Science*, vol.264, pp.1102–5.

Damasio, H., Grabowski, T.J., Tranel, D., Hichwa, R.D. and Damasio, A.R. (1996) 'A neural basis for lexical retrieval', *Nature*, vol.380, pp.499–505.

Ellis, A.W. and Young, A.W. (1988) *Human Cognitive Neuropsychology*, Hove, London, Erlbaum.

Farah, M.J. and McClelland, J.L. (1991) 'A computational model of semantic memory impairment: modality specificity and emergent category specificity', *Journal of Experimental Psychology: General*, vol.120, pp.339–57.

Gaffan, D. and Heywood, C.A. (1993) 'A spurious category specific visual agnosia for living things in normal human and nonhuman primates', *Journal of Cognitive Neuroscience*, vol.5, pp.118–28.

Gall, F. and Spurzheim, G. (1970) 'Research on the nervous system in general and on that of the brain in particular' in Pribram, K. (ed.) *Brain and Behavior: Vol. 1. Mood States and Mind*, Harmondsworth, Penguin Books.

Gazzaniga, M.S., Bogen, J.E. and Sperry, R.W. (1962) 'Some functional effects of sectioning the cerebral commisures in man', *Proceedings of the National Academy of Sciences USA*, vol.48, pp.1765–9.

Gazzaniga, M.S., Ivry, R.B. and Mangun, G.R. (1998) *Cognitive Neuroscience: The Biology of the Mind*, New York, London, W.W. Norton.

Glymour, C. (1994) 'On the methods of cognitive neuropsychology', *British Journal for the Philosophy of Science*, vol.45, pp.815–35.

Goodglass, H. and Kaplan, E. (1972) *The Assessment of Aphasia and Related Disorders*, Philadelphia, PA, Lea & Febiger.

Grant, D.A. and Berg, E.A. (1948) 'A behavioral analysis of degree reinforcement and ease of shifting to new responses in a Weigl-type card-sorting problem', *Journal of Experimental Psychology*, vol.38, pp.404–11.

Harlow, J. (1868) 'Recovery after severe injury to the head', *Publications of the Massachusetts Medical Society*, vol.2, pp.327–46.

Hillis, A.E. and Caramazza, A. (1991) 'Mechanisms for accessing lexical representations for output: evidence from a category-specific semantic deficit', *Brain and Language*, vol.40, pp.208–35.

Hitch, G.J. (2005) 'Working memory' in Braisby, N.R. and Gellatly, A. (eds) *Cognitive Psychology*, Oxford, Oxford University Press/The Open University.

Humphreys, G.W. and Riddoch, M.J. (1987) *To See But Not to See: A Case Study of Visual Agnosia*, London, Erlbaum.

Humphreys, G.W., Riddoch, M.J. and Quinlan, P.T. (1988) 'Cognitive processes in picture identification', *Cognitive Neuropsychology*, vol.5, pp.67–104.

Hunkin, N.M., Squires, E.J., Aldrich, F.K. and Parkin, A.J. (1998) 'Errorless learning and the acquisition of word processing skills', *Neuropsychological Rehabilitation*, vol.8, pp.433–49.

Jansari, A., Davis, K. and Kapur, N. (2003) 'When long-term memory does not necessarily mean "forever": evidence of long-term amnesia (LTA) in a patient with temporal lobe epilepsy', *British Psychological Society (BPS) Cognitive Section Conference Abstracts*, Leicester, British Psychological Society.

Juola, P. and Plunkett, K. (1998) 'Why double dissociations don't mean much', *Proceedings of the 20th Annual Conference of the Cognitive Science Society, Vol.1–6*, Mahweh, NJ, Lawrence Erlbaum Associates.

Kopelman, M.D. (1989) 'Remote and autobiographical memory, temporal context memory and frontal atrophy in Korsakoff and Alzheimer patients', *Neuropsychologia*, vol.27, pp.437–60.

Lhermitte, F. and Beauvois, M.F. (1973) 'A visual–speech disconnection syndrome. Report of a case with optic aphasia, agnosic alexia and colour agnosia', *Brain*, vol.96, pp.695–714.

Lichteim, L. (1885) 'On aphasia', *Brain*, vol.7, pp.433–84.

Luck, S.J., Hillyard, S.A., Mangun, G.R. and Gazzaniga, M.S. (1994) 'Independent attentional scanning in the separated hemispheres of split-brain patients', *Journal of Cognitive Neuroscience*, vol.6, pp.84–91.

Marshall, J.C. and Newcombe, F. (1973) 'Patterns of paralexia: a psycholinguistic approach', *Journal of Psycholinguistic Research*, vol.2, pp.175–99.

McCarthy, R.A. and Warrington, E.K. (1990) *Cognitive Neuropsychology. A Clinical Introduction*, San Diego, Academic Press.

Pike, G. and Brace, N. (2005) 'Recognition' in Braisby, N.R. and Gellatly, A. (eds) *Cognitive Psychology, Oxford, Oxford University Press/The Open University*.

Pisella, L. Rode, G., Farne, A., Boisson, D. and Rossetti, Y. (2002) 'Dissociated long lasting improvements of straight-ahead pointing and line bisection tasks in two hemineglect patients', *Neuropsychologia*, vol.40, pp.327–34.

Ramachandran, V.S., Cronin-Golomb, A. and Myers, J.J. (1986) 'Perception of apparent motion by commissurotomy patients', *Nature*, vol.320, pp.358–9.

Rose, F.D. and Johnson, D.A. (1996) 'Brains, injuries and outcomes' in Rose, F.D. and Johnson, D.A. (eds) *Brain Injury and After*, Chichester, John Wiley and Sons.

Rutherford, A. (2005) 'Long-term memory: encoding to retrieval' in Braisby, N.R. and Gellatly, A. (eds) *Cognitive Psychology, Oxford, Oxford University Press/The Open University*.

Sacchett, C. and Humphreys, G.W. (1992) 'Calling a squirrel a squirrel but a canoe a wigwam: a category-specific deficit for artefactual objects and body parts', *Cognitive Neuropsychology*, vol.9, pp.73–86.

Sacks, O. (1985) *The Man who Mistook his Wife for a Hat*, New York, Summit Books.

Scoville, W.B. and Milner, B. (1957) 'Loss of recent memory after bilateral hippocampal lesions', *Journal of Neurology, Neurosurgery and Psychiatry*, vol.20, pp.11–21.

Selnes, O.A. (2001) 'A historical overview of contributions from the study of deficits' in Rapp, B. (ed.) *The Handbook of Cognitive Neuropsychology*, Hove, Psychology Press.

Shallice, T. and Warrington, E.K. (1970) 'Independent functioning of the verbal memory stores: a neuropsychological study', *Quarterly Journal of Experimental Psychology*, vol.22, pp.261–73.

Sperry, R.W. and Gazzaniga, M.S. (1967) *Language Following Surgical Disconnection of the Hemispheres*, New York, Grune, Stratton.

Sutherland, N.S. (1989) *A Dictionary of Psychology*, London, MacMillan.

Tranel, E., Damasio, H. and Damasio, A.R. (1997) 'A neural basis for the retrieval of conceptual knowledge', *Neuropsychologia*, vol.35, pp.1319–27.

Vargha-Khadem, F., Gadian, D.C., Watkins, K.E., Connelly, A., Van Paesschen, W. and Mishkin, M. (1997) 'Differential effects of early hippocampal pathology on episodic and semantic memory', *Science*, vol.277, pp.376–80.

Warrington, E.K. and Shallice, T. (1984) 'Category specific semantic impairments', *Brain*, vol.107, pp.829–53.

Weiskrantz, L. (1986) *Blindsight: A Case Study and Implications*, Oxford, Clarendon Press.

Weiskrantz, L. (1987) 'Blindsight' in Boller, F. and Grafman, J. (eds) *Handbook of Neuropsychology*, vol.2, pp.375–85, Amsterdam, Elsevier Publishers.

Wernicke, K. (1874) 'Der aphasische Symptomenkomplex' (trans.) in *Boston Studies in Philosophy of Science*, vol.4, pp.34–97.

Wilson, B.A., J.C. and Hughes, E. (1997) 'Coping with amnesia: the natural history of a compensatory memory system' in Parkin, A.J. (ed.) *Case Studies in the Neuropsychology of Memory*, pp.179–90, Hove, Psychology Press.

Wilson, B.A., Ernslie, H.C., Quirk, K. and Evans, J.J. (2001) 'Reducing everyday memory and planning problems by means of a paging system: a randomised control crossover study', *Journal of Neurology, Neurosurgery and Psychiatry*, vol.70, pp.477–82.

Wilson, B.A. and Wearing, D. (1995) 'Amnesia in a musician' in Campbell, R. and Conway, M. (eds) *Broken Memories*, Oxford, Blackwell.

Young, A.W., Hay, D.C. and Ellis, A.W. (1985) 'The faces that launched a thousand slips: everyday difficulties and errors in recognizing people', *British Journal of Psychology*, vol.76, pp.495–523.

Young, A.W., Newcombe, F., de Hann, E.H.F., Small, M. and Hay, D.C. (1993) 'Face perception after brain injury', *Brain*, vol.116, pp.941–59.

Quantitative methods Chapter 6

Martin Le Voi

1 Introduction

In this chapter you will learn about parametric univariate statistics, for which computer packages (such as SPSS, Statistical Package for Social Sciences) are available to take the grind out of the mathematics. You only need to understand what these statistics do, not all of the mathematics behind them. Univariate statistics are about tests with a single dependent variable.

This chapter assumes a previous understanding of probability and statistics corresponding to what you should have studied in a second-level course in psychology. It may help you to revise that work if you feel you are not entirely familiar with those concepts, although we do begin by covering some fundamentals. This chapter will assist you with understanding statistical concepts by presenting alternative and additional conceptualizations of these statistical ideas. Different students respond better to different ways of presenting statistical concepts, so it is hoped that presenting these ideas in various ways will help all students to understand them.

The chapter will specify exercises for you to carry out. Some are optional to help you understand points. Others should be considered to be the minimum you need to ensure you understand the concepts.

Starting with two fundamentals, the chapter moves on to consider the conceptual basis for analysis of variance, leading into a number of related topics.

2 Two fundamentals

2.1 Why do we do statistics?

Suppose I want to test the Stroop effect, in which people are expected to take longer to name the ink colour of a word if that word is the name of a different colour. I get one person and time him as he names the colour of 50 words which spell out non-colour words. I get another person and time her as she names the colour of 50 words, all of which are colour names which differ from the actual colour of the ink. The first participant takes 15 seconds, and the second takes 20 seconds. Have I proved my hypothesis? Do I even have evidence in support of it?

Well, I suppose the evidence is in support, but this evidence isn't much use because of the obvious problem that I have little idea what would happen if I tried it out on two new (different) people. The problem is that individual scores on the naming task will naturally vary, even if the colour words have no effect, because some people just do things faster than others. I want results which can be true of *general* human cognition, not just true of the particular participants I happened to pick on one day. In other words, I want to be able to generalize from the people who did my experiment to the general population of humans. How do I do this?

I could find another two people, and ask them to try the experiment. Trying it out on two more doesn't seem to be a specially satisfactory measure to ensure generalizability. So, I could try another 20 participants. Is this enough? How will I know if I can correctly generalize from my experiment to make statements about human cognition in general?

This is what statistics is all about. In the early twentieth century, scientists were casting around for arithmetically defined concepts which would permit this kind of generalization. Not just any mathematical idea would do. The essential feature of such an idea is that its value behaves in a systematic way when it is calculated from many samples from a population. In particular, it needs to have a defined **sampling distribution** (like that in Figure 6.4 in Section 3.2.1 of this chapter), so that we can see how its value varies from sample to sample in an expected way. We shall look at a demonstration of such systematic behaviour of a sampling distribution in Section 3.2.1.

Scientists came up with a number of concepts, called *statistics*, which have the required behaviour and allow us to draw conclusions (make *inferences*) about the population from the data in our sample. It is these **inferential statistics** that you will learn about here, so that you can find out how to make valid scientific judgements about theories and hypotheses from experimental data.

2.2   Estimating the mean: reducing error

One way of looking at statistical analysis is to consider it as an exercise in *prediction*. This will be particularly useful when we look at multiple regression later on. For now, consider the situation where I have measured the height of everyone in my country. If I was then asked to predict the height of one individual, who could be anyone at all from the population, what would be my best guess, my best *estimate*? You may well be thinking that the best estimate would be the average or **mean** height, and you would be right. But what is so special about the mean that makes it a good single estimate (in statistics we call it a **point estimate**)?

Table 6.1

Data values
6
2
1

Let's look at a smaller problem than the whole population of my country. Take the three numbers in Table 6.1. How do I decide what would be a good point estimate of these numbers? What we need to think of is *error*. The estimate I choose will, if applied to individuals, usually show some error, because it is, after all, an informed guess. So it's agreed, by definition, that the best estimate is the one which, when applied to *all* the individuals in my sample, ends up producing the **least error** when the total error is added up over all the numbers. Suppose I try the number 3 as an estimate for the numbers in Table 6.1. Guessing that number gives errors for all three numbers: 6 is higher by 3, 2 is lower by 1, 1 is lower by 2. We calculate the **total error** by adding up these numbers (ignoring whether they are higher or lower), so the total error for this estimate is 6 (3 + 1 + 2). Is this the best estimate (i.e. the one with the lowest total error) that we can find? Try another number to see what happens to the error.

Spreadsheet exercise 1

For this and subsequent exercises, details of how to access the relevant files and software are given in the Introduction to this book.

You can try this very quickly by opening the spreadsheet exercise 1 file. It is in two different versions to be able to run on Microsoft Excel and StarOffice spreadsheet applications (the latter is a widely available free spreadsheet package). The exercise works best if you can use Microsoft Excel.

Instructions for Microsoft Excel users

Open the spreadsheet EX1 (Excel).xls. You will see three data points in a graph and an estimate value represented as a line with a circle at one end. The circle is a 'handle' that you can click on to move the estimate up and down. You click on the handle (small circle) to select it, then you can drag it up and down to change the estimate. A number pops up to show what value you are choosing. When you 'let go' of the handle, the graph updates to show the new value of the estimate, and above the graph the value of the Total (or Sum) Absolute Error changes. Try moving the estimate up and down to see how the Total Absolute Error changes (see Figure 6.1).

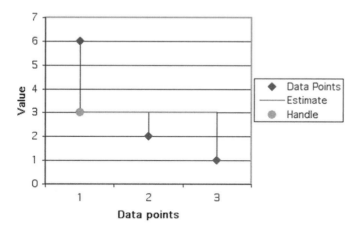

Absolute Error

Figure 6.1

Instructions for StarOffice spreadsheet users

Open the spreadsheet EX1 (Star).sxc. You can see the three data points and a line representing the estimate. You move the estimate by typing a new value in the cell indicated by 'estimate: change this value'. As soon as you put a new value in and tell the spreadsheet to accept the value (often by pressing 'return'), the line representing the estimate will move and the value of the Total Absolute Error changes.

If you try this, you find there are better estimates than 3. Let's try 2. 6 is higher by 4, 2 is the same (0), while 1 is lower by 1. The total error is now only (4 + 0 + 1) = 5. So this is a better estimate. Actually, it can be proved that this is the best estimate for these three data points, and reduces the Total Absolute Error to the smallest value.

Table 6.2

Data values
8
5
2
1

Before we get excited that we've found a good definition of error and hence a good estimate, consider the numbers in Table 6.2. Measuring error as we have just specified, what is our best estimate? 3 might be good: the total error is 5 + 2 + 1 + 2 = 10. How about 2? Here error is 6 + 3 + 0 + 1, also 10. Let's try 4. Error is 4 + 1 + 2 + 3 = 10 again. In fact there is no *unique* number between 2 and 5 (inclusive) which gives less error than any other number, so the estimate is no longer a point estimate, because any number between 2 and 5 is as good as any other.

Spreadsheet exercise 2

This is the same as spreadsheet exercise 1, but using the four data points in Table 6.2.

Instructions for Microsoft Excel users

Open the file EX2 (Excel).xls. Again, select the 'handle' (a circular blob) and move it up and down. See how the Total Absolute Error changes for different values of the estimate.

Instructions for StarOffice spreadsheet users

Open the file EX2 (Star).sxc. You can change the estimate value by typing a new value in the cell marked 'estimate: change this value'. See how the Total Absolute Error changes for different values of the estimate.

The lack of a unique point estimate is rather undesirable. So mathematicians came up with another definition of error. (There were other reasons, too, which will come up as you learn more about statistics.) The new error measure involves *squaring* the error of each individual score before adding them up. (You square a number by multiplying it by itself.) So if we estimate 2 for the numbers in Table 6.1, the errors are:

6	$(6-2)^2 =$	$4^2 = 4 \times 4$	$=$	16
		$+$		
2	$(2-2)^2 =$	$0^2 = 0 \times 0$	$=$	0
		$+$		
1	$(1-2)^2 =$	$1^2 = 1 \times 1$	$=$	1
Total			$=$	17

This gives an error of 17. Is 2 the best estimate?

Spreadsheet exercise 3

Using spreadsheet exercise 3, can you find an estimate which gives a better (lower) total squared error? Again, there are two versions of the spreadsheet, EX3 (Excel).xls for Microsoft Excel users, and EX3 (Star).sxc for StarOffice spreadsheet users. Use the same procedures as in spreadsheet exercises 1 and 2.

Let's try the estimate 3. The errors are 3, 1 and 2, so total squared error is: $3^2 + 1^2 + 2^2 = 14$. So 3 is much better than 2 (or 4)! (Again, it can be proved that this is the best estimate for these numbers, although we do not burden you with that proof here.) Note that the best estimate depends on the choice we make about the error calculation. Using squared error gives a different best estimate from using absolute (non-squared) error. For the numbers in Table 6.2, 3 gives total squared error $5^2 + 2^2 + 1^2 + 2^2 = 34$. While for the estimate 4, the error is $4^2 + 1^2 + 2^2 + 3^2 = 30$. With 4, the error is reduced, and in fact 4 does give a *unique* point estimate which has less error than any other estimate. So the special property of this point estimate is that it gives the **least squared error** across all the scores being estimated.

Spreadsheet exercise 4

Use this spreadsheet exercise to explore values of the estimator to see the effect on squared error. The version for Microsoft Excel users is EX4 (Excel).xls, the version for StarOffice users is EX4 (Star).sxd.

What is this point estimate with least squared error? It is, in fact, the **mean** (or average). The mean is a point estimator of a population which has the special property of having the least squared error to all the scores being estimated. The concept of estimates having the least squared error is the *fundamental concept* behind an entire family of statistics called **parametric statistics**, which is the family of statistics you will learn about here.

To tidy up, what about the first estimate we considered in spreadsheet exercises 1 and 2? It had the special property that it was an estimate with the least 'non-squared' error (also known as the Least Absolute Deviation), and it is known as the **median**. The median, and statistics based on the Least Absolute Deviation, are fundamental to a family of statistics called **distribution-free** statistics, which you can learn about elsewhere, if you are curious. We will not cover them here.

Summary of Section 2

- Statistics are used to allow us to generalize our results beyond the participants in our sample.
- Parametric statistics are based on estimating parameters (such as the mean) which have the least squared error.

- Statistics based on Least Absolute Deviation, such as the median, make up a family of statistics called distribution-free statistics.
- Analysis of variance, multiple regression and analysis of covariance are all types of parametric statistics.

3 Analysis of variance

3.1 The conceptual basis for analysis of variance

This section provides an entirely intuitive description of analysis of variance (ANOVA), without using algebra, formulae, or even arithmetic. The intention is to ensure you have an intuitive grasp of what analysis of variance tries to do, so that you are not disturbed by the mathematical treatment frequently found in statistics books. We are assuming you know some basic concepts in statistics: four of them are covered in Box 6.1.

6.1

A revision of statistical inference

Key concepts: **null hypothesis**; **alpha (α) level**; **significance**; **Type I error**.

Statistical inference is a decision-making process based on the results of experiments. When your experiment has included a number of conditions, you need to decide (infer from the data) whether there is any difference between the conditions.

Your starting point is the **null hypothesis**. This states that there is no effect of conditions, so when it is true any difference between conditions must be because you were unlucky in your sampling, and the results are due to random chance. It is important to remember that this can be a valid explanation of *any* set of results, no matter how large the difference between the conditions (we shall see in Section 3.2.1 that a big effect can occasionally be produced from a purely random sampling of conditions which were known not to differ).

By chance, some variations between conditions are more likely than others. Eventually, however, the difference between the conditions can be so unlikely that we allow ourselves the luxury of rejecting the null hypothesis. Usually, we say that when the chance of finding such a large difference between conditions in a sample, were the null hypothesis to be true, has fallen to one in 20 (5 per cent, or 0.05) or less, we believe that the difference is a real one, and *decide* (remember this is a decision-making procedure) to reject the null hypothesis. We then say that we have decided that the difference between our conditions results from a real (factual) difference, not one due to chance.

The chance level (or probability) at which we make that decision is the **alpha (α) level**. Another description of this is the *p value*. We have suggested its normal setting is 5 per cent: this is simply a *convention* that scientists adhere to (so is often referred to as 'a conventional level of **significance**'). If the alpha level has been exceeded (i.e. p value < 0.05), the result is known as a **significant** result.

Being ready to make this decision introduces a problem, however. The random nature of results has not gone away. With α set to 5 per cent, even when there really is no difference between conditions, 5 per cent of the time you will allow yourself to decide that there *is* a difference. This is a **Type I error**. It is a mistake (a Type I *error*) to decide your conditions are different when really they are not. But sometimes you are bound to make such mistakes if you allow yourself to decide there is a difference when the alpha level is exceeded. The intention of setting α to 1 in 20 (or 5 per cent) is to make such mistakes rare events, so that you (mostly) draw correct conclusions and don't get misled (often) by your errors.

3.2 What is analysis of variance?

Why do we do analysis of variance? Usually psychologists run experiments in which there are a number of different conditions, which they hope will affect the behaviour of experimental participants on a given dependent variable. The psychologist usually calculates the mean of the participants' performance within each condition, and what the experimenter wants to know is whether the difference between the means can be trusted. If the psychologist is interested in these differences between the means, then what is the justification for doing an analysis of the variance, which is apparently not focusing on the mean of the data? Indeed, what is the variance that is being analysed?

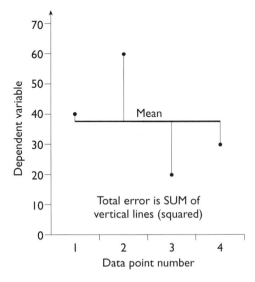

Figure 6.2

Look at Figure 6.2. Each datum – the singular form of the plural word 'data' – on this graph represents the response from one participant. Four participants were run. The experimenter has calculated the mean of these four participants on the dependent variable measured, and that mean is drawn horizontally across the figure. None of the data points in the figure lies exactly on this mean. Instead, they are all some distance away from it, shown in the figure by the line running from each data point to the mean. In general, data will be scattered around the mean like this, and that scatter can be measured by squared error, as described in Section 2.2. In parametric statistics, the measure of scatter used is called the **variance**, which is arrived at simply by taking the distance by which each datum varies from the mean and squaring it before adding all the squared differences together. This is known as the **sum of squares (SS)**, from which the variance is calculated by dividing by degrees of freedom (N − 1) (see Box 6.2).

6.2

Degrees of freedom (1)

As mentioned in Section 2.2, in parametric tests variance is measured by using the squared error of each datum. These are all added up to create a 'sum of squares' and divided by a number to arrive at an average error for each point (a 'mean square'). This is very like calculating the mean (when you add up all the numbers, and divide by the number of numbers you have), except that the total sum of squares is divided by a number called the **degrees of freedom**. If the total number of numbers is N, the degrees of freedom is *one less* than this number (N − 1). So:

$$\text{Variance or mean square} = \frac{\text{Total sum of squares}}{\text{N} - 1 \text{ (degrees of freedom)}}$$

The mean square is the usual definition of variance, in preference to the total sum of squares looked at in Section 2.

Why are the degrees of freedom one less than the total number of data points? The reason comes partly from the way the total sum of squares is calculated. The sum of squares is calculated by subtracting the mean from each data point before squaring it:

$$\text{Sum of squares} = \text{Sum (data point} - \text{mean)}^2$$

The problem is that the mean is itself calculated from the *same* data. When this happens you 'lose' a degree of freedom. Consider the case when you have three numbers 6, 8, and 10. The mean is 8. Suppose you are allowed to change any of these numbers, as long as the mean is kept constant at 8. How many numbers are free to vary? Perhaps counterintuitively, all three numbers cannot vary freely. If you change all three numbers haphazardly, most of the time the mean will no longer be 8. The point is that only two numbers can be *freely* changed if the mean is to stay the same. For example, if you change the 6 to a 7 and the 10 to a 13, the remaining number is *fixed* (not free): it must be a 4 to keep the mean as 8. The same argument applies for larger collections of numbers; with 50 numbers you can vary 49, the last number is always determined. So degrees of freedom are N − 1. Fortunately, statistics packages (such as SPSS) always calculate degrees of freedom correctly for you.

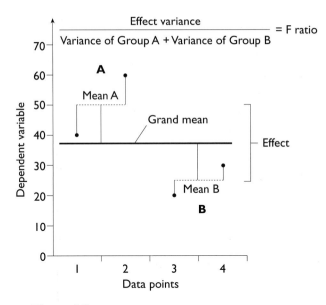

Figure 6.3

So what do we do when we analyse this variance? Look at Figure 6.3. In this figure, the same four data points from Figure 6.2 are plotted on the graph. The original mean of those data points, usually called the **grand mean**, is still plotted across the graph. However, there is now additional information available about the four data points. The data in fact belong to two groups, group A and group B. We can calculate means for each group, shown as mean A and mean B on Figure 6.3. Now, instead of measuring the distance of each datum from the grand mean, we can measure the distance by which each datum differs from its own group mean. These distances are shown on Figure 6.3. We can now add up this variability of the data points around the group means to give a new total variance.

However, you can see from Figure 6.3 that generally the distance each datum finds itself from the group mean is smaller than the distance each datum found itself from the grand mean. For data sets with many data points, it isn't necessarily the case that every datum will be nearer to its own group mean than it is to the grand mean. However, it is inevitable that as a whole the total distances of the data points from their own group means will be less than the total distances that the data are from the grand mean. In other words, this new variance that we have calculated (by measuring the distance from each datum to its own group mean) is less than the total variance calculated using the distance of each datum from the grand mean. Introducing the additional information that the data are divided into two groups, has resulted in a **reduction of variance** in the data. The results of many statistical tests, especially parametric ones, are frequently described in terms of the reduction in variance produced by the separation of the data into various groups etc. This is a very important concept in parametric statistics. The remaining variance of the data points around their group means (i.e. after separating the data points into the various groups) is called the **residual variance** (also referred to as **error variance**), and it is *always* less than the total variance.

So we have reduced the variance of the data points by measuring their distance from the group means instead of the grand mean. What has happened to the 'missing' variance? The missing variance has not disappeared. Instead of looking at the data points on Figure 6.3, look at the two group means. Each of the group means is itself some distance away from the grand mean. In other words, the group means themselves vary by some amount around the grand mean. Again, we can take the distance by which each group mean finds itself from the grand mean, and add up these squared distances to arrive at a total variance due to the dispersion of the group means around the grand mean. This variance is known as the **effect variance** or variance due to conditions. The arithmetic is carefully constructed so that the effect variance measured in this way is exactly the amount by which the total variance of the data points was reduced by measuring their distance from the group means rather than the grand means (this results from using squared distances and is another advantage of using squared error as the measure of dispersion).

Now, instead of having one value for the total variance of the data, we have two measures, or *sources*, of variance. One is the effect variance, and the other the residual variance. We have essentially **analysed the variance** by separating it, or **partitioning** it, into two sources. The final step is to perform a comparison to tell us whether the differences between the group means may have arisen by chance or not. Statisticians have worked out that a simple way to make this comparison is to compare the two variances we have just calculated by dividing one by the other. We divide the effect variance by the residual variance and the result is called a ratio – the **F ratio**, to be precise:

$$\frac{\text{Effect variance}}{\text{Residual variance}} = \text{F ratio}$$

You can see from Figure 6.3 that as the two group means get further and further apart the effect variance will get larger and larger. Similarly, if the data are found to cluster closer and closer to their own group means, then the residual variance gets smaller and smaller. *So the larger the effect size is compared to the dispersion of the data points around the group means, the bigger will be the F ratio.*

3.2.1 The F distribution

Now we've got an F ratio, what does it mean? We can see that as it gets bigger, the variance due to the conditions is large compared to the variance within the groups. Eventually, it will become large enough that we can decide to reject the null hypothesis (that there is no difference between the groups) and accept that our conditions had a real effect. How big does the F ratio need to be to make this decision?

When the F ratio was investigated in the first half of the last century, there were no computers. Also, the precise (mathematical) form of the distribution was unknown. Instead, the distribution had to be plotted by 'Monte Carlo' simulation. In this method, distributions are found by repeatedly using random procedures to sample, rather like throwing dice at casinos in Monte Carlo. I will show how this works with a demonstration. In this demonstration, I have three groups making up three conditions. I have created a population of 300 individuals, 100 in each of the groups. These three populations have different individual scores, but all three have the same mean; that is, the null hypothesis (of no difference) is *known* to be true of the population.

The Monte Carlo procedure works by taking a **random sample** of fifteen individuals, five from each group, and calculating the F ratio from that sample. This is then repeated with a new random sample a large number of times. I did it 10,000 times. Tables 6.3 and 6.4 show two of the samples.

Table 6.3   A sample of 15 participants in three groups

Condition		
1	**2**	**3**
5.47	9.73	7.69
1.24	−2.43	19.93
5.82	9.23	9.28
27.92	27.38	16.57
2.19	−1.11	20.38

Table 6.4   A second sample of 15 participants in three groups

Condition		
1	**2**	**3**
26.27	13.99	28.71
27.12	14.10	26.03
25.00	13.20	24.21
25.10	14.72	23.10
25.40	14.05	25.05

6.3

Degrees of freedom (2)

The F ratio has two degrees of freedom: one for the effect variance (numerator) and one for the residual variance (denominator). In our example with three conditions, there are 3 − 1 (N − 1), i.e. 2 degrees of freedom on the top (numerator) of the F ratio. Residual (or error) variance goes on the bottom. In our example of a Monte Carlo simulation, there are five individuals in each condition. Since we calculate the mean for *each* condition, we lose a degree of freedom each time, so there are four degrees of freedom among the five participants in *each* condition. Again, there are three conditions, so the total error degrees of freedom is 4 + 4 + 4 = 12. So the bottom (denominator) of the F ratio has 12 degrees of freedom.

The two degrees of freedom are conventionally written top first, then bottom. So the F ratio in our example would be written $F_{(2,12)}$.

You may notice that the degrees of freedom here add up to 14 (12 + 2), which is one less (N − 1) than the total number of participants (15). So it all adds up nicely.

These two samples in Tables 6.3 and 6.4 respectively produce two different F ratios, one quite small ($F_{(2,12)} = 0.647$) and one very large ($F_{(2,12)} = 117$) (see Box 6.3 for an explanation of the subscripted degrees of freedom for these ratios). We have 10,000 of these F ratios, varying in size (and remember, all these samples came from a population in which the null hypothesis is known to be true). So we can plot a distribution of these values of F.

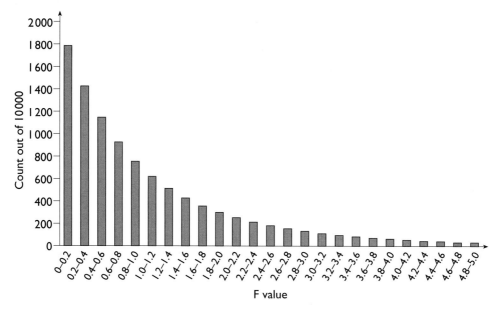

Figure 6.4 Count of F values

Figure 6.4 shows the distribution of these F values by counting how many F values in the 10,000 samples fall into each range. So, for example, 1,785 F values fell in the range 0 to 0.2, while only 30 fell in the range 4.8 to 5. The best way to use this distribution is to plot a **cumulative distribution**. A cumulative distribution counts all the values of F which are less than a certain value. So, for example, I found that the number of F values between 0 and 0.2 is 1,785, and in this sample 1,424 F values lie between 0.2 and 0.4. So the cumulative number of F values up to 0.4 is 3,209. The counts are also converted to a **probability**, by dividing the count (e.g. 3,209) by the total number of samples (10,000): so the cumulative probability is 0.3209. We can plot these cumulative values on a graph.

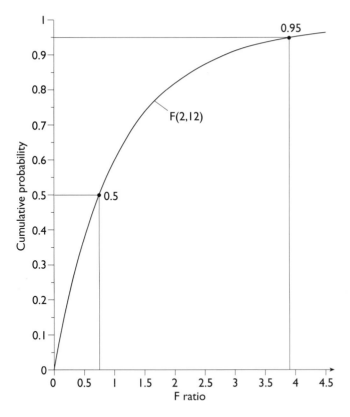

Figure 6.5 Cumulative F distribution

Figure 6.5 shows the cumulative probability of the F values in my sample of 10,000. Plotting the distribution in this way makes it easy to find values for F which correspond to the lower part of the distribution. For example, 50 per cent of the F values fall below the number 0.74. A much more useful cut-off is the 95 per cent point. Here we see that the F value at the 95 per cent point is 3.89.

You should remember that we reject the null hypothesis if the statistic we calculate has a less than 5 per cent (0.05) chance of being as big as it is when the null hypothesis is known to be true (see Box 6.1 at the start of Section 3.1). So if the cumulative probability between 0 and 3.89 is 95 per cent, there is only a 5 per cent chance of getting an F ratio larger than 3.89. This therefore is the **critical value** above which, in an experiment, we would reject the null hypothesis and accept that our conditions differ.

This critical value is only true for the particular F distribution we have looked at. This is because the F distribution changes with the number of groups and the number of participants in each group. This is expressed in the degrees of freedom for the F ratio. Figure 6.6 plots two cumulative F distributions, one with (2,12) degrees of freedom, one with (1,4) degrees of freedom. You can see the distributions are different, and they cut the critical 95 per cent value at different points (critical values at 95 per cent are $F_{(2,12)} = 3.89$, $F_{(1,4)} = 7.71$).

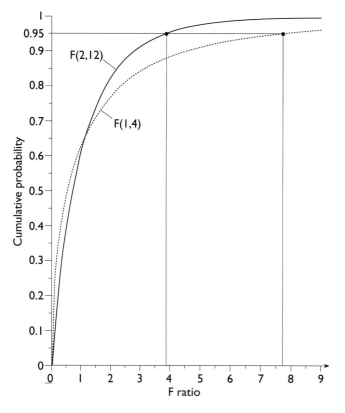

Figure 6.6 Two cumulative F distributions: $F_{2,12)}$ and $F_{(1,4)}$

In the last century, these critical values were placed in large tables so that scientists could look them up to see if the value of F from their experiment fell above (in the 5 per cent region) or below (in the 95 per cent region) the critical value for their experiment. Nowadays, we have equations for the F distributions and computers calculate the exact point on the cumulative F distribution on which a particular value falls. For example, my spreadsheet package has an FDIST function, and if I give this function the $F_{(2,8)} = 8.9$ value, it tells me it falls at the 0.00924 level, so it is easily in the 5 per cent rejection region (this function is used in the spreadsheet exercises). In fact the function prints the p value 0.00924 showing how unlikely it is to have occurred by chance. Statistical analysis packages such as SPSS also automatically print this probability.[*]

SPSS exercise 1: One-way between-subjects ANOVA

Analyse the data file 1-WayBetween-SubjectsAnova.sav. You may wish to consult a book to guide you through the analysis in SPSS. For example, you may read

---

[*] I must confess here that the graphs in Figures 6.4 and 6.5 used the spreadsheet function, not a Monte Carlo method. The Monte Carlo simulation for repeated measures (Section 5.1) is genuine, however.

Section 2 of Chapter 7 in Brace *et al*. (2003), and check your results against those they report.

The psychologist, therefore, is able to analyse the variance of his or her data into two sources (effect variance, and residual (or error) variance), and, by comparing them, discover whether the reduction in variance of the data produced by separating them into several groups can be considered to be due to chance or not.

3.3 Analysis of variance with more than two conditions

The example discussed above had only two conditions. However, the discussion can be directly extended to the case where there are more than two treatments. Let us consider a simple one-way analysis of variance. The data in Table 6.5 have been taken from eight participants in an experiment. The eight participants are divided into four groups, producing two participants in each group. Two participants may not seem very much to give a result for each group. However, any number of participants greater than one is sufficient to give a calculation of the variance. You can see the data plotted out in Figure 6.7.

Table 6.5

Group	A		B		C		D	
	Participant	Data	Participant	Data	Participant	Data	Participant	Data
	1	35	3	65	5	25	7	25
	2	45	4	55	6	15	8	35
Group mean		40		60		20		30

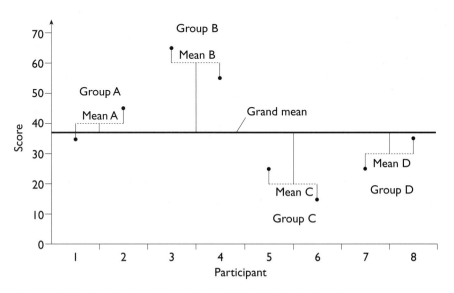

Figure 6.7 The eight data points from Table 6.5 divided into four groups

Given the information that these eight data points are divided into four groups, A, B, C and D, we can analyse the variance in exactly the same way as we did in Section 3.2. The group mean for each of the four groups is calculated, and the distance of each datum from its own group mean is measured. Once again, putting each datum into a group results in the residual variance of the data points about their own group means being less than the total variance. There has been a reduction in the variance of the data. The missing variance has not gone away. Again, each of the group means can be said to vary about the grand mean, and the amount by which each group mean differs from the grand mean can be measured. This distance is shown for each group mean in Figure 6.7. The effect variance is calculated by adding up all of these squared distances from each of the group means (and dividing by degrees of freedom). Again, the analysis of variance proceeds by comparing the effect variance against the residual variance to see if the effect variance is so much larger that the discrepancy cannot be attributed to chance. Having calculated the F ratio it is an easy matter to look in the appropriate part of the statistical tables to see the probability that it arose by chance.

In this example, an analysis of variance produces an F ratio (with three and four degrees of freedom – see Box 6.3) of 11.67. What does this F ratio mean?

If you look in a table of F ratios, the chance of getting an $F_{(3,4)}$ ratio as high as 11.67 when there is no difference between the means (the null hypothesis is true) is less than 0.05. In these circumstances, we usually decide to reject the null hypothesis, and conclude that there actually is a real difference between the means which is not due to chance variation. So, in the scientific context of the experiment that we discussed in this section, we consider that there are some real measurable differences between the four groups used in this experiment. In other words, the null hypothesis, that there are no differences between any of the conditions, is false.

In this example, there are four treatment groups being compared. However, any number of treatment groups greater than one can be used in the analysis of variance.

Spreadsheet exercise 5

Spreadsheet exercise 5 contains the data for this analysis of variance (for Microsoft Excel: EX5 (Excel).xls; for StarOffice spreadsheet users: EX5 (Star).sxc). You may find it useful to try changing the data to see what happens and give you a 'feel' for analysis of variance (ANOVA).

Instructions for Microsoft Excel users

You can change the data by selecting a point in the first graph, and dragging it up or down, just as you selected the 'handle' in earlier exercises.

1   Select the first point (the one on the far left).

Drag it downwards. Sometimes Excel takes a bit of 'persuading' to let you drag the data points around. You need to click exactly on the data point itself. If you miss (even slightly) you end up selecting the wrong part of the graph. You know when the data point itself is selected because when you hold the pointer over the data point it changes shape to this [ ].

When you release it, you will see the grand mean change on graphs 1 and 3, and the mean of group A change on graphs 2 and 3. You will also see new values for the sum of squares appear. The total sum of squares will have gone up, because you moved the point *away* from the grand mean. The error (residual) sum of squares will also go up, because you moved the point away from its group mean. Because of this, the F ratio will have gone down. As the F ratio reduces, the p value goes up. If you moved the point far enough, the p value will have gone higher than 0.05, making the result non-significant.

2   For each of the four groups, select the lower data point and move it up towards the other data point in each group. Watch what happens to the error (residual) sum of squares as you do this. The closer the points in each group get together, the smaller the error sum of squares becomes. This is because you are reducing the disagreement (error) between the data in each group and its own group mean. As the squared error falls, the F ratio rises. This can rise indefinitely. However, you will notice η^2 (eta-squared) does not rise higher than 1 (more on this in Section 6.3).

So the more the data cluster tightly around the group means and therefore agree on the effect of conditions, the higher the F ratio and the more likely it is that we will get a significant result.

Instructions for StarOffice spreadsheet users

In this spreadsheet, you can see a table containing the participants scores. You can change the data for any participant by selecting that cell and typing in a new value.

1   Choose the point with the highest value in the first group. Enter a smaller value (e.g. 40). Make sure the value has been accepted by pressing return. Read the discussion under 'Instructions for Microsoft Excel users' above about how the mean and sums of squares change.

2   In each group, select the smaller value and enter a number which is nearer in value to the data point for the other participant in the same group. Read the discussion under 'Instructions for Microsoft Excel users' above about how the sums of squares change as the two points in each group get closer together.

Summary of Section 3

- Analysing variance means partitioning the total variance of a series of data points into different sources of variance, such as the effect variance and the residual variance.
- The information introduced into the analysis by dividing the data into the appropriate groups (conditions) is evaluated by comparing the effect variance with the residual variance.
- If the reduction in the variance of the data points produced by grouping them in conditions is large, the F ratio calculated by dividing the effect variance by the

residual variance may be larger than expected by chance alone, and we would feel justified in concluding that the division of the data points into those groups had a meaningful basis.

4   Multiple factor analysis of variance

The main conceptualization above, namely the partitioning of total variance in order to arrive at values for different sources of variance, is the fundamental concept in the analysis of variance. We now go on to consider how these concepts are extended into multi-factor or multiple factor analysis of variance.

If you look back at Figure 6.7, you will recall that in that analysis of variance there were eight individual data points which we then considered to be grouped into four different groups. An analysis of variance performed in that way would have found whether locating the data in the four different groups resulted in a significant reduction in the residual variance. One of the sources of variance identified, therefore, was the amount by which the four group means vary from the grand mean. That was known as the effect variance.

However, there is an analogy between Figure 6.7 and Figure 6.2. In Figure 6.7, the means of the four different groups vary about the grand mean. In Figure 6.2, four individual participants were varying around the grand mean. From Figure 6.2 to Figure 6.3 we discovered what happened if we partitioned the variance of the four participants into the effect variance resulting from knowing that two of the participants belonged to one group and two of the participants to another group. This left the residual variance and an effect variance due to the grouping. Exactly the same operation can be achieved with the group means in Figure 6.7. Suppose I give you the additional information that groups A and B are in fact data from only men and groups C and D are data from only women. Therefore, we could consider groups A and B together and groups C and D together (see Figure 6.8).

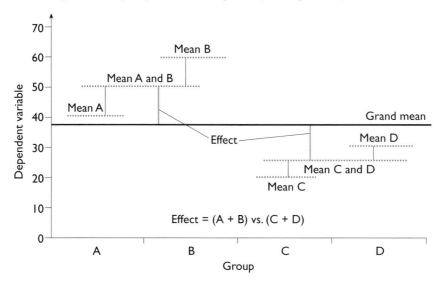

Figure 6.8   Main effect from men (A and B) versus women (C and D)

In Figure 6.8 we are ignoring the data from the participants for the moment, and have simply plotted the four group means. The two groups A and B taken together have a mean overall. This could be described as the mean for the men. Similarly groups C and D themselves have a common mean which could be called the mean for the women. These two overall means differ from the grand mean. The amount by which these means differ from the grand mean is the effect variance of the comparison between the men and the women. We have performed precisely the same operation as that between Figure 6.2 and Figure 6.3. Between Figure 6.7 and Figure 6.8, the treatment variance has been partitioned into an overall effect variance, men compared to women, leaving some residual variance.

In a multi-factor experiment, separating the group means into just two conditions is often not the only way of partitioning the variance. In this case, suppose I told you that groups A and C consisted only of left-handed participants whereas groups B and D comprised only right-handed participants. We could then calculate the overall mean for groups A and C taken together and the overall means for groups B and D taken together (see Figure 6.9).

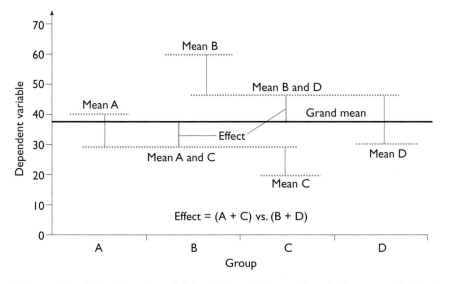

Figure 6.9 Main effect from left-handed participants (A and C) versus right-handers (B and D)

Once again, the means for groups A and C and the means for groups B and D differ from the grand mean. Again, this comprises a source of variance which we have partitioned from the overall variance of the treatment effects.

This is an example of a multi-factor experiment. There are two **factors**, the sex of the participant and the handedness of the participant. Each factor has a number of **levels**; in this case, sex has two levels (male and female), and handedness has two levels (right- and left-handed). These two factors, each with two levels, form four groups (the four groups are male left-handers, male right-handers, female left-handers and female right-handers). A simple 'one-way' analysis of variance simply partitions the variance into the effect variance due to these four groups and the residual variance of the participants. A multi-factor analysis of variance involves partitioning the variance of the four treatments into the two factors; that is, the male versus the female groups, and the left-handed versus the right-handed groups. In addition to these **main effects** the two factors combine in an **interaction**.

4.1 Interactions

What is an interaction? We saw with Figures 6.7, 6.8 and 6.9 that four groups of subjects A, B, C and D could in fact be meaningfully grouped into two factors, sex and handedness. These two factors allowed a way of grouping the four means in two different ways. First, A was grouped with B and compared with the remaining two groups. Second, A was grouped with C and compared with the other two groups together. This leaves a third grouping where group A is grouped with D and compared with the other two together (group B with group C). This is the interaction comparison. What does it mean?

The main factors, sex and handedness, were easy to understand, since sex effectively compared men against women, and handedness compared left handers against right handers. In the interaction grouping, however, male right-handers are paired with female left-handers and compared against the group of male-left handers with female right-handers. You can see from this pairing that different levels of each factor are paired with their opposite. The factors are said to be **crossed** with each other. What is this interaction term testing? Let's look more closely at the pattern of data.

Suppose the four group means were those shown in Figure 6.10. You can see that the value for left-handers is always above the value for right-handers and the values for men are always above the values for women. So the main factors produce a difference between their group means. To emphasize, there is a measured *difference* between the scores for left-handers and the scores for right-handers. Similarly, there is a measured difference between the scores for men compared with the scores for women. Look at Table 6.6.

Table 6.6 Table showing the overall differences due to the main effects (handedness and gender)

	Men	Women	Both sexes taken together
Left-handers	60	40	50
Right-handers	50	30	40
Left- and right-handedness taken together	55	35	

Overall difference for left-handers vs. right handers: 50 − 40 = 10

Overall difference for men vs. women: 55 − 35 = 20

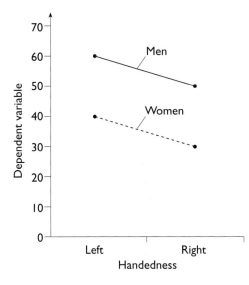

Figure 6.10 Data from Table 6.6

The main effects in the multi-factor analysis of variance evaluate these overall differences: is the difference of 10 between left-handers and right-handers more than you would expect by chance? Is the difference of 20 between men and women more than would be expected by chance?

The interaction takes this analysis a stage further. It looks at the differences found in the sub-cells of the table (see Table 6.7).

Table 6.7 Table showing the differences due to handedness within the two sexes

	Men	Women
Differences between handedness scores	10 (60 – 50)	10 (40 – 30)

Difference of the differences scores: 10 – 10 = 0

It then asks, are these two differences between handedness scores *different from each other*. So is the difference between male left-handers and male right-handers (10) different from the difference between female left-handers and female right-handers (10)? In this case, the two differences are identical, so there is no 'difference of the differences': there is no interaction.

Previously, we noted that the interaction combines A + D (left-handed men + right-handed women), and compares with B + C (right-handed men + left-handed women). You can see from Table 6.6 that A + D = 90, and B + C = 90: the same result of 'no difference'.

Suppose the data were as in Table 6.8 (plotted in Figure 6.11).

Table 6.8 New (fictitious) data for the interaction test

	Men	Women
Left-handers	60	40
Right-handers	40	50

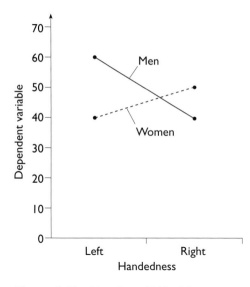

Figure 6.11   Data from Table 6.8

What is the 'difference of the differences' now? For men, left-handers score greater than right-handers by +20. However, for women, left-handers score 10 less than right-handers, so the difference is −10. These two differences, +20 and −10, are not identical so there may well be a 'difference of the differences' (i.e. an interaction is found). Again, comparing A + D (110) with B + C (80), the same difference of 30 is found.

An interaction means that the effect of handedness for men is somehow different from the effect for women. In this case, there is a clear difference, since male left-handers have higher scores, while female right-handers have the higher scores. Therefore, in this (fictional) example, *understanding the effect of handedness can only be understood if the context of gender is considered because there is an interaction.*

The idea of 'difference of differences' is most easily seen in the graphs of results. When the 'difference of differences' is zero, the lines will be parallel, as in Figure 6.10. But when the interaction is significant the lines are not parallel, since the differences change. This is true also when the experiment has more than two levels in one of the factors. Figure 6.12 illustrates several sets of results with lines not parallel (showing different interaction patterns).

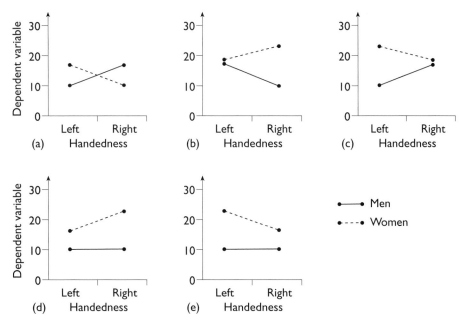

Figure 6.12 Graphs showing different interaction patterns

SPSS exercise 2

Analyse the data file 2-WayBetween-SubjectsAnova.sav. You may wish to consult a book to guide you through the analysis in SPSS. For example, you may read Section 3 of Chapter 7 in Brace *et al.* (2003), and check your results against those they report.

4.2   Degrees of freedom

With the four groups of participants we were talking about above in relation to gender and handedness, we looked at all three possible pairings that group A can join and be tested against the remaining two groups (A with B, A with C, and A with D). There are no more possible pairings because we have used up all the three degrees of freedom available in the set of four data points (see Box 6.3).

Summary of Section 4

- The concept of partitioning variance (see Section 3.2) extends to creating partitions based on independent factors, of which there may be more than one.
- Each factor has an effect variance component unique to itself, which can be tested for significance by an appropriate F ratio.
- When more than one factor is involved, the effect of that factor may depend on the context of the other factors. If it does, then an interaction between the factors has been found.

- Interactions are made visible by looking at graphs of main effects. Lines connecting levels in one factor are found not to be parallel across levels of the other factor when an interaction is present.

5 The assumptions underlying analysis of variance and most parametric statistics

You should now understand the underlying logic of analysis of variance, which results in the generation of an F ratio to test whether conditions have an effect which cannot be ascribed to chance. Calculating the F ratio is a numerical procedure, and the F ratio is defined simply as the ratio of two variances. I commented in Section 3.3 above that, having calculated the F ratio, we use tables calculated by statisticians to see whether the value of this statistic allows us to reject the interpretation that the results were due to chance. We now have to look closely at what statisticians had to do to create those tables. This is because the creation of those tables is only possible if certain restrictive assumptions about the data are made. Those assumptions are as follows:

1   The data points are distributed around means according to the normal distribution (the normality assumption).

2   The variance of the data points within each of the groups (such as the four groups A, B, C and D in Figure 6.7) is the same (the homogeneity of variance assumption).

3   The observations are independent: knowing the value of one observation should tell us nothing about the value of another observation (the independence assumption).

These assumptions are very important. This chapter assumes you are familiar with what a normal distribution is, and under what conditions it may be found.

If the data which are being analysed are not normally distributed, then the tables of the F statistic found in statistics books are inaccurate. If those tables are inaccurate, then the scientific judgements being based on the analytical results are suspect. In other words, scientists doing analysis of variance with data that are not from a normal distribution are liable to make mistakes by drawing the wrong conclusions.

In general, most modern psychologists make few corrections for violating assumptions. This is because the F test is 'robust' to some violations: i.e. our decisions remain reasonably reliable even when assumptions do not hold. However, you should be aware of these assumptions and ready to act if necessary. When it comes to repeated measures ANOVA, however, violation of one of the assumptions is routinely handled in the analysis.

5.1   Repeated measures

So far, we have discussed experiments when each participant serves in one experimental condition. These are between-participants designs. These are excellent research designs. However, some consider that these designs may be weakened by large individual differences between participants. These individual differences create some of the residual error which the experiment must overcome in order to detect a difference between the treatments.

Table 6.9 Three participants with repeated measures

		Conditions			Participant mean
		1	**2**	**3**	
	1	40	37	39	38.6
Participants	2	20	16	18	18
	3	10	4	7	7
Condition mean		23.3	19	21.3	

In another experimental design, the participants do all of the conditions in one or more factor(s), meaning that empirical measurements are repeated on each participant; this is known as a **repeated measures** design. Three participants in a repeated measures design are shown in Table 6.9. You can see that there are large individual differences between the participants, and (in this case) smaller differences between the treatments. In the analysis of variance, it is the three differences between the treatments (1 vs. 2, 1 vs. 3 and 2 vs. 3) for *each* individual which are used to measure the error variance. The idea is that this bypasses the individual differences and eliminates them (at least in part) from the error term.

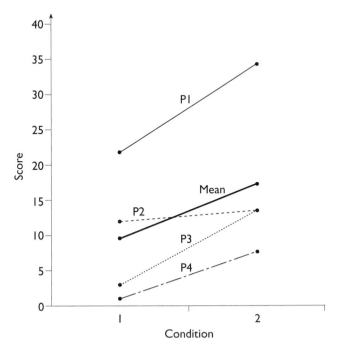

Figure 6.13 Repeated measures analysis

Figure 6.13 is another illustration of repeated measures analysis. Four participants have been measured in two conditions. The data for each participant have been joined together with a line. The figure also shows the mean for the two conditions, also joined by a line. You can see that the data for participant 1 (P1) are much higher overall than the others. But this *overall* difference between participants does not matter for the analysis. What matters is the lines joining the two conditions. If these lines mostly agree that one condition is better than the other, then the repeated measures analysis will allow us to conclude that the two means do differ. Here, the four participants all have lines which slope upwards (left to right), and additionally these slopes are in reasonable agreement, so that the statistical analysis ($F_{(1,3)}$ = 12.86) is significant (see spreadsheet exercise 6).

Spreadsheet exercise 6

Spreadsheet exercise 6 uses the data which created Figure 6.13. You can use this to explore how repeated measures analysis is sensitive to agreement between the participants. Example exercises follow.

Instructions for Microsoft Excel users

Open the spreadsheet EX6 (Excel).xls. You can manipulate the data by clicking on data points in the graph. Then you can move the data points up and down by dragging them (the same way you can drag files around inside folders).

Instructions for StarOffice spreadsheet users

If you use the StarOffice spreadsheet, open the spreadsheet EX6 (Star).sxc. The data points of the four participants are in a table at the top. Select the correct one (the biggest number in exercise 6.1, the smallest ones in exercise 6.2). Type in a new value (lower values for exercise 6.1; in exercise 6.2, 'play' with the values until the lines become more parallel).

Exercise 6.1
Select the highest data point (it is in condition 2) and pull it down to below the data point for condition 1 for that participant. When you 'let go', the analysis of variance table updates, and you should see that the mean square (MS) for the condition has reduced, while the MS for the error term has increased. As a result the F ratio, on which the statistical test depends, has reduced a lot, and the probability level (Prob) is not significant.

What has happened is that there is now quite a lot of disagreement between the participants about whether condition 2 is better than condition 1, since three participants have condition 2 better than condition 1, unlike the fourth participant. With so much disagreement between the participants, the result is not significant.

Exercise 6.2
In this exercise, which is a bit fiddly, try to move the data points for three participants so they are all parallel to the fourth. You can do this by moving one datum for each participant.

As you make the slopes all more parallel, you are increasing the agreement between the participants. The more you do this, the MS error term will get smaller and smaller. Meanwhile the F ratio will get larger, so the result is more significant. Indeed, if all four lines are *exactly* parallel, the MS error term will be zero! What happens to the F ratio then?

You can try other patterns of agreement between the lines to see the effect on the F ratio. For example, you could try moving *both* data points for one participant (e.g. participant 1) the same amount in the same direction. If you do this accurately, so that the slope does not change, the MS values for condition and error should not change, leaving the result as it was before.

What does change? The mean square (MS) value for the between-subjects term changes. A statistical test is not usually performed on this source of variance.

Note that the degrees of freedom change in repeated measures. Suppose I decide to measure three treatments five times each. In the between-subjects design, I need fifteen participants, five in each group, and my F ratio will have 12 degrees of freedom (four from each group) in the denominator. However, in the repeated-measures design, I will use five participants repeatedly to give the fifteen measures. Because it is the differences between the treatments which is analysed, or (equivalently) because we discard the individual differences between the five participants (and hence lose four, $N-1$, degrees of freedom), we only have 8 degrees of freedom in the denominator. This means we have to have a higher F ratio in the repeated measures design to reach significance. The 5 per cent critical value for the between-groups design $F_{(2,12)}$ is 3.89, while the 5 per cent critical value of the repeated measures design $F_{(2,8)}$ is 4.46. The F ratio needs to be 15 per cent higher in the second case. Of course, we may decide to run more participants in the repeated measures design, which would increase the degrees of freedom.

A real problem is the fact that one of the assumptions behind analysis of variance has been violated. This is the independence assumption. Because we measure the same participant repeatedly, the data are no longer independent. Consider the example in Table 6.9. You can see that knowing the score from one condition for one participant gives us a good guess about the values of scores on the other two treatments for the same participant. The result is that the scores on the three conditions are **correlated** with each other: a clear violation of independence.

Fortunately, statisticians have used a mathematical analysis to show that the independence assumption can be replaced with an assumption called **sphericity**. The sphericity assumption is made about the correlations between the conditions. In Table 6.9, there are three correlations, between Condition 1 and Condition 2, Condition 1 and Condition 3, Condition 2 and Condition 3. *The sphericity assumption is that these correlations are the same.* If they are the same, we can use the F distribution appropriate for the normal degrees of freedom (such as F(2,8) in the example above). But what if they are not?

5.1.1 Approximating the F distribution

Let's take a look at a situation where these correlations are different. I've created a dataset based on a population of 100 participants, with repeated measurements across three conditions. In this data set, the correlations between the conditions are very different (see Table 6.10).

Table 6.10   Correlations between conditions in a population of measurements

Condition pairs	Correlation
Condition 1 with Condition 2	0.7
Condition 1 with Condition 3	0.1
Condition 2 with Condition 3	−0.6

As before, the *means* of the three conditions are exactly the same, so the null hypothesis is *known* to be true. After sampling five participants from this population 10,000 times, and calculating the F ratio for each sample, we can plot the cumulative F distribution.

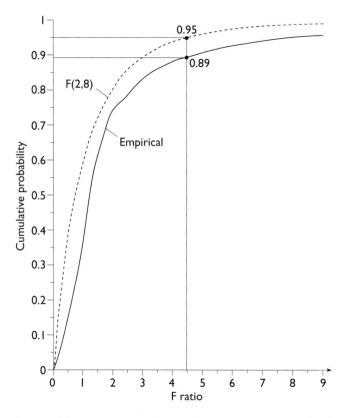

Figure 6.14   Empirical and exact $F_{(2,8)}$ cumulative F distributions

Figure 6.14 plots our empirical $F_{(2,8)}$ distribution against the theoretical $F_{(2,8)}$ distribution which would apply if the sphericity assumption held. You can see the empirical distribution is everywhere systematically lower than the ideal $F_{(2,8)}$ distribution. If we were to use the ideal $F_{(2,8)}$ distribution, we would make many more Type I errors than we would expect. This is because the 5 per cent $F_{(2,8)}$ critical value we would normally use is 4.46. Looking at the empirical distribution, we find that this value gives an actual Type I error rate of 11 per cent. This represents the 0.89 point on the cumulative distribution. We are quite a long way out. Therefore, our Type I error rate has risen from 5 per cent to 11 per cent, and we would only know this by doing a Monte Carlo test: not something to be done routinely. So we can't use the usual critical value found in our F tables. What can we do?

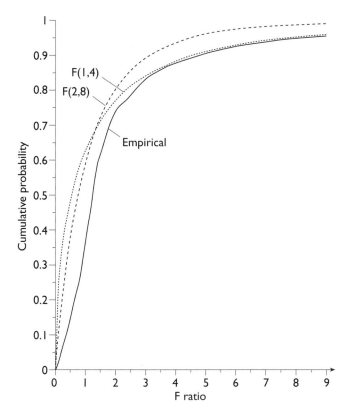

Figure 6.15 One empirical and two theoretical F distributions

We need to try to approximate the empirical F distribution. Figure 6.15 has another cumulative F distribution added: $F_{(1,4)}$. You can see, in comparison with the $F_{(2,8)}$ distribution, that it lies above it at the left-hand (lower) end, and below it at the right-hand (upper) end. Compared with the empirical F distribution, it doesn't look like a good approximation. It is quite a long way away at the lower end. But that doesn't really matter, it is the top end that matters. Around the 95 per cent area, the $F_{(1,4)}$ distribution is very close to the empirical distribution. The 5 per cent $F_{(1,4)}$ critical value is 7.7, which is at the 6 per cent point on the empirical distribution. This is obviously a big improvement.

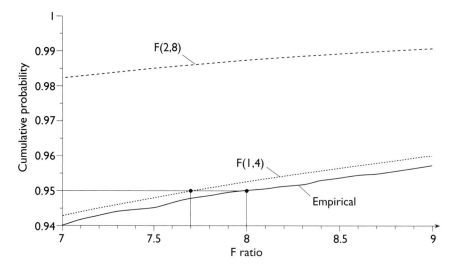

Figure 6.16 Three cumulative F distributions at the 95 per cent point

You can see from Figure 6.16 how close the $F_{(1,4)}$ distribution is as an approximation to the empirical distribution over the important area around the 95 per cent level.

So the trick to approximating the empirical distribution is to choose another F distribution which is close to it. A mathematical analysis shows this can be done by calculating a correction factor, epsilon (ε), from the correlations between the treatments. There are two ways of calculating epsilon, one due to Greenhouse-Geisser, the other worked out by Huynh-Feldt (because we are approximating, there is no ideal solution). Epsilon is then used to calculate new values for the degrees of freedom, and these provide the new F distribution which is an approximation to the empirical one. This is then used to calculate the p value. When you do an analysis of variance using SPSS, the epsilon calculation is done automatically and the corrected p values are given. The simplest rule is to always use the Greenhouse-Geisser correction for the p value. Sometimes it is a little conservative, but not excessively so. By conservative we mean that, instead of holding Type I error at 5 per cent, it holds it at a *lower* value (e.g. 4 per cent).

SPSS exercise 3: one-way repeated measures ANOVA

Analyse the data file 1-WayWithin-SubjectsAnova.sav. You may wish to consult a book to guide you through the analysis in SPSS. For example, you may read Section 4 of Chapter 7 in Brace *et al.* (2003), and check your results against those they report. Look at the epsilon corrections in the ANOVA table.

Summary of Section 5

- Analysis of variance assumes:
  - The data points are distributed according to the normal distribution (the normality assumption).

- The variance between groups is the same (the homogeneity of variance assumption.

- The observations are independent of each other (the independence assumption).

- Repeated measures analysis of variance is appropriate when a subject is tested several times in different conditions.

- Repeated measures make the additional assumption of sphericity.

- When the sphericity assumption does not hold, repeated measures analyses can be corrected using adjustments to degrees of freedom.

6   Making decisions under uncertainty

6.1   Drawing conclusions from statistical tests

You should be familiar with the basic idea behind using statistical tests. Inferential statistics such as are normally taught in psychology departments are based on the testing of null hypotheses.

The actual values of variance found in any random sample will always differ from other samples. As we saw in Section 3.3, an F ratio can take any value, even when there is no effect of conditions, and the null hypothesis is true. As you saw, there is a particular sampling distribution for the F statistic, which shows how likely it is that you will get a certain value or greater when comparing two sources of variance drawn at random from the same population. These F distributions are called the **central F distributions**. These are the F distributions normally tabulated in statistics books or calculated by computers, and they are the ones we use to look up the 'significance' of a result.

The basis of the null hypothesis test, therefore, is that we consider the value of our calculated F ratio against these central F distributions to see whether it is likely or unlikely that we have obtained such a result by chance. By fixing a certain level of probability, known as the α or Type I error probability, the number of times that a decision is made in error – which means rejecting the null hypothesis when it is in fact true – is held at a certain level.

I will now develop the idea of Type I error further by considering multiple comparison techniques.

6.2   Multiple comparison techniques

The discussion of Type I errors so far in this chapter has focused on a scientific decision being made in a single comparison. This we can call the **error rate per comparison (PC)**. When we are doing more than one comparison, each one has a chance of producing a Type I error. Across all the comparisons we do (i.e. the complete **family** of comparisons), each one increases the chance that we will make at least one Type I error. This is known as the **familywise error rate (FW)**. If you are doing very many comparisons, this familywise error rate can become large indeed.

We need to find ways of doing lots of comparisons if we are really interested in them, yet avoid making lots of erroneous decisions.

As well as the issue of multiple comparisons, frequently we plan in advance (according to our scientific predictions) to do a certain set of analytical comparisons of the data. These tests which we have specified in advance are known as **a priori comparisons** (the 'a' is often, depending on your view of Latin, pronounced 'ah' as when the doctor asks you to say 'ah').

Sometimes however we have a set of data and we have little idea in advance of, or are simply surprised by, the kind of results that emerge. We then find ourselves doing comparisons which we didn't think of in advance in response to the data we have collected. These new comparisons, devised after finding the data from an experiment, are known as **post-hoc comparisons**.

Let us consider this a little more. Suppose we have the four groups as we discussed in Section 3.3 of this chapter. There are 25 possible (simple) inter-group contrasts. These are listed in Table 6.11.

Table 6.11 All possible comparisons for four treatments

Pairwise comparisons	1 vs 2 comparisons	1 vs 3 comparisons	2 vs 2 comparisons
A vs. B	A vs. (B + C)	A vs. (B + C + D)	(A + B) vs. (C + D)
A vs. C	A vs. (B + D)	B vs. (A + C + D)	(A + C) vs. (B + D)
A vs. D	A vs. (C + D)	C vs. (A + B + D)	(A + D) vs. (B + C)
B vs. C	B vs. (A + C)	D vs. (A + B + C)	
B vs. D	B vs. (A + D)		
C vs. D	B vs. (C + D)		
	C vs. (A + B)		
	C vs. (A + D)		
	C vs. (B + D)		
	D vs. (A + B)		
	D vs. (A + C)		
	D vs. (B + C)		

With four treatment groups we can see in Table 6.11 that there are as many as 25 different contrasts, all of which can be tested. Indeed, if you were to do 25 such comparisons (and the comparisons were all independent) your chance of making at least one Type I error would have risen from 5 per cent to 72 per cent (72 per cent is calculated from $1 - 0.95^{25}$). Such a high chance of making a Type I error is clearly unacceptable, especially if tests are being done wildly and without having been planned in advance of the experiment. Even so, Scheffé has modified the analysis of variance to allow such multiple comparisons to be done. Basically, his procedure (the **Scheffé test**) calculates a new critical value for the F ratio against which the comparisons are tested. For four treatments, the new critical value is equivalent to a single comparison being performed at $\alpha = 0.052^*$. Using this critical value instead of the normal one ensures that the familywise Type I error rate is at most 5 per cent. So, if you felt like it, all 25 contrasts in Table 6.11 could be done and tested. However, such a procedure is highly unusual, and the Scheffé test is so conservative in order to deal with this extreme case that it is rarely used. This is because the new critical value is very high, and thus it is hard for any individual comparison to reach it. Most statistical packages continue to print its results however.

The majority of post-hoc comparison techniques don't attempt to cover the possibility of doing all possible contrasts. They usually concentrate on doing just the **pairwise comparisons** (these are the six in the first column in Table 6.11). The problem of the rising familywise error rate for doing several comparisons has been much reduced because only six tests are to be performed, rather than 25. Instead of the familywise error rate for the complete set of comparisons performed at $\alpha = 0.05$ being 0.72, it is only 0.26 (26 per cent is calculated from $1 - 0.95^6$) for the six. This is still a high value, but the problem of dealing with it is obviously much reduced.

One way to deal with this is to change the α level for each comparison. Suppose, with six comparisons, the alpha level for each one is set to 0.0085. This succeeds in keeping familywise Type I errors at 5 per cent. This is because $(1 - 0.9915^6) = 5$ per cent. The downside again is that the individual comparison level is conservative: so it is harder for the individual comparison to be significant. Indeed, the test is often little better than the Scheffé. There is a neat way of avoiding this problem, however, which relies on using sequential, conditional tests.

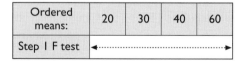

Step 2 continues in two 'halves':

Note: Tests are conditional: subsequent tests are only made if tests in previous stages are significant

Figure 6.17 Sequential conditional testing (REGW-F) procedure

I will illustrate how this works with what is called the Ryan-Einolt-Gabriel-Welsh F procedure (usually referred to as the **REGW-F**, and you'll find it as that in SPSS). The means from the simple analysis of variance example (see Table 6.5, Section 3.3) are ordered as in Figure 6.17, lowest at the left and largest at the right. The procedure works by calculating the ANOVA F test across all four of the means (Step 1 in Figure 6.17), then if (*and only if*) that test is significant, the next step of the procedure is

---

* This is an asymptotic value (i.e. it is increasingly accurate as df (error) approaches infinity).

performed, which is to do another two F tests across sets of three adjacent means (Step 2 in Figure 6.17). If one of those tests is not significant, the procedure stops and those three means are declared equivalent. If the Step 2 F test is significant, the procedure moves to the next step and tests the two adjacent pairwise comparisons to see where the differences lie (Step 3 in Figure 6.17). Fortunately, SPSS does this procedure automatically when asked (see 'SPSS exercise 4').

Protection from familywise Type I errors comes from the sequential, conditional procedure. For example, the very first test is performed at $\alpha = 0.05$. If the complete null hypothesis is true (that there are no differences between *any* of the means), the procedure will stop 95 per cent of the time with a declaration of no significant differences. Only 5 per cent of the time will we proceed to do more tests, so we have held Type I error rates to 5 per cent (it doesn't matter if our subsequent tests erroneously identify more than one pair of means as different, the familywise error rate is defined as 'at least one' Type I error). The REGW-F procedure uses adjusted p values at each step to compensate for the sequential testing procedure, but this is all handled automatically by SPSS so we don't need to worry about how that is done.

The net effect of this analytical procedure is that we have searched for significant pairwise comparisons using an efficient sequential procedure.

SPSS exercise 4

Analyse the data file 1-WayBetween-SubjectsAnova.sav as a one-way ANOVA and ask for the post-hoc comparison REGW-F. You may wish to consult a book to guide you through the analysis in SPSS. For example, you may read Section 8 of Chapter 7 in Brace *et al.* (2003), and check your results against those they report. Instead of selecting *Bonferroni* tests, select *R-E-G-W-F* instead.

6.2.1 Historical note on pairwise comparison techniques

The sequential procedure set out here can use any **omnibus test** procedure for differences among means. (Analysis of variance is an 'omnibus' test because it simultaneously tests for *any* differences between *all* the treatment means.) Another omnibus test is called the **Studentized Range** statistic which is very similar to the t test, but designed to work across a range of ordered means such as in Figure 6.17. The statistic it calculates is known as q. In SPSS, you will see a post-hoc procedure called REGW-Q. This is exactly the same analytical procedure as REGW-F, except it uses the Studentized Range q statistic instead of the ANOVA F statistic. In addition, there are several other tests suggested by SPSS for post-hoc comparisons. The following tests all use the same analytical procedure as REGW-Q: Neuman-Keuls, Tukey HSD and Duncan's range. The only difference between these procedures is their approach to making corrections to the p values during the steps. The REGW tests are recognized as being the most powerful tests which accurately keep the familywise Type 1 error rate low under all conditions. REGW-F and REGW-Q are very similar in power, perhaps with REGW-F just shading out REGW-Q, so the former test is my recommendation.

6.2.2 Special case: comparing multiple treatments to a single control (Dunnett's test)

If we want to restrict the post-hoc comparisons still further, there is a specialist test which is a little more powerful. If our experiments had a single control condition, and all the treatments need comparing to it, then we would be making fewer of the pairwise comparisons. For the data in Figure 6.7, if one mean was a control, we would only have three pairwise comparisons, instead of six as in Table 6.11. Again, we have reduced the opportunity for making Type I errors and that will assist us in controlling the familywise Type I error rate.

Dunnett's test (based on the t test) is a specialist test for this situation, in which Dunnett has developed a special t distribution (t_d) for the comparisons. Again, SPSS will perform this test automatically if requested.

6.2.3 Planned comparisons

Planned, a priori comparisons are those in which the analysis is dictated by scientific considerations. In other words, theoretical considerations have dictated which comparisons between treatments are being tested, rather than feelings which have arisen due to you seeing the means after the experiment has been completed.

Post-hoc comparisons are useful when you couldn't predict in advance what differences will appear between your conditions. But psychologists are often a little more insightful! If you know what you are looking for, you can be clear in advance which are the important *planned comparisons* out of all the possible ones (e.g. see Table 6.11), and this allows you to perform these few comparisons at the normal 5 per cent α level of significance.

Usually, the prediction made in advance involves some form of comparison between the conditions in the experiment. This is most easily seen by looking at an example. We shall look at the example from 'SPSS exercise 1: One-Way Between-Subjects ANOVA'. This used an experiment by Towell *et al.* (1986) in which participants, pretending to be jurors, were shown the testimony of an alleged victim of rape, and afterwards had to try to recall facts from the testimony. So the level of recall was measured. However, in three of the four conditions, the face of the witness was obscured: one condition covered her face with a grey blob, a second condition covered her face with pixelation, and the third negated her face (white and black reversed like a photographic negative). In the fourth condition the witness's face was unmasked (normal).

Since the hypothesis was that the masking would reduce recall, the most powerful a priori (planned) comparison is the unmasked condition compared with the other three conditions taken together. This requires the use of **coefficients** to define the contrast, in this case −3, 1, 1, 1. The −3 coefficient is applied to the unmasked condition, and the 1 coefficients are applied to the three masking conditions.

SPSS exercise 5: planned comparisons

Perform a set of comparisons on the file 1-WayBetween-SubjectsAnova.sav.

You may find it helpful to consult a book to guide you in doing this in SPSS. For example, the second half of Section 8 in Chapter 7 of Brace *et al.* (2003) discusses planned comparisons; the authors explain how coefficients can be used to compare (contrast) other combinations of means. You might well find these useful for your own projects. They also refer to preset contrasts in SPSS; these can be used for special analyses in advanced statistical testing.

6.3   Type II errors, effect size and power

We have dwelt a lot on *controlling* Type I errors, making sure we don't make too many erroneous scientific decisions such that we wrongly conclude there is a difference between conditions when really there is none. The emphasis here is on *control*, because we as scientists take control over how many such errors we are prepared to make: usually it is 5 per cent of the time when the null hypothesis is true. When the null hypothesis is true, the size of the effect is zero, so a conclusion that there is a difference is an error.

But what if there is really an effect, so that the effect size is greater than zero? If so, we can't make a Type I error, since the null hypothesis is false. Are we therefore sure to find a significant effect? Unfortunately not. There is one more source of error, called a Type II error, in which we fail to detect a significant effect and erroneously accept the null hypothesis.

Unlike Type I errors, we don't have control over Type II errors, at least not in the same way. How often are we likely to make Type II errors? It depends on how big the effect is (the **effect size**) and how many participants we run. Large effects are easy to detect and mean we make few Type II errors even with modest numbers of participants. Small effects are hard to detect and mean we would need many participants (sometimes hundreds or even thousands) to give us a good chance of avoiding Type II errors.

Effect sizes are often measured by values related to correlation (r). A very common measure is **squared correlation** (r^2). In analysis of variance, the equivalent of r^2 is η^2 (eta-squared). It can take any value between zero (no effect, the null hypothesis is true) and 1 (all the variability between our measures has come from the conditions). It is worth paying attention to the effect size as it can tell us how big our effect is, and it is even possible to calculate the likely Type II error rate for an experiment. For example, the analysis of variance in 'SPSS exercise 1' produced an effect size of $\eta^2 = 0.3$. From this it is possible to calculate that an experiment which ran 80 participants in each group would have a Type II error rate of 20 per cent. In other words, such experiments would fail to get a significant result once in every five replications. This may seem to be a high failure rate, but is actually quite common among psychology experiments. For the Type II error rate to fall to 5 per cent, the experiment would have to run 120 participants per group.

Another way of looking at Type II errors is to consider **power**. Power is 1 – (Type II error rate). So if Type II error rate is 20 per cent, power is 80 per cent. We say an experiment has power of 80 per cent if it has an 80 per cent chance of detecting an effect of a given size. When we design experiments, it is obviously desirable to increase our power as much as possible, though this usually means running lots of participants, which can be very inconvenient.

Calculation of power is quite technical and usually done at advanced levels (beyond undergraduate degrees). Computer programmes are available to assist, however. A good one is G Power (Erdfelder *et al.*, 1996), which is available on the internet. Calculation of power is described well by the Erdfelder *et al.* article.

Summary of Section 6

- Type I decision errors are set at a particular level by the experimenter choosing a value for the alpha probability.
- Multiple comparison procedures are designed to reduce the total number of Type I errors to an acceptable rate for a family of comparisons. This is known as the **familywise error rate**.
- The different kinds of multiple comparison techniques differ in the number of different comparisons which they are testing, though all attempt to retain the same familywise error rate.
- Type II errors are failures to reject the null hypothesis even when there is truly a treatment effect.
- The sample measure of the effect size can be used to give an idea of the Type II error rate of an experiment.
- The power of an experiment is simply the converse of the Type II error rate (1 – Type II error rate).

7 Analysing data for the case where the independent variables are continuous

7.1 Simple linear regression

Analysis of variance involves partitioning the variance found for a dependent variable according to independent variables (factors) which are categorical (such as gender, handedness, or treatment situations such as drug treatments etc.). However, partitioning variance can also be applied when the independent variables are continuous (e.g. age of participant). The principles are almost identical to those in an analysis of variance, which is why regression and analysis of variance are considered to be two sides of the same coin. I shall illustrate this with a simple example for linear regression.

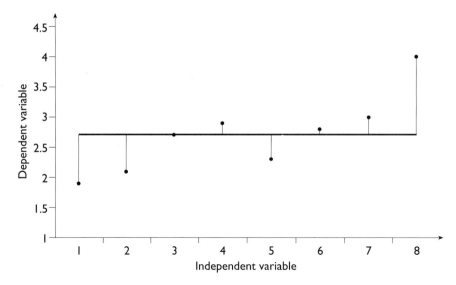

Figure 6.18 Eight data points from an experiment

Figure 6.18 shows another eight data points which have been measured on a dependent variable. Again, each data point varies from the grand mean by a certain amount. The variance of those data points about the grand mean can be calculated as before. As in Section 3.2 (Figures 6.2 and 6.3) of this chapter, giving you the information that these eight data points in Figure 6.18 fall into two groups would allow them to be measured according to Figure 6.19.

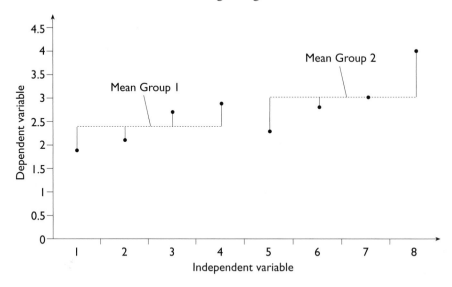

Figure 6.19 The eight data points treated as two groups

Here, with the data in two groups, each data point is found to vary about the mean for its own group. The residual variance can be calculated, and the reduction in variance tested with an appropriate F ratio. In regression, we are still interested in the reduction of variance, but now with information rather different from the categorical (group) information in Figure 6.19. Instead, we are told that the eight data points are in fact serially ordered from left to right across an independent variable.

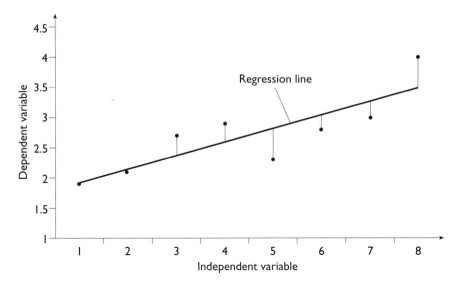

Figure 6.20 The eight data points treated as a continuous series

In Figure 6.20 the same eight data points represent measures taken at different points across a continuous independent variable along the horizontal X axis. Because the independent variable is continuous, we now want to know whether there is a continuous rise in performance on the dependent variable as we measure at different points on the independent variable. That is, we want to know if the data are well fitted by an upward-sloping straight line as shown in Figure 6.20. If we calculate a good straight line across the data points, we can then measure the distance by which each data point differs from that line. These distances, shown in Figure 6.20, are used to calculate the residual variance in the case of regression, just as differences from the individual group means were used in the categorical case (ANOVA). Once again, the residual variance will be somewhat less than the total variance around the grand mean, and an F ratio is calculated to test whether the reduction in variance found should be attributed to chance or not.

Spreadsheet exercise 7

Spreadsheet exercise 7 uses data for a linear regression over four points. The residual (error) sum of squares over the four points is shown. As in spreadsheet exercise 1, you can move the regression line, this time at both ends, so you can change its slope as well as its position.

Instructions for Microsoft Excel users

Open spreadsheet EX7 (Excel).xls. Select the handle on each end of the regression line in turn, and drag it *towards* the nearest point (above or below).

When you let go, you should see the error sum of squares go down, at least to begin with. As the error sum of squares goes down the F ratio rises, eventually becoming significant. See if you can find the line with the least squared error (this is when the Error Sum of Squares = 1.2).

Instructions for StarOffice spreadsheet users

Open spreadsheet EX7 (Star).sxc. At the top there are two values which specify the two ends of the estimated regression line. They are labelled as 'Estimate: Left-hand point' and 'Estimate: Right-hand point'. Select each one and type in a new value. Increase the value of the left-hand point (e.g. to 7) and decrease the value of the right-hand point (e.g. to 2). Read the description above about what happens to the error sum of squares.

Thinking back to the fundamentals we considered in Section 3, as the above exercise illustrates, linear regression constructs a regression line that minimizes the squared error between the data points and the line: again the method is *least squared error*. Whereas in ANOVA we were using means (in groups) to minimize error, in regression we use a sloping straight line to minimize error. Both techniques use least squared error (Section 2.2) to arrive at estimates, and in both the variance is partitioned into that due to the independent variables and that due to remaining (residual) error. (This is because they are examples of what is called General Linear Modelling.)

7.2 Multiple linear regression

Simple linear regression measures the amount by which predicting from a linear function of a single independent variable reduces the variance in one dependent variable. Multiple linear regression is still concerned with reducing the variance in a single dependent variable, but in multiple regression there are several independent variables which are used to predict its values. The same principle, that of reducing (or conversely predicting) the variance in the data, still holds. You can perhaps begin to imagine how the concept of multiple regression is linked to analysis of variance, which we have also described as a mechanism for partitioning the variance in the data.

The extension from single linear regression to multiple linear regression is similar to the extension of one-way ANOVA (which has one 'factor') to multiple factor analysis of variance. Several predictor (independent) variables are used to predict the dependent variable, using least squares estimation of the slopes for each one. Let's look at a special example in which three predictors, which are overall measures extracted from rating scales, are used to predict a dependent variable.

Students at a large university in the USA were asked to rate the overall quality of lecturers on various courses, using a scale of 1–5 (5 being good).

We shall use this overall rating as the dependent variable, i.e. the one we want to predict from the independent variables.

For this exercise, we are using specially constructed independent variables calculated from a set of other ratings and data from the students. The first independent variable is general quality, which is a combination of several other ratings of quality that the students made. The second independent variable is knowledge and popularity, which combines the rating of lecturer's knowledge with the popularity of the course. The third independent variable comes mainly from the expected grade for the student (1 = low grade, 5 = high grade). How will these three independent variables predict the dependent variable?

When you perform the multiple regression using SPSS, you'll see that you include these independent variables in the same way as you include factors in between-subjects analysis of variance.

SPSS exercise 6

Do a multiple regression on the file courfact.sav. You may wish to consult a book to guide you through the analysis in SPSS. For example, you may read Section 2 of Chapter 8 in Brace *et al.* (2003) (but use the courfact.sav file rather than the file suggested by Brace *et al.*).

When you do the multiple regression, make sure you specify:

Dependent variable = Overall

Independent variables = Genqual
Knowpop
Gradesiz

You should use the 'Enter' method, as Brace *et al.* recommend. Also make sure you select *Descriptives* as they recommend.

Table 6.12 Multiple regression results

Coefficients [a]

Model		Unstandardized Coefficients		Standardized Coefficients	t	Sig.
		B	Std. Error	Beta		
1	(Constant)	3.550	.050		71.574	.000
	General Quality	.432	.050	.705	8.627	.000
	Knowledge and Popularity	.265	.050	.431	5.282	.000
	Expected Grade	6.381E-02	.050	.104	1.274	.209

a. Dependent Variable: OVERALL

The table of results (see Table 6.12) gives several numbers for each independent variable. There are the main coefficients B and Beta. These are the *slopes* of regression lines (see Figure 6.20), as estimated by the least squares procedure. The B value is the slope of the regression line calculated on raw data. The Beta coefficient is the slope of the regression line calculated on the data after each variable has been *standardized* (a standardized variable has been changed so that its mean is 0 and its variance is 1). We shall see in a moment that the Beta coefficient has special properties.

Each independent variable is tested for significance by a t test. This, also, is exactly like analysis of variance in which every factor is tested with an F test. However, in regression each independent variable involves a single line (slope), and can only have one degree of freedom. In fact $F_{(1,n)}$ is the same numerically as $t(n)^2$, so the t test is used equivalently. If you want to stay working with F values, you can square the t value: it won't affect the p value at all. Finally, you will also see an 'R square' (r^2) value in the Model Summary. This is an effect size measure equivalent to eta-square (η^2) in analysis of variance. So multiple regression operates in basically the same way as analysis of variance, giving statistical tests for each independent variable. In this case, the statistical tests for the independent variables 'genqual' and 'knowpop' are both significant, so these factors had an effect. However, the third independent variable ('gradesiz') was not significant. The only thing missing, compared with ANOVA, is interactions between independent variables, and if you go on to do advanced statistics, you will find that these can also be evaluated.

7.2.1 Correlations and orthogonality

The above example is a special case of multiple regression, because the independent variables are **orthogonal**. This means the correlation between any of the independent variables is exactly zero.

Your analysis in 'SPSS exercise 6' produced the correlations between all the variables. Take a look at those correlations (see Table 6.13).

Table 6.13 Correlations between the variables

Correlations

		OVERALL	General Quality	Knowledge and Popularity	Expected Grade
Pearson Correlation	OVERALL	1.000	.705	.431	.104
	General Quality	.705	1.000	.000	.000
	Knowledge and Popularity	.431	.000	1.000	.000
	Expected Grade	.104	.000	.000	1.000
Sig. (1-tailed)	OVERALL	.	.000	.001	.236
	General Quality	.000	.	.500	.500
	Knowledge and Popularity	.001	.500	.	.500
	Expected Grade	.236	.500	.500	.
N	OVERALL	50	50	50	50
	General Quality	50	50	50	50
	Knowledge and Popularity	50	50	50	50
	Expected Grade	50	50	50	50

As you can see, the three predictors do not correlate with each other at all (the correlations are zero). However, they do all correlate with the dependent variable. What do you notice about those correlations?

The correlations between each independent variable and the dependent variable are exactly the same as the Beta values. This only happens when the independent variables are orthogonal. In this special case, the Beta values are equal to the correlations between variables.

7.2.2 A more realistic regression problem

In reality, multiple regression analyses are almost always done when the independent variables are correlated with each other (i.e. they are not orthogonal). Let's look at a typical example. An investigation of children's spelling might examine the relationship between several psycholinguistic variables on spelling performance. It may attempt to predict children's spelling performance from chronological age, reading age, a standardized measure of reading ability and a standardized measure of spelling ability. These measures are all correlated with each other: we certainly expect chronological age to correlate with reading age, and the standardized scores are likely to correlate with each other too.

SPSS exercise 7

Once again, do a multiple regression, this time on the file multipleregression.sav. You may wish to consult a book to guide you through the analysis in SPSS. For example, you may read Section 2 of Chapter 8 in Brace *et al.* (2003), and check your results against those they report (multipleregression.sav is the same file that Brace *et al.* analyse).

Make sure you get the correlations as well as the coefficients table. Do *not* use the Stepwise Method (which has fallen into disrepute as a misleading technique for regression analysis).

Again, each independent variable is tested by a t test, and has both a B and Beta value. You can see from the correlations that the independent variables are correlated with each other. Now, the Beta values are *not* the same as the correlations. Why is this?

The correlations and Beta values are estimated in different ways. Correlations are estimated by correlating two variables directly: other variables are ignored as if they aren't there. But Beta values are calculated in a different way. The Beta value for each independent variable is calculated from the relationship with the dependent variable only after *all* the other variables have had their contribution removed. And if those other variables are correlated with the independent variable in question, it means some of its contribution has been removed with them. Only in the special case we looked at first, when the independent variables are not correlated at all, does the effect of an independent variable on a dependent variable stay the same whether other independent variables are being taken account of or not. So the correlations between the independent variables can be very important. In this case the correlations between the independent variables range from 0.124 to 0.793. Brace *et al.* (2003) suggest such correlations are acceptable, but the higher correlations are worrying: we don't really want to use variables which correlate as strongly as 0.793. All sorts of problems can arise; for example, the Beta values are 'unstable' and fluctuate wildly with only slightly different data. We could do with something that helps us decide whether there are grounds for excluding a variable.

7.2.3 Tolerance

The correlation matrix shows how two variables are correlated. To see if there is a problem with a particular variable, it would be more useful to have a measure of the correlation between one independent variable and all the other independent variables taken together. For example, in this case the standardized reading score has a multiple correlation with the other variables, taken together, of 0.859. This is a high value, and we probably would consider excluding this variable from the model. High multiple correlations can result in instability in the regression solution, sometimes resulting in no solution being found at all. In short, it gets harder to trust the results from the analysis.

I just said that the multiple correlation of the standardized reading score with the other independent variables was 0.859. How did I know that? Unfortunately, this obvious figure isn't provided by SPSS. Instead, we are given something called **tolerance**.

Tolerance is calculated directly from the multiple correlation, by squaring it (0.859 squared gives 0.738) and subtracting from 1 ($1 - 0.738 = 0.262$). So the tolerance for the standardized reading score is 0.262. As we've subtracted from 1, low tolerance values are bad news, and we ought to worry if they are less than about 0.3.

Tolerance gives a *statistical* reason for excluding a variable from an analysis. However, statistical reasons shouldn't automatically be used to override theoretical reasons. If we have reason (i.e. a theory or results from other experiments) to believe a particular variable is important, we should retain it and look elsewhere for problems or solutions. In particular, if we want to retain independent variables which have low tolerance, we will need large numbers of participants to try to increase stability in the estimates of the Beta coefficients. This is because independent variables with low tolerance make these estimates very unstable, which means the estimates vary widely from one set of data to the next.

So multiple regression allows us to consider continuous independent variables rather like factors in analysis of variance, but we need to be careful because, unlike ANOVA, these independent variables can be correlated, leading to potential problems with our results.

7.3   Analysis of covariance

You can think of analysis of covariance as simply a way of combining into one analysis effects due to continuous and categorical variables. It is worth pointing out the importance when constructing an analysis of using the appropriate forms for the factors and variables. It is a common practice amongst psychologists to treat continuous factors as if they are discrete purely for the convenience of being able to run an analysis of variance. For example, even when the data for the age of subjects are available, such as when running experiments on child development where children's ages are known, frequently the sample is cut into two or three groups such as 5 to 7-year-olds, 8 to 10-year-olds, and 11 to 15-year-olds. This produces a categorical factor with three levels which may easily be used in analysis of variance. However, as we shall see, this is a poor way of entering a continuous variable such as age which is certainly very easy to measure precisely (though, of course, there may be theoretical reasons for grouping children by age). Let us consider the data which are used to create the graphs in Figures 6.18, 6.19 and 6.20 in Section 7.1 of this chapter. The eight data points may represent eight subjects of different ages. The actual data are shown in Table 6.14.

Table 6.14

X	Y
1	1.9
2	2.1
3	2.7
4	2.9
5	2.3
6	2.8
7	3
8	4

If these data are appropriately analysed using linear regression, the F value for predicting the dependent variable Y from the continuous predictor X is 6.8, which with one and six degrees of freedom is significant at more than the 1 per cent level. But suppose the psychologist had chosen simply to divide the data according to a dichotomous classification as in Figure 6.19, whereby the first four data points are grouped together and the second four data points are grouped together. Now, the F statistic produced by this grouping is only 3.1, which with one and six degrees of freedom is not even significant at the 5 per cent level. Artificially constructing groups from something that is really a continuous dependent variable is a sure way to lose information in a set of data, and prejudices the likelihood of finding results in the analysis. Analysis of covariance allows the introduction of continuous dependent variables alongside categorical ones, which will allow easy interpretation by the psychologist. We shall look at an example of this in a computer exercise.

Let us first finish considering what in fact happens when the data in Table 6.14 are categorized into two groups. Effectively, the continuous variable is recoded with only two levels, such as in Table 6.15.

Table 6.15

1	1.9
1	2.1
1	2.7
1	2.9
2	2.3
2	2.8
2	3
2	4

This makes it obvious how the continuous variable has been collapsed to only two values. Indeed, you may consider it instructive to treat this as a simple linear regression and perform the regression predicting the values of the dependent variable from the new X values, even though there are only two possible numbers. If you do such a regression, you will find exactly the same result as you get from the analysis of variance (or t test) with a dichotomous factor. This again emphasizes the correspondence between analysis of variance and linear regression. Indeed, in effect what happens in analysis of variance is that a regression line is drawn between the two groups, as you can see in Figure 6.21.

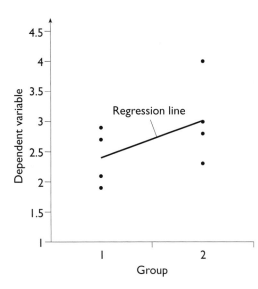

Figure 6.21   A regression line drawn through two groups

The regression based on the categorical variable formed in the analysis of variance is calculated in the same way as regression lines on the continuous variables in multiple regression. Therefore, when at all possible make sure that all the information in a continuous variable is used in the analysis.

SPSS exercise 8

Do an analysis of covariance on the file ancova.sav. You may wish to consult a book to guide you through the analysis in SPSS. For example, you may read Sections 1 and 2 only in Chapter 9 in Brace *et al.* (2003), and check your results against those they report.

One final point about linear regression models. If we evaluate models with continuous variables directly in the analysis, we are only looking for linear relationships. If the actual relationship between the predictor and the criterion variable is not a straight line but a curve, then our model will be less able to detect the relationship (in much the same way that incorrectly analysing a linear trend, such as Figure 6.18 in this chapter, as a dichotomous variable – as in Figure 6.19 – weakens the analysis). It may result in no relationship being found at all. So you should always do scatter plots of your data to see if the trends are linear or decidedly curved. If they are curved, you'll need to come up with a more sophisticated analysis. Brace *et al.* (2003) explain at length how to check if the relationship is linear (see Chapter 9, Section 2).

Summary of Section 7

- Multiple linear regression, analysis of variance and analysis of covariance are all techniques for partitioning the variance of a dependent variable according to a number of predictor variables.

- These predictor variables may be categorical ('discrete') or continuous. Analysis of variance deals with designs involving factors which are all discrete. Multiple regression and analysis of covariance are ways of analysing the variance with predictor variables which are both continuous and discrete.
- Where possible, if a dependent variable has been measured continuously, it should be used in a statistical model in a way which retains that measurement.
- In many regression problems, especially multiple linear regression, the predictor (continuous) variables are correlated with each other – that is, they are not orthogonal.
- Non-orthogonality amongst predictor variables means that results of the analyses must be interpreted with care, and may make it necessary to exclude variables if tolerance is low.

8 Conclusion

In this chapter you have learned that the basis of parametric statistics is to produce parameters (or estimates, such as the mean) which have least squared error. From this concept emerge the analytical techniques of analysis of variance, multiple regression and analysis of covariance. All these techniques are ways to formalize how we make decisions on the basis of experimental data. We always want to make the best decisions we can, but don't forget that we are engaged in a scientific endeavour, and the result of a statistical test is always only a part of the information we use.

Always make sure you are using these tests in the most appropriate way. As the old adage says, there are lies, damned lies, and statistics ...

Further reading

Howell, D.C. (2002) *Statistical Methods for Psychology* (5th edn), Belmont, CA, Duxbury Press (imprint of Wadsworth Publishing Company/a division of International Thompson Publishing Inc.).

References

Brace, N., Kemp, R. and Snelgar, R. (2003) *SPSS for Psychologists* (2nd edn), Basingstoke, Palgrave Macmillan.

Erdfelder, E., Faul, F. and Buchner, A. (1996) 'G Power: a general purpose power analysis program', *Behavior Research Methods, Instruments and Computers,* vol.28, no.1, pp.1–11.

Towell, N., Kemp, R. and Pike, G. (1996) 'The effects of witness identity masking on memory and person perception', *Psychology, Crime and Law,* vol.2, pp.333–46.

Appendix 1: Psychological ethical codes

Research in the UK must normally conform to BPS standards, although work published in journals in the USA may also need to comply with APA (American Psychological Association) codes. Limited extracts from both are reproduced below. Ethical codes are reviewed and updated regularly; check the relevant websites for up-to-date versions (BPS: http://www.bps.org.uk; APA: http://www.apa.org).

(A) British Psychological Society (BPS): Extracts from 'Ethical Principles for Conducting Research with Human Participants'

1 Introduction

1.1 The principles given below are intended to apply to research with human participants. Principles of conduct in professional practice are to be found in the Society's Code of Conduct and in the advisory documents prepared by the Divisions, Sections and Special Groups of the Society.

1.2 Participants in psychological research should have confidence in the investigators. Good psychological research is possibly only if there is mutual respect and confidence between investigators and participants. Psychological investigators are potentially interested in all aspects of human behaviour and conscious experience. However, for ethical reasons, some areas of human experience and behaviour may be beyond the reach of experiment, observation or other form of psychological investigation. Ethical guidelines are necessary to clarify the conditions under which psychological research is acceptable.

1.3 The principles given below supplement for researchers with human participants the general ethical principles of members of the Society as stated in The British Psychological Society's Code of Conduct (q.v.). Members of The British Psychological society are expected to abide by both the Code of Conduct and the fuller principles expressed here. Members should also draw the principles to the attention of research colleagues who are not members of the Society. Members should encourage colleagues to adopt them and ensure that they are followed by all researchers whom they supervise (e.g. research assistants, postgraduate, undergraduate, A-Level and GCSE students).

1.4 In recent years, there has been an increase in legal actions by members of the general public against professionals for alleged misconduct. Researchers must recognize the possibility of such legal action if they infringe the rights and dignity of participants in their research.

2 General

2.1   In all circumstances, investigators must consider the ethical implications and psychological consequences for the participants in their research. The essential principle is that the investigation should be considered from the standpoint of all participants; foreseeable threats to their psychological well-being, health, value or dignity should be eliminated. Investigators should recognize that, in our multi-cultural and multi-ethnic society and where investigations involve individuals of different ages, gender and social background, the investigators may not have sufficient knowledge of the implications of any investigation for the participants. It should be borne in mind that the best judge of whether an investigation will cause offence may be members of the population from which the participants in the research are to be drawn.

3 Consent

3.1   Whenever possible, the investigator should inform all participants of the objectives of the investigation. The investigator should inform the participants of all aspects of the research or intervention that might reasonably be expected to influence willingness to participate. The investigator should, normally, explain all other aspects of the research or intervention about which the participants enquire. Failure to make full disclosure prior to obtaining informed consent requires additional safeguards to protect the welfare and dignity of the participants (see Section 4).

3.2   Research with children or with participants who have impairments that will limit understanding and/or communication such that they are unable to give their consent requires special safe-guarding procedures.

3.3   Where possible, the real consent of children and of adults with impairments in understanding or communication should be obtained. In addition, where research involves any persons under 16 years of age, consent should be obtained from parents or from those in loco parentis. If the nature of the research precludes consent being obtained from parents or permission being obtained from teachers, before proceeding with the research, the investigator must obtain approval from an Ethics Committee.

3.4   Where real consent cannot be obtained from adults with impairments in understanding or communication, wherever possible the investigator should consult a person well-placed to appreciate the participant's reaction, such as a member of the person's family, and must obtain the disinterested approval of the research from independent advisors.

3.5   When research is being conducted with detained persons, particular care should be taken over informed consent, paying attention to the special circumstances which may affect the person's ability to give free informed consent.

3.6 Investigators should realize that they are often in a position of authority or influence over participants who may be their students, employees or clients. This relationship must not be allowed to pressurize the participants to take part in, or remain in, an investigation.

3.7 The payment of participants must not be used to induce them to risk harm beyond that which they risk without payment in their normal lifestyle.

3.8 If harm, unusual discomfort, or other negative consequences for the individual's future life might occur, the investigator must obtain the disinterested approval of independent advisors, inform the participants, and obtain informed, real consent from each of them.

3.9 In longitudinal research, consent may need to be obtained on more than one occasion.

4 Deception

4.1 The withholding of information or the misleading of participants is unacceptable if the participants are typically likely to object or show unease once debriefed. Where this is in any doubt, appropriate consultation must precede the investigation. Consultation is best carried out with individuals who share the social and cultural background of the participants in the research, but the advice of ethics committees or experienced and disinterested colleagues may be sufficient.

4.2 Intentional deception of the participants over the purpose and general nature of the investigation should be avoided whenever possible. Participants should never be deliberately misled without extremely strong scientific or medical justification. Even then there should be strict controls and the disinterested approval of independent advisors.

4.3 It may be impossible to study some psychological processes without withholding information about the true object of the study or deliberately misleading the participants. Before conducting such a study, the investigator has a special responsibility to (a) determine that alternative procedures avoiding concealment or deception are not available; (b) ensure that the participants are provided with sufficient information at the earliest stage; and (c) consult appropriately upon the way that the withholding of information or deliberate deception will be received.

5 Debriefing

5.1 In studies where the participants are aware that they have taken part in an investigation, when the data have been collected, the investigator should provide the participants with any necessary information to complete their understanding of the nature of the research. The investigator should discuss with the participants their experience of the research in order to monitor any unforeseen negative effects or misconceptions.

5.2 Debriefing does not provide a justification for unethical aspects of any investigation.

5.3   Some effects which may be produced by an experiment will not be negated by a verbal description following the research. Investigators have a responsibility to ensure that participants receive any necessary debriefing in the form of active intervention before they leave the research setting.

6   Withdrawal from the investigation

6.1   At the onset of the investigation investigators should make plain to participants their right to withdraw from the research at any time, irrespective of whether or not payment or other inducement has been offered. It is recognized that this may be difficult in certain observational or organizational settings, but nevertheless the investigator must attempt to ensure that participants (including children) know of their right to withdraw. When testing children, avoidance of the testing situation may be taken as evidence of failure to consent to the procedure and should be acknowledged.

6.2   In the light of experience of the investigation, or as a result of debriefing, the participant has the right to withdraw retrospectively any consent given, and to require that their own data, including recordings, be destroyed.

7   Confidentiality

7.1   Subject to the requirements of legislation, including the Data Protection Act, information obtained about a participant during an investigation is confidential unless otherwise agreed in advance. Investigators who are put under pressure to disclose confidential information should draw this point to the attention of those exerting such pressure. Participants in psychological research have a right to expect that information they provide will be treated confidentially and, if published, will not be identifiable as theirs. In the event that confidentiality and/or anonymity cannot be guaranteed, the participants must be warned of this in advance of agreeing to participate.

8   Protection of participants

8.1   Investigators have a primary responsibility to protect participants from physical and mental harm during the investigation. Normally, the risk of harm must be no greater than in ordinary life, i.e. participants should not be exposed to risks greater than or additional to those encountered in their normal lifestyles. Where the risk of harm is greater than in ordinary life the provisions of 3.8 should apply. Participants must be asked about any factors in the procedure that might create a risk, such as pre-existing medical conditions, and must be advised of any special action they should take to avoid risk.

8.2   Participants should be informed of procedures for contacting the investigator within a reasonable time period following participation should stress, potential harm, or related questions or concern arise despite the precautions required by the Principles. Where research procedures might result in undesirable consequences for participants, the investigator has the responsibility to detect and remove or correct these consequences.

8.3 Where research may involve behaviour or experiences that participants may regard as personal and private the participants must be protected from stress by all appropriate measures, including the assurance that answers to personal questions need not be given. There should be no concealment or deception when seeking information that might encroach on privacy.

8.4 In research involving children, great caution should be exercised when discussing the results with parents, teachers or others in loco parentis, since evaluative statements may carry unintended weight.

9 Observational research

9.1 Studies based upon observation must respect the privacy and psychological well-being of the individuals studied. Unless those observed give their consent to being observed, observational research is only acceptable in situations where those observed would expect to be observed by strangers. Additionally, particular account should be taken of local cultural values and of the possibility of intruding upon the privacy of individuals who, even while in a normally public space, may believe they are unobserved.

10 Giving advice

10.1 During research, an investigator may obtain evidence of psychological or physical problems of which a participant is, apparently, unaware. In such a case, the investigator has a responsibility to inform the participant if the investigator believes that by not doing so the participant's future well-being may be endangered.

10.2 If, in the normal course of psychological research, or as a result of problems detected as in 10.1, a participant solicits advice concerning educational, personality, behavioural or health issues, caution should be exercised. If the issue is serious and the investigator is not qualified to offer assistance, the appropriate source of professional advice should be recommended. Further details on the giving of advice will be found in the Society's Code of Conduct.

10.3 In some kinds of investigation the giving of advice is appropriate if this forms an intrinsic part of the research and has been agreed in advance.

11 Colleagues

11.1 Investigators share responsibility for the ethical treatment of research participants with their collaborators, assistants, students and employees. A psychologist who believes that another psychologist or investigator may be conducting research that is not in accordance with the principles above should encourage that investigator or re-evaluate the research.

Source: The British Psychological Society (2000) *Code of Conduct, Ethical Principles and Guidelines*, Leicester, The British Psychological Society, pp.8–11

(B) American Psychological Association (APA): Extracts from 'Ethical Principles of Psychologists and Code of Conduct 2002'

Note: Items marked with an asterisk (*) are referred to in this extract but not reproduced here. They may be found in the complete code of conduct.

Introduction and Applicability

The American Psychological Association's (APA's) Ethical Principles of Psychologists and Code of Conduct (hereinafter referred to as the Ethics Code) consists of an Introduction, a Preamble, five General Principles (A–E), and specific Ethical Standards. The Introduction discusses the intent, organization, procedural considerations, and scope of application of the Ethics Code. The Preamble and General Principles are aspirational goals to guide psychologists toward the highest ideals of psychology. Although the Preamble and General Principles are not themselves enforceable rules, they should be considered by psychologists in arriving at an ethical course of action. The Ethical Standards set forth enforceable rules for conduct as psychologists. Most of the Ethical Standards are written broadly, in order to apply to psychologists in varied roles, although the application of an Ethical Standard may vary depending on the context. The Ethical Standards are not exhaustive. The fact that a given conduct is not specifically addressed by an Ethical Standard does not mean that it is necessarily either ethical or unethical.

This Ethics Code applies only to psychologists' activities that are part of their scientific, educational, or professional roles as psychologists. Areas covered include but are not limited to the clinical, counseling, and school practice of psychology; research; teaching; supervision of trainees; public service; policy development; social intervention; development of assessment instruments; conducting assessments; educational counseling; organizational consulting; forensic activities; program design and evaluation; and administration. This Ethics Code applies to these activities across a variety of contexts, such as in person, postal, telephone, internet, and other electronic transmissions. These activities shall be distinguished from the purely private conduct of psychologists, which is not within the purview of the Ethics Code.

Membership in the APA commits members and student affiliates to comply with the standards of the APA Ethics Code and to the rules and procedures used to enforce them. Lack of awareness or misunderstanding of an Ethical Standard is not itself a defense to a charge of unethical conduct.

The Ethics Code is intended to provide guidance for psychologists and standards of professional conduct that can be applied by the APA and by other bodies that choose to adopt them. The Ethics Code is not intended to be a basis of civil liability. Whether a psychologist has violated the Ethics Code standards does not by itself determine whether the psychologist is legally liable in a court action, whether a contract is enforceable, or whether other legal consequences occur.

The modifiers used in some of the standards of this Ethics Code (e.g., *reasonably, appropriate, potentially*) are included in the standards when they would (1) allow professional judgment on the part of psychologists, (2) eliminate injustice or inequality that would occur without the modifier, (3) ensure applicability across the broad range of activities conducted by psychologists, or (4) guard against a set of rigid rules that might be quickly outdated. As used in this Ethics Code, the term *reasonable* means the prevailing professional judgment of psychologists engaged in similar activities in similar circumstances, given the knowledge the psychologist had or should have had at the time.

Preamble

Psychologists are committed to increasing scientific and professional knowledge of behavior and people's understanding of themselves and others and to the use of such knowledge to improve the condition of individuals, organizations, and society. Psychologists respect and protect civil and human rights and the central importance of freedom of inquiry and expression in research, teaching, and publication. They strive to help the public in developing informed judgments and choices concerning human behavior. In doing so, they perform many roles, such as researcher, educator, diagnostician, therapist, supervisor, consultant, administrator, social interventionist, and expert witness. This Ethics Code provides a common set of principles and standards upon which psychologists build their professional and scientific work.

This Ethics Code is intended to provide specific standards to cover most situations encountered by psychologists. It has as its goals the welfare and protection of the individuals and groups with whom psychologists work and the education of members, students, and the public regarding ethical standards of the discipline.

The development of a dynamic set of ethical standards for psychologists' work-related conduct requires a personal commitment and lifelong effort to act ethically; to encourage ethical behavior by students, supervisees, employees, and colleagues; and to consult with others concerning ethical problems.

General Principles

This section consists of General Principles. General Principles, as opposed to Ethical Standards, are aspirational in nature. Their intent is to guide and inspire psychologists toward the very highest ethical ideals of the profession. General Principles, in contrast to Ethical Standards, do not represent obligations and should not form the basis for imposing sanctions. Relying upon General Principles for either of these reasons distorts both their meaning and purpose.

Principle A: Beneficence and Nonmaleficence

Psychologists strive to benefit those with whom they work and take care to do no harm. In their professional actions, psychologists seek to safeguard the welfare and rights of those with whom they interact professionally and other affected persons, and the welfare of animal subjects of research. When conflicts occur among psychologists' obligations or concerns, they attempt to resolve these conflicts in a responsible fashion that avoids or minimizes harm. Because psychologists' scientific and professional judgments and actions may affect the lives of others, they are alert to and guard against personal, financial, social, organizational, or political factors that might lead to misuse of their influence. Psychologists strive to be aware of the possible effect of their own physical and mental health on their ability to help those with whom they work.

Principle B: Fidelity and Responsibility

Psychologists establish relationships of trust with those with whom they work. They are aware of their professional and scientific responsibilities to society and to the specific communities in which they work. Psychologists uphold professional standards of conduct, clarify their professional roles and obligations, accept appropriate responsibility for their behavior, and seek to manage conflicts of interest that could lead to exploitation or harm. Psychologists consult with, refer to, or cooperate with other professionals and institutions to the extent needed to serve the best interests of those with whom they work. They are concerned about the ethical compliance of their colleagues' scientific and professional conduct. Psychologists strive to contribute a portion of their professional time for little or no compensation or personal advantage.

Principle C: Integrity

Psychologists seek to promote accuracy, honesty, and truthfulness in the science, teaching, and practice of psychology. In these activities psychologists do not steal, cheat, or engage in fraud, subterfuge, or intentional misrepresentation of fact. Psychologists strive to keep their promises and to avoid unwise or unclear commitments. In situations in which deception may be ethically justifiable to maximize benefits and minimize harm, psychologists have a serious obligation to consider the need for, the possible consequences of, and their responsibility to correct any resulting mistrust or other harmful effects that arise from the use of such techniques.

Principle D: Justice

Psychologists recognize that fairness and justice entitle all persons to access to and benefit from the contributions of psychology and to equal quality in the processes, procedures, and services being conducted by psychologists. Psychologists exercise reasonable judgment and take precautions to ensure that their potential biases, the boundaries of their competence, and the limitations of their expertise do not lead to or condone unjust practices.

Principle E: Respect for People's Rights and Dignity

Psychologists respect the dignity and worth of all people, and the rights of individuals to privacy, confidentiality, and self-determination. Psychologists are aware that special safeguards may be necessary to protect the rights and welfare of persons or communities whose vulnerabilities impair autonomous decision making. Psychologists are aware of and respect cultural, individual, and role differences, including those based on age, gender, gender identity, race, ethnicity, culture, national origin, religion, sexual orientation, disability, language, and socioeconomic status and consider these factors when working with members of such groups. Psychologists try to eliminate the effect on their work of biases based on those factors, and they do not knowingly participate in or condone activities of others based upon such prejudices.

Ethical Standards

2. Competence

2.01 Boundaries of Competence

(a) Psychologists provide services, teach, and conduct research with populations and in areas only within the boundaries of their competence, based on their education, training, supervised experience, consultation, study, or professional experience.

(b) Where scientific or professional knowledge in the discipline of psychology establishes that an understanding of factors associated with age, gender, gender identity, race, ethnicity, culture, national origin, religion, sexual orientation, disability, language, or socioeconomic status is essential for effective implementation of their services or research, psychologists have or obtain the training, experience, consultation, or supervision necessary to ensure the competence of their services, or they make appropriate referrals, except as provided in Standard 2.02, Providing Services in Emergencies*.

(c) Psychologists planning to provide services, teach, or conduct research involving populations, areas, techniques, or technologies new to them undertake relevant education, training, supervised experience, consultation, or study.

(d) When psychologists are asked to provide services to individuals for whom appropriate mental health services are not available and for which psychologists have not obtained the competence necessary, psychologists with closely related prior training or experience may provide such services in order to ensure that services are not denied if they make a reasonable effort to obtain the competence required by using relevant research, training, consultation, or study.

(e) In those emerging areas in which generally recognized standards for preparatory training do not yet exist, psychologists nevertheless take reasonable steps to ensure the competence of their work and to protect clients/patients, students, supervisees, research participants, organizational clients, and others from harm.

(f) When assuming forensic roles, psychologists are or become reasonably familiar with the judicial or administrative rules governing their roles.

5. Advertising and Other Public Statements

5.04 Media Presentations

When psychologists provide public advice or comment via print, internet, or other electronic transmission, they take precautions to ensure that statements (1) are based on their professional knowledge, training, or experience in accord with appropriate psychological literature and practice; (2) are otherwise consistent with this Ethics Code; and (3) do not indicate that a professional relationship has been established with the recipient. (See also Standard 2.04, Bases for Scientific and Professional Judgments*.)

8. Research and Publication

8.01 Institutional Approval

When institutional approval is required, psychologists provide accurate information about their research proposals and obtain approval prior to conducting the research. They conduct the research in accordance with the approved research protocol.

8.02 Informed Consent to Research

(a)   When obtaining informed consent as required in Standard 3.10, Informed Consent, psychologists inform participants about (1) the purpose of the research, expected duration, and procedures; (2) their right to decline to participate and to withdraw from the research once participation has begun; (3) the foreseeable consequences of declining or withdrawing; (4) reasonably foreseeable factors that may be expected to influence their willingness to participate such as potential risks, discomfort, or adverse effects; (5) any prospective research benefits; (6) limits of confidentiality; (7) incentives for participation; and (8) whom to contact for questions about the research and research participants' rights. They provide opportunity for the prospective participants to ask questions and receive answers. (See also Standards 8.03, Informed Consent for Recording Voices and Images in Research; 8.05, Dispensing With Informed Consent for Research; and 8.07, Deception in Research.)

(b)   Psychologists conducting intervention research involving the use of experimental treatments clarify to participants at the outset of the research (1) the experimental nature of the treatment; (2) the services that will or will not be available to the control group(s) if appropriate; (3) the means by which assignment to treatment and control groups will be made; (4) available treatment alternatives if an individual does not wish to participate in the research or wishes to withdraw once a study has begun; and (5) compensation for or monetary costs of participating including, if appropriate, whether reimbursement from the participant or a third-party payor will be sought. (See also Standard 8.02a, Informed Consent to Research.)

8.03 Informed Consent for Recording Voices and Images in Research

Psychologists obtain informed consent from research participants prior to recording their voices or images for data collection unless (1) the research consists solely of naturalistic observations in public places, and it is not anticipated that the recording will be used in a manner that could cause personal identification or harm, or (2) the research design includes deception, and consent for the use of the recording is obtained during debriefing. (See also Standard 8.07, Deception in Research.)

8.04 Client/Patient, Student, and Subordinate Research Participants

(a) When psychologists conduct research with clients/patients, students, or subordinates as participants, psychologists take steps to protect the prospective participants from adverse consequences of declining or withdrawing from participation.

(b) When research participation is a course requirement or an opportunity for extra credit, the prospective participant is given the choice of equitable alternative activities.

8.05 Dispensing With Informed Consent for Research

Psychologists may dispense with informed consent only (1) where research would not reasonably be assumed to create distress or harm and involves (a) the study of normal educational practices, curricula, or classroom management methods conducted in educational settings; (b) only anonymous questionnaires, naturalistic observations, or archival research for which disclosure of responses would not place participants at risk of criminal or civil liability or damage their financial standing, employability, or reputation, and confidentiality is protected; or (c) the study of factors related to job or organization effectiveness conducted in organizational settings for which there is no risk to participants' employability, and confidentiality is protected or (2) where otherwise permitted by law or federal or institutional regulations.

8.06 Offering Inducements for Research Participation

(a) Psychologists make reasonable efforts to avoid offering excessive or inappropriate financial or other inducements for research participation when such inducements are likely to coerce participation.

(b) When offering professional services as an inducement for research participation, psychologists clarify the nature of the services, as well as the risks, obligations, and limitations. (See also Standard 6.05, Barter With Clients/Patients*.)

8.07 Deception in Research

(a) Psychologists do not conduct a study involving deception unless they have determined that the use of deceptive techniques is justified by the study's significant prospective scientific, educational, or applied value and that effective nondeceptive alternative procedures are not feasible.

(b) Psychologists do not deceive prospective participants about research that is reasonably expected to cause physical pain or severe emotional distress.

(c) Psychologists explain any deception that is an integral feature of the design and conduct of an experiment to participants as early as is feasible, preferably at the conclusion of their participation, but no later than at the conclusion of the data collection, and permit participants to withdraw their data. (See also Standard 8.08, Debriefing.)

8.08 Debriefing

(a) Psychologists provide a prompt opportunity for participants to obtain appropriate information about the nature, results, and conclusions of the research, and they take reasonable steps to correct any misconceptions that participants may have of which the psychologists are aware.

(b) If scientific or humane values justify delaying or withholding this information, psychologists take reasonable measures to reduce the risk of harm.

(c) When psychologists become aware that research procedures have harmed a participant, they take reasonable steps to minimize the harm.

8.10 Reporting Research Results

(a) Psychologists do not fabricate data. (See also Standard 5.01a, Avoidance of False or Deceptive Statements*.)

(b) If psychologists discover significant errors in their published data, they take reasonable steps to correct such errors in a correction, retraction, erratum, or other appropriate publication means.

8.11 Plagiarism

Psychologists do not present portions of another's work or data as their own, even if the other work or data source is cited occasionally.

8.12 Publication Credit

(a) Psychologists take responsibility and credit, including authorship credit, only for work they have actually performed or to which they have substantially contributed. (See also Standard 8.12b, Publication Credit.)

(b) Principal authorship and other publication credits accurately reflect the relative scientific or professional contributions of the individuals involved, regardless of their relative status. Mere possession of an institutional position, such as department chair, does not justify authorship credit. Minor contributions to the research or to the writing for publications are acknowledged appropriately, such as in footnotes or in an introductory statement.

(c) Except under exceptional circumstances, a student is listed as principal author on any multiple-authored article that is substantially based on the student's doctoral dissertation. Faculty advisors discuss publication credit with students as early as feasible and throughout the research and publication process as appropriate. (See also Standard 8.12b, Publication Credit.)

8.13 Duplicate Publication of Data

Psychologists do not publish, as original data, data that have been previously published. This does not preclude republishing data when they are accompanied by proper acknowledgment.

8.14 Sharing Research Data for Verification

(a) After research results are published, psychologists do not withhold the data on which their conclusions are based from other competent professionals who seek to verify the substantive claims through reanalysis and who intend to use such data only for that purpose, provided that the confidentiality of the participants can be protected and unless legal rights concerning proprietary data preclude their release. This does not preclude psychologists from requiring that such individuals or groups be responsible for costs associated with the provision of such information.

(b) Psychologists who request data from other psychologists to verify the substantive claims through reanalysis may use shared data only for the declared purpose. Requesting psychologists obtain prior written agreement for all other uses of the data.

8.15 Reviewers

Psychologists who review material submitted for presentation, publication, grant, or research proposal review respect the confidentiality of and the proprietary rights in such information of those who submitted it.

History and Effective Date Footnote

This version of the APA Ethics Code was adopted by the American Psychological Association's Council of Representatives during its meeting, August 21, 2002, and is effective beginning June 1, 2003. The Ethics Code and information regarding the Code can be found on the APA website, http://www.apa.org/ethics

Request copies of the APA's Ethical Principles of Psychologists and Code of Conduct from the APA Order Department, 750 First Street, NE, Washington, DC 20002-4242, or phone (202) 336-5510.

© 2002 American Psychological Association

Source: American Psychological Association (2002) *Ethical Principles of Psychologists and Code of Conduct 2002*, Washington, DC, American Psychological Association.

Appendix 2: Sample Data Protection Act information sheet

DATA PROTECTION ACT

Security of data

The 1998 Act states that appropriate security measures should be taken against unauthorized or unlawful processing of personal data and against accidental loss or destruction of, or damage to, personal data. The Act extends the rights of the data subject to recompense if their data is processed in any way that might cause them damage or distress.

The following principles apply to all personal data processed:

1   Access to the data, both those which are electronically stored and in hardcopy, should be restricted to staff who need those data for their 'name of institution' work.

2   Staff should not leave screens that can access personal data unattended when signed on, should use a (short time-out) password-controlled screen saver, and should log-off correctly at the end of a session. Screens should always be cleared of personal data after use.

3   Staff who may have contact with personal data must take care that personal data is kept away from people not entitled to see it (including authorized visitors) and that casual sight of screens is avoided.

4   Passwords should not be easily guessable and should be changed regularly. They should be kept secure and not be disclosed to unauthorized persons.

5   Floppy disc files with personal data must be removed from the PC and stored securely when not in use. When they are no longer required they should be erased and reformatted.

6   Personal data on workstation fixed hard discs must have adequate protection, e.g. password access to files to prevent unauthorized access. Where personal data is held on a shared area of a server, the list of people with access rights to that area must be:

- Strictly limited to those who need to know all of it

- Be reviewed regularly to ensure that it reflects current need to know.

7   Print-outs and microfiche containing personal data should be stored securely and disposed of using confidential waste disposal services. It is the institution's responsibility to see that external contractors disposing of personal data (or processing it in any other way) on the 'name of institution's' behalf, comply with the Act.

8   Data no longer required should be destroyed. If a PC is passed to another area, measures must be taken to ensure that personal data files not relevant to the receiving area are destroyed or removed.

Disclosures

1   There are a limited number of circumstances in which personal data should be disclosed outside the institution other than to the data subject themselves (although disclosures may already be made with the consent of the data subject). Personal data should not be disclosed over the telephone, except in predefined circumstances and very exceptionally on the authority of a senior officer.

2   Personal data may be disclosed to staff of the institution but only if they need to see and handle it as part of their 'name of institution' work.

NB: If in doubt about either of the above two cases do not disclose and seek further advice.

3   Personal data sent by post should only be sent to validated addresses (eg a registered address).

4   Accidental disclosures may be made in transmissions using email and conference facilities as these are insecure. Avoid the use of these means therefore if the transmission is of sensitive personal data.

Source: adapted from an Open University information sheet

Index

Acknowledgements

Grateful acknowledgement is made to the following sources for permission to reproduce material within this book:

Cover image
Face icon based on image supplied by Getty Images.

Colour plates
Plate 6: George, M.S. 'Transcranial Magnetic Stimulation', *Scientific American,* vol.289, no.3, September 2003. Scientific American, Inc.; *Plate 8:* Damasio, H., Grabowski, T., Frank, R., Galaburda, A.M., Damasio, A.R., 'The return of Phineas Gage: Clues about the brain from a famous patient', *Science,* 264: 1102–1105, 1994, with permission of Hanna Damasio, Department of Neurology and Image Analysis Facility, University of Iowa. © 1994 AAAS; *Plate 9:* Tranel, D., *et al.* 'A neural basis for the retrieval of conceptual knowledge', *Neuropsychologia,* vol.35, no.10, 1997. Elsevier Science Ltd.

Figures
Figures 2.20, 2.21 and 2.22: Seidenberg, M.S. and McClelland, J.L. (1989) 'A distributed, developmental model of word recognition and naming', *Psychological Review,* vol.96. American Psychological Association; *Figures 3.2, 3.13, 3.14 and 3.16:* Anderson, J.R. and Lebiere, C. (1998) *The Atomic Components of Thought,* Lawrence Erlbaum Associates, Inc.; *Figure 4.2:* Courtesy of Ingrid Johnsrude; *Figure 4.3:* Opitz, B. *et al.* (1999) 'Combining electrophysiological and hemodynamic measures of the auditory oddball', *Psychophysiology,* vol.36, Blackwell Publishing Ltd; *Figure 4.8:* Adapted from 'Brief Introduction to FMRI', http://www.fmrib.ox.ac.uk

Appendices
Appendix 1(A): The British Psychological Society (2000) 'Ethical Principles for Conducting Research with Human Participants', *Code of Conduct, Ethical Principles and Guidelines.* The British Psychological Society; *Appendix 1(B):* American Psychological Association (2002) *Ethical Principles of Psychologists and Code of Conduct 2002.* American Psychological Association.

Every effort has been made to contact copyright owners. If any have been inadvertently overlooked, the publishers will be pleased to make the necessary arrangements at the first opportunity.